CROSSING THE BOUNDARY

D0806552

7/2069141

CROSSING THE BOUNDARY

KEVIN PIETERSEN

EBURY
PRESS

1 3 5 7 9 10 8 6 4 2

This edition published in 2007
First published in 2006 by Ebury Press, an imprint of Ebury Publishing

Ebury Publishing is a division of the Random House Group

The Random House Group Limited Reg. No. 954009

Addresses for companies within the Random House Group can be found at
www.randomhouse.co.uk

A CIP catalogue record for this book is available from the British Library

Printed and bound in 2007 by CPI Cox & Wyman, Reading, RG1 8EX

ISBN 9780091912062

Mixed Sources
Product group from well-managed
forests and other controlled sources
www.fsc.org Cert no. TT-COC-2139
FSC © 1996 Forest Stewardship Council

Acknowledgements

I would like to thank my editor Claire Kingston and everyone at Ebury for all their work on this book. Thanks to my agent Adam Wheatley for his guidance and to Paul Newman for his help with this project. Thanks also to Philip Brown for the great photos and to Tim Nichols for the stats.

But above all, my wholehearted thanks to my family for their support through everything that has happened so far. This is just the beginning.

Paul Newman is Deputy Sports Editor of the *Daily Mail*. He collaborated with Kevin Pietersen on *Crossing The Boundary* and has worked on numerous cricket books, notably the award-winning *Playing With Fire* by Nasser Hussain. He is a huge fan of both the England cricket team and Tottenham Hotspur FC, and considered having a KP haircut while working on this project but thought better of it.

CONTENTS

FOREWORD
by Shane Warne

When I was asked to write the foreword for Kevin Pietersen's book I thought, what the hell is he doing a book for after only a year in the game at the highest level? Then, when I thought about it a bit more, I quickly recognised that the KP story has already been a complex and interesting one.

Kevin has been through an awful lot in a short space of time. He left the country of his birth to find his fame and fortune in the land of his mother and then had to endure all sorts of things as a young man in a new environment while still learning the game.

All the usual learning processes had to be achieved away from what he was used to, his home environment and his friends and family, but he was still able to explode on to international cricket in a spectacular manner. It took quite something for him to help England regain the Ashes in his first Test series, especially considering that England had not achieved an Ashes victory in almost 20 years. It is just the beginning. The KP story can go on and on, just like England's celebrations did!

I first met KP in a game at the Rose Bowl when I was playing for Hampshire and he was playing for Nottinghamshire. My first impressions, I suppose, were like everyone else's in the game. 'Who the hell is this cocky little upstart?' From memory he got about 40-odd and played OK.

Kevin was a little different in the way he played. He used his reach pretty well and was trying to be positive, which is always better than being scared to play a shot. I did not really mix with him on that occasion, so did not get to know him, but there were whispers that he was a bit of an individual and did his own thing. I know how people can jump to conclusions too quickly but, as an opposition player at that time, I decided to keep my distance.

When the teams met again later that season I decided it was time to test this kid out. When he came out to bat I stood at the top of my mark and gave him some serious verbals. I wanted to see how he would react, and it was just how I thought he would. When I was coming in to bowl, KP pulled away and, well, it really started then. I gave it to him again verbally and then, second ball, he was out, caught at bat pad. Nothing needed to be said.

At the end of that season we spoke on the phone and, through the chairman of his management company, our friend Ian 'Beefy' Botham, Kevin said he was keen to have a chat about the possibility of leaving Trent Bridge and joining us at Hampshire.

We organised a lunch at a local pub in Southampton and I think we hit it off straight away. KP was an impressive guy. He was confident and knew what he wanted, which I liked straight away. There were a few counties chasing him at the time so we chatted about life, Hampshire and where I thought the club was going. I told Kevin that I thought Hampshire would be a good learning place for him, both on and off the field. I believed his technique would improve playing at the Rose Bowl and he would enjoy himself at the club. We have created a wonderful environment for players to become the best they possibly can and to his credit he decided to take on a contract at Hampshire.

We spoke lots and talked about so much stuff and became very close. I think I understood him, and as his captain I think he enjoyed that and it made a change from where he had come from.

Throughout the 2005 season we talked about the temptations and pitfalls of being successful and how to handle expectations, both his and other people's. There was talk about him being selected for England, and the more I saw KP play the more I thought, wow, this guy could be something special. It is no secret that's how I felt, as I am on record as saying at that time that England would be crazy not to select him.

As a man I think Kevin Pietersen is very loyal and is a kind and generous guy who just wants to be liked and play cricket. He loves the scene of being an international cricketer and the scene suits him. KP, I think, could go down as one of the most talented players ever to play the game. He has everything in his favour. It will be up to him how far he goes and what he wants to achieve. My view is that once he goes through his failure period then this will be the making of KP.

There really has only been one player in the history of the game who has never really failed for any length of time: the one and only Sir Don Bradman. When KP goes through this he will work out how to play different situations, he will work out who his real friends are, and he will remember what his feelings were when everything was going well. This will make him hungry and, as I said, look out when this happens because we will see some very, very special innings.

By the way, we have seen some pretty special ones so far from the big fella! The one at the Oval which secured the Ashes for England should not have happened. If one of his two chances were taken early, especially the catch that yours truly grassed, I think we would have seen a very different outcome to that epic Ashes battle and, quite possibly, to Kevin's life. It's amazing how things happen, and that innings made KP believe that he was good enough at this level. Since then he has got better and better and become one of the most dangerous players in the world.

The Ashes series coming up, as I write, in Australia in the 2006/07 season will be amazing for the players and for the public and media. I think everybody is anticipating another special series but let's hope there is a different result!

The Aussie crowds will give KP massive stick and he will enjoy that. By the end of the series I'm sure KP will have earned the respect of the crowds through the way he plays the game, both with his batting and the spirit he shows. He plays the game in the right spirit and has good sportsmanship, and this will make him popular with everyone.

In finishing I would just like to say that this book will be a very interesting read and I'm sure it will give you a good insight into what makes KP tick. It's my pleasure to write the foreword. Good luck, buddy – except against Australia! I hope this book is a huge success.

Shane Warne, June 2006

When talent announces itself these days we rush to buy tickets for the burn-out. This modern scepticism attached itself to Kevin Pietersen long before his bludgeoning and decisive innings of 158 on the final day of the Ashes 2005.

The genre for Pietersen's rise as cricketer and celebrity is one known to David Beckham, Jenson Button of Formula One and the self-basting Gavin Henson, Welsh rugby's icon for the iPod generation. With all these ubiquitous idols we observe the billboard competing with the scoreboard. It's a truism of modern sport that many young athletes have the party before they have fully done the work. In fact, there are those who worry that sport now exists as a fame academy – a factory for the making of deals – with the game itself an incidental part of the manufacturing process.

Pietersen certainly did the work at the Oval and he sure as hell had the party afterwards. But when Pietersen stopped the victory bus to dive into Starbucks to relieve himself, cynics expected him to come out clutching a deal establishing him as the new face of the caramel macchiato.

He wasted no time affirming his status as cricket's first rock star. 'Get your hair cut, Pietersen!' one MCC member barked as Michael Vaughan's men finally made it back to the Long Room after a long day of handshakes, hangovers and grins. The heckler was expressing the prejudices of those who regarded the lurching hero with suspicion.

The talent is the thing. Always the talent. If the gift is authentic it's easier to ignore the peripheral ringing of tills and vacuous celebrity chatter. On that front, Pietersen struck 473 runs in five Tests against Australia. This after KP – as in 'the nuts' – had recorded an average in 23 one-day internationals of 73.09.

These are the figures of a resoundingly good cricketer. The ICC anointed him both Emerging Player and One-day Player of the Year. His belligerent and fearless innings at the Oval lit the imagination's touch-paper way beyond cricket. His team-mate Ashley Giles observed: 'It was real grandchildren stuff. Gather round and I'll tell you about the innings I played with Pietersen, with the white stripe and the earrings.' In the ensuing tide of English euphoria it was swiftly forgotten that KP had been dropped three times, most calamitously by Shane Warne, his Hampshire colleague and friend. That simple error turned Pietersen into a household name and millionaire. Sport's soundtrack is the music of chance.

The game has never seen anything like this. Pietersen is surely the first man in flannels who chose to be famous. Who set out to be world-renowned, just as Beckham and Henson have in their chosen fields. So now we stand back to find out whether he will be remembered as the cricketer who ate himself or a legend of the willow. Take your eyes off him if you can.

Paul Hayward writing in *Wisden Cricketers' Almanack* 2006 after Kevin Pietersen was named as one of the Five Cricketers of the Year

INTRODUCTION

THE DAY THAT CHANGED MY LIFE

Monday 12 September 2005, The Oval

It has come down to this. All the drama. All the excitement. All the nail-biting tension. All the blood, sweat and tears. From the humiliation of the first Test at Lord's, to the sheer joy of the 'greatest Test of all time' at Edgbaston, the agony of Old Trafford and the exhilaration of Trent Bridge.

Here we are at the Oval, with the nation's eyes upon us, needing to bat through this final day of one of the most epic series of Test cricket of all time. And here I am, Kevin Pietersen, in my first Test series, a South-African born Englishman needing to bat the whole day if England, my country, are going to win the biggest prize in cricket after a wait of 18 years.

It has been quite a journey to reach this stage. I have crossed many boundaries to get here and the ride has been eventful. But how can anything prepare you for this? We are 2–1 up in the series and need only to draw to achieve our holy grail. We score a respectable 373 all out in our first innings at the Oval but see Australia race to 277 for two by the close of the third day. A monumental bowling effort, led by one Andrew Flintoff, sees them bowled out for 367 and now it is up to us, England's batsmen, to complete the job.

The weather had helped us in this match and now we have a dull, but dry, last day. We have lost one wicket, that of Andrew Strauss, overnight and now Michael Vaughan and Marcus Trescothick go out with the whole country watching to take on two of the greatest bowlers of all time, Shane Warne and Glenn McGrath, and their colleagues for the last time in this monumental summer.

There is a stillness in the dressing room as we watch our captain and his deputy make a good, confident, positive start. No alarms. Is it possible we will just calmly bat through to the ultimate prize? After all that has happened this summer? No, it cannot be that simple. At 67 for one the captain, who had looked so good, pushed at McGrath and sees Adam Gilchrist produce a spectacular catch.

Time for me, batting at number five, to get padded up. All we need to do, I keep on telling myself, is bat for 60 or 70 overs. That's all. Then the Ashes would be ours. I calmly put my first pad on but as I reach for my second Ian Bell is dismissed first ball, touching a superb McGrath delivery to Warne at slip. Now I have to rush. I chuck my second pad on, grab my gloves and hurry out to the middle.

We are so close. We know we have done enough, just about, to get home over the course of the summer. We can't throw it away now. I don't have any time to think about my innings or get nervous. The butterflies have been there all morning but, strangely, they ease as I go out to face the hat-trick ball from Glenn McGrath, perhaps the greatest pace bowler of them all.

It's a brute of a delivery. It hits the pitch and homes in on me, like a missile. It strikes me on the shoulder, perilously close to bat and glove, as I attempt to take evasive action. The ball flies to slip and the Aussies, as one, leap up and acclaim the hat-trick, the hat-trick that will win them the Ashes. I know I haven't touched it but my heart is in my mouth. You always know as a batsman if you've hit the ball. But how is the umpire going to react? Thankfully, Billy Bowden is the calmest man in the ground and firmly says not out. Relief. I smile at Glenn and just mouth 'no'. Stay calm. Focus.

Deep breath. Now, in the next over, I'm facing Warne, who has become a close friend and who has had the better, just, of our exchanges this summer on the biggest stage of them all. The ball is angled in around off-stump, I push at it, it turns, takes my edge, takes a slight deflection off Gilchrist's glove and Matt Hayden at slip drops it.

Warne is turning it big time. How to play this genius? Concentrate. Trescothick survives a big lbw appeal. God, it looks close. The nerves have returned. Just keep reminding myself to play for time. It's such a big day. I need a score. I've had a bit of criticism in the build-up to the game, particularly from Geoff Boycott and Mike Gatting, over off-field matters. Basically, they don't seem to like my lifestyle. Don't seem to like the fact that I enjoy myself off the pitch, that I have a sponsorship with a jewellery company, that I have a distinctive hairstyle and wear earrings.

I'm not your conventional cricketer and they don't seem to like that. But times have changed. Cricket is fashionable, after this series, and I am at the forefront of that. It bugs me because no one trains harder or works harder at their game than me. Nothing I do off the field does ever or will ever detract from the way I play cricket. Peripheral matters that bring publicity to this great game are fine as far as I'm concerned, as long as they don't get in the way of the main business. And they don't.

Yet I can't help feeling that I need to contribute today. To silence any doubters. To convince people that I can play this game, that I'm worthy of playing Test cricket for England. This is all whirling around my mind before the most significant moment in my career so far and, it turns out, the most significant moment in the destiny of the Ashes.

There are eight overs to go before lunch when, with me on 15, I drive hard at the extreme pace of Brett Lee and the ball flies to slip at neck height. There stands Shane Warne. It goes straight into his upturned hands and straight out again.

Shane would tell me later that it didn't come to him as quickly as he expected, but it looked pretty quick to me. I nicked it, turned round and he had dropped it. I think it was too quick for him. I can't believe my good fortune.

Then the words of Greg Matthews, former Australian cricketer and friend of mine, come back to me. Greg had rung me a couple of nights before the game and said, 'You're not playing your normal game. Go out there, be positive, be confident, be arrogant, stop messing about!' He pretty much knows my game. Now is the moment to take that on board. It's true. I haven't been playing my normal game. I've been pushing and prodding. And I have been dropped twice.

So I think: to hell with this. I'm going to take the attack to them and play my natural game. Why change now? Remember what got you here in the first place. Don't try to bat out 70 overs by being negative, do it by being positive.

I walk down the wicket to Marcus and tell him, 'I'm just going to whack it now.'

I notice that, for the first time in three Tests, Shane did not have a cow corner in place for me in the field. We had joked about it before the match. He said, 'Why are you not taking me on?' and I replied, 'Bring your cow corner up and I will hit you.' He has. So I hit him for two sixes and the complexity of the situation changes. I find myself feeling more focused. I have no particular plans for individual bowlers. I just like to keep things simple. Watch the ball. The most basic truism in the game but it's amazing how easy it is to forget it. Just watch the ball. Play the situation. And the situation now is telling me to be positive.

But a big setback is just around the corner. Trescothick falls to Warne. Shane is turning it and turning it large. It is his 168th wicket against England, beating Dennis Lillee's record, and no man deserves it more. Freddie Flintoff emerges. Ever since my arrival as an England cricketer people have been talking about the bar-emptying prospect of Flintoff and Pietersen batting together. Fred has had an heroic summer, become a national hero. Our partnerships have been reasonably brief up to now but, on this occasion, no spectator needs any incentive to stay glued to his seat. There is so much at stake.

Fred and I tell each other to play our normal games but we both know it is an abnormal situation. Then, all too soon, Fred is deceived by Warne and he's out, just before lunch. It is a huge blow. The Test, and the Ashes, are in the balance again. Brett Lee comes back. He is a rapid bowler at the best of times but now he bowls me what I consider to be the fastest over I've ever faced. Two key men have gone just before lunch and I can't afford to join them in the dressing room. Brett hits me. I call for treatment from the physio, Kirk Russell. Perhaps I'm being a bit of a drama queen but I need to get us off the field, need to stop Shane bowling another over at new batsman Paul Collingwood before we have the chance to get in the dressing room and regroup.

This is do-or-die cricket. Win the Ashes or lose the Ashes. It's always in the back of my mind. What I do here can win or lose the Ashes. We manage to get through to lunch, at the hardly safe position of 127 for five, still only 133 ahead. Not nearly enough. Michael Vaughan remains calm in the dressing room. He tells us to bat the next session and we'll be OK. Easier said than done. I spend much of the interval receiving treatment for the back injury I've been feeling all summer. Brett hit me in the ribs so I have them taped up and get ready to go back on. No time for any food. I try to play things down. Try to relax. Try not to get too wound up about the importance of the next couple of hours. I know the next session will decide the summer, the Ashes and, in all probability, change my life. But I can't think of that now.

Brett is seriously quick again after lunch but I know I must still be positive. No pushing and prodding now. I think to myself: if I can get any bat on these short balls, with these short boundaries, they are going to go for six. If I top edge Lee it will go for six and if I hit it properly it will go for six. I'm not thinking about getting out at all. No negative thoughts. But I also know that if Colly or I get out it's trouble. We are not far enough ahead. We need to keep on hammering nails in the Aussie coffin with each boundary we hit.

Brett bowls faster and faster. Anyone who says they enjoy facing fast bowling is a liar. I hit him for two sixes. He hits me on the body three times. Colly later says that my eyes have gone but he tells me to keep on going. There is no point reining in now. This is high-risk cricket but it is working in our favour. I give a half chance to Shaun Tait diving on the boundary but it would have been the catch of the century if he had taken it.

Then comes a shot that people were later to pick out as perhaps the shot of my innings. Brett bowls fast, just outside off-stump, it is not quite short enough to pull so I somehow flat bat straight past the bowler, like a rocket, for a straight boundary. I have no idea how I play it. It is pure instinct. By this time I'm in a zone, a boundary zone, and it feels good. I'm hardly saying a word to Collingwood. I'm just so focused and really and truly don't know what I'm doing now. Nothing is planned. Nothing is premeditated.

Now another significant moment. Shane is bowling round the wicket to me. This means I've won a huge psychological battle as far as I'm concerned. On day five of a Test match, with the ball turning, the greatest spin bowler in the history of the game is resorting to negative tactics. Because I don't think Shane Warne can dismiss me bowling round the wicket. For him to bowl me round my legs would take the most monumental delivery or a huge error of judgement from me. I think about the angles and the degrees of spin, and I don't think he can get me this way. I know he has got people out like this, but not me. I'm sure of it.

Mind you, I do play a stupid sweep, which I seem to hit straight onto my boot and it balloons up and is easily caught. It's a heart-stopping moment. Because I know if it is referred to the third umpire I might be in trouble. Rudi Koertzen, the umpire, walks over to square leg to consult with Billy Bowden. Warne says to me, 'Let's get it referred and get the right decision.' I tell him to do what he wants.

This time I knew I might genuinely be out but Billy is insistent the ball has hit the ground rather than my boot and we play on with no call to the third umpire. I'm not sure how he can be so sure from square leg but thank goodness he made that decision. I tell myself off. Don't ruin it now. Shane is coming round the wicket. Don't throw it away. I've got this far. See it through.

Colly is out, at 186 for six, and then Shaun Tait knocks over Geraint Jones. Tea is approaching, we are now 200 ahead, but there are still more than 50 overs to go. Enough time for Australia to win this match. Now, however, comes the arrival of George Clooney!

Ashley Giles has become my biggest mate in the England team, going back to my first short tour of Zimbabwe when we were designated official 'buddies'. This is the day, the partnership, when I nickname him George. I think he looks like the American actor. The grey hair has been getting more noticeable as the summer wears on. Maybe the name is flattering to him. But it sticks.

Now we back each other in the most important partnership either of us will ever feature in. 'Shot, George,' I say each time he defies the Aussies. We speak to each other after every single ball. Gilo has had a rollercoaster summer. Criticised heavily after Lord's, he has hit back to play a huge part in our success, notable when scoring the winning runs at Trent Bridge. But nothing can compare to this.

Tait has some pace about him but he bowls a lot of four balls and I see this as an opportunity to score runs. I'm still in boundary mode. Thank God I'm not sitting in the dressing room watching this. I would have been an absolute bundle of nerves. While I'm batting I always feel in control. When I'm in the dressing room I feel completely helpless. It's a case now of hitting Tait's bad balls for four and getting that total up beyond Australia's reach. No way are we going to declare. Not today. We are not even going to leave them 300 in 10 overs.

I'm quickly through the nineties. Then the big moment arrives. I cover drive Tait for four. It's my first Test hundred. Pandemonium. That's a heck of a release of pressure. What a time to get it. I signal to the dressing room. Then I point my bat to my mum, Penny, and my younger brother Bryan on the families' balcony. I know where they are and locate them in an instant. I celebrate, the noise is enormous, but I know the game isn't safe yet.

I embrace Gilo and he tells me, over and over, 'The job isn't done, the job isn't done.' But now we are counting down every over. At the start of each one we say to each other, 'Let's talk again in six balls' time. Make sure you are here.' Ash is a cool dude. He's batting fantastically well. This is turning into one of the best days of my life. Playing the sport I love, millions of people watching, so much at stake. As you're growing up you want to score Test hundreds. This is what it's all about, what all the dreams have been about, the sacrifices and the huge decisions in my life to get this far.

But stop thinking about that. Shane Warne is now coming over the wicket again and I edge a couple of balls to short third man so he brings in a second slip. I have to get rid of him and I do so by attacking Shane again. I keep on expressing myself. When it gets to 35 overs left we think we are nearly there. Shane is real tired now. I get to 150, signal to Mum and Bryan again, and the match, dare I believe it, is safe.

They take the new ball and Glenn bowls me a pretty good pill, which he probably wishes he'd bowled me a few hours earlier. I'm out. It's over. I just smile at him, say, 'Good ball,' and start to walk off. Shane runs after me, catches me up and says, 'Savour this moment.' What a gesture. It sums up the spirit this series has been played in.

I wish I could live this moment again, over and over, every day. I do savour it. The crowd are going nuts. I can hardly hear myself think. Lots of screaming and shouting. I'm just trying to take it all in. My body is so pumped but I feel drained. It is two or three minutes of 'I just don't know what's happening to me here'. It's like an out-of-body experience. It's special. The public are amazing.

I get to the dressing room where I'm hugged and kissed and hugged and kissed again. I make sure I get myself changed real quick because I know Ashley is close to 50 and I want to be on the balcony for him when he gets there. I am just as happy, even more happy, for him than I am for myself. When he's out he gets the biggest hug from me because I know how big our partnership was. More importantly, we know now that the Ashes are ours.

We are all out for 335 and there is barely any time left. Along with everybody I clap Warney off the field. He's had such a fantastic series and this is probably the last time he'll play in an Ashes series in England. We take to the field, briefly, and Vaughan tells us to all wear our England caps and enjoy every second we are on the field. We are off for light but we know it is all over. The umpires want to remove the bails ceremonially and it is confirmed. We have done it.

I'm man of the match for the first time in a Test match but we have all done this together. An individual has always put up his hand when it has been needed this summer. It has been an amazing day, an amazing summer and everyone has put in the hard yards to get us to where we are now.

My innings has been called the most significant by an England player in a Test. How does that make me feel? Immensely proud. It's a massive honour for people to say that. But it's also like, please let's get this into proportion. I haven't been around very long and I want to savour a few more days like this. It is one day in my life and I want to be gracious and humble about it. I want to play for England for another ten years and have plenty of good days.

In all I have faced 187 balls for my 158, hitting over a century in boundaries (seven sixes and 15 fours) and by the end was on my third Woodworm Torch bat, having broken two in the process of the innings. Is it the best I've ever batted? No, because I gave three chances but, at times, when I was positive against Warne and positive against Lee, it was as good as I have ever felt with a cricket bat in my hands. Let's just say I'll take that innings any day! We soak it all in. Enjoy the adulation of the crowd. And it dawns on me that this has been a life-changing day. Things may never be quite the same again.

Throughout this book I am going to invite those closest to me, those who know me best and those who know cricket best to share their memories of our time together and their opinions of me. Who better to start than the man I call George Clooney? The man who shared that decisive partnership with me at the Oval. Step up, Ashley Giles.

Ashley Giles: *My mind was still open – that's the way I like to be with everyone – the day I met Kevin Pietersen. We, in the England dressing room, had heard a lot about him, much of it negative, but I wanted to make my own mind up. Some had said he was a destructive influence, others that he wasn't a team man. I think it's fair to say that a lot of us in the England dressing room were ready for him. We thought, if he wants to be big time around us then he's in for a shock.*

Also, when someone comes from another country and plays for England I think it's inevitable that you wonder about their commitment.

But I found him to be completely different to what I had been expecting. The exact opposite. Kevin was great in the dressing room, he was a team player and he was a great influence on those around him. Also, he played with such passion and determination that no one could be left in any doubt as to how much it means to him to play for England. I was pleasantly surprised, to say the least!

I first saw him bat at close quarters in Zimbabwe and everybody thought he looked like a class act straight away.

The cleanliness with which he hit the ball was what stood out. Just as importantly, he became a good friend of mine from the start.

Kevin is a bit different, certainly. He has a huge desire for success and will not let anything get in the way of that. He sees what he wants to achieve and where he wants to go. Nothing is going to stop him.

In county cricket you can get dragged down by those who are jealous and those who say things like, 'What gives you the right to act like that and say things like that?' Kevin can put some noses out of joint, people who have been around a long time and maybe don't share his depth of ambition, but in the England dressing room we all want to be the best we possibly can and he fitted in with us straight away.

Good for Duncan Fletcher and Michael Vaughan. They saw this guy and realised he could add something to our team while some might have been suspicious of him. He added something to our team that we just didn't have to the point where people were saying, 'Where has this guy been?' I had heard that he could hit the ball even cleaner than Andrew Flintoff and my reaction to that was: 'Bollocks. That's a huge thing to say.' Then after Kevin had played in those spectacular one-day internationals in South Africa I was saying the same thing myself! I couldn't believe how hard he could hit the ball.

Underneath the bravado and bullshit of Kevin Pietersen there is a very professional cricketer who works hard and has a huge desire to succeed. He hides that intensity very well. He can be as fragile and insecure as the rest of us deep down, perhaps even more than the rest of us, but he loves being in the limelight and I'm afraid there are a lot of people in the media who don't like that.

Fact is, if KP ever slips up slightly there are people who will point the finger at his lifestyle but he's got to take that and take the rough with the smooth. I think he can handle that.

Our partnership at the Oval was special. He helped me through those three hours in a way I will never forget and the memories will last for ever. 'Come on, George,' he kept on saying. When Brett Lee came back all I could think about was surviving with my life intact but Kev was flat-batting deliveries around 96mph past Lee and straight to the boundary like a rocket. I was just standing at the other end in awe, saying to myself: how does he do that? Kev made it look so simple but being at the other end when he played that innings will stay with me for ever.

I started the George Clooney thing in the dressing room. I started noticing more and more grey in my hair but I announced to everybody, 'I'm not going to colour it. I'm going to go natural and have a new look, the Clooney look.' So I left myself open to banter and Kevin seized on that. He still calls me George now.

The world is Kevin's oyster. Because of the way he plays there will always be people who want to criticise him if gets out to an attacking shot but it's playing in an extravagant way that has got him to where he is now. As he matures he may curb his natural game a little. He may become a little bit more like a mere mortal as he develops but I don't think he should or will change too much.

Kevin Pietersen is the man who took on the Aussies and won us the Ashes. That's good enough for me, hairstyles, jewellery and all.

1

WHO'S WATCHING ME?

'I asked Kevin, after a purple patch, what he thought about when the bowler was running in. He just looked at me with a wry grin and said, "I feel sorry for the bowler."'

Adam Wheatley, Kevin Pietersen's agent

I have since realised beyond all doubt that my innings at the Oval and the aftermath of England winning the Ashes has changed my life forever. I'm glad I didn't realise quite how much things would change at the time because it would probably have freaked me out and stopped me performing the way I did.

My life has changed in so many ways, the majority of them good but also in some ways not so good. The scrutiny is the biggest thing. Yes, I am a sociable person and yes I like going out, meeting people and having a good time, but I have discovered that that can be a double-edged sword.

There is a lot more media interest in the things I do now. When you're 'on duty' that is pretty easy to deal with, but when you are walking out with your girlfriend, going clothes shopping or even having your hair cut, it can be a bit intrusive. I try as much as possible to behave in a way that is acceptable for a professional sportsman but I am still young and sometimes make mistakes. A lot has changed for me since that day at the Oval but I still love going out and having fun. What I do know now is that if I do anything really silly there is a good chance it will appear in the paper the next day.

We were successful in the summer of 2005 and I was successful at my job. I take it as a massive compliment that people are interested in me, and as a positive confidence booster that people want to know me and want to talk to me. Essentially, being in the public eye is fun and I would rather things be this way than just be a county cricketer who is never noticed and who doesn't know what to do with his life every winter.

I'm a hyperactive person. I can't sit still for two minutes so I definitely have no intention of changing my life and staying in more because of the additional scrutiny. Yet, every time I go out now, I find myself asking who's watching me, and there's no doubt that some people can be intrusive and can cause problems for you in the street or in a club with their attitude towards you.

I do know I must always be on my best behaviour and endeavour never to be rude or unpleasant to anyone, even if they are not particularly nice to me. That can be difficult after the end of a hard day's play or a poor performance but I think I do a pretty good job generally. The importance of good manners is something my parents always instilled in me anyway, but it is particularly relevant when you are in the public eye. If you are rude to just one person, that is the impression they will always have of Kevin Pietersen, even if they have just happened to catch you at a bad moment or haven't respected your privacy.

Before my life changed in 2005 I could relax a little more and behave like a normal young person. During the course of that momentous summer I had some unpleasant things written about me and was the victim of a couple of kiss-and-tells in the papers, and it made me have a long hard think about my personal life.

The worst thing about it all is that so many lies get written and you don't appear to be able to do anything about it. On one occasion a girl sold 'her story' about me when we had never even been out as a couple. I was staggered how such blatant inaccuracies could be taken at face value without any checks being made by the newspaper concerned.

That sort of thing is definitely the worst aspect of fame, but it can be funny, too. On a couple of occasions during Test matches

I've got up on a Sunday, seen a pack of lies written about my love life in a paper and then arrived at the England dressing room to be greeted by the whole team taking the mickey out of me. I can see how that's funny and I'd almost certainly join in with the joke if it wasn't at my expense, but the fact is, it's your name, your reputation and your family that gets affected by these sorts of things. Some of the things I'm supposed to have done make quite bizarre reading and I have no respect at all for the type of girls who fabricate these articles, often on the back of a brief meeting in a bar or club somewhere.

That's why I'm a lot more careful now with the girls I meet and the things I do and I was extremely fortunate, towards the end of 2005, to meet a very special girl who has added a new dimension to my life. Her name is Jessica Taylor and you will be hearing a lot more about her later in the book. I arrived on the England cricket scene as, I guess, a flamboyant, larger-than-life character who is something of an extrovert with a penchant for jewellery and different hairstyles. That won't change, I see no reason why it should, but I have come to the slightly sad conclusion that the only people I can really trust are my family and very close friends. Now, I am happy to say, I can include Jess on that list.

You find yourself analysing everyone you meet, asking yourself if they can be trusted or in what way they might come back to haunt you if you are not ultra-careful in what you say to them. Don't get me wrong. I'm not going to stop going out, but you won't see me pictured leaving a club with a girl now, unless it's Jess. She is someone I can trust and who I want to be with.

What do I make of being a recognisable face? You become one because you are successful. It goes with the territory. So, in that way, it is a positive thing and there is nothing you can really do about that.

There are of course huge benefits to success, like being very well looked after in restaurants and not having to queue as much as I did before, and people generally go out of their way to help me. I'm still not used to people staring at me as it can be very disconcerting sometimes. In the team hotel in India, I was talking to my agent, Adam in reception when three Indian fans just walked up to us and stood 1 yard from me and stared at me without saying anything. We both burst out laughing as it looked totally bizarre. It's not quite that bad in England!

Commercially my image has been enhanced 100 per cent and I find myself sitting down a lot with my agent Adam Wheatley to decide which of the offers I receive fit my personality and are right for me. We tried to build up an image that suited me when I first started out and I'm pretty happy with the way it has worked out.

Since the Oval Adam has been even busier than me because he takes all the phone calls. His life has changed quite a bit too. Yes, this is the man who is in charge of Ian Botham's commercial dealings so he is used to being busy, but my dealings have gone through the roof in recent times. Before I played for England Adam would ring people, trying to launch me, saying, 'Would you be interested in Kevin Pietersen?'

But during the Ashes people started ringing Adam and it has moved on from there. Now he will ring me and ask if I'm interested in going on this TV show or in doing this deal and it's amazing how, in two years, Adam has gone from trying to get people interested in me to turning loads of stuff away.

I'm careful over what I choose. We've turned down a lot. Cricket is what I do. All these other things are fun but I don't want anything to interfere with my cricket or my training. I want my commercial life to be as little, but also as much, as possible, if you see what I mean. A case of maximising the amount of time I have at my disposal. We are working with some really good partners and there are more in the pipeline. I have chosen Barnardo's as my charity because I have a particular affinity with kids. One of my more pleasing and fulfilling extra-curricular activities came at the start of the 2006 season when I was chosen as the face of the npower Urban Cricket scheme, which is aimed at getting kids from poor areas interested in the game and playing it on the streets and in the parks. That's a wonderful campaign – I just had to listen to how many more young people are said to be interested in cricket now after the Ashes to want to get involved in that one. I launched the campaign in Peckham and took Jess, who is a member of the Liberty X pop group, along for our first public appearance together. It was an excellent day and just the sort of thing I like to get involved in. I am busy away from cricket but it's manageable. None of these take up too much of my time.

I wouldn't say I'm set up financially for life yet but the Ashes have definitely helped, which is good because I like spending money! I particularly like spending money on clothes and I will have the odd spending spree and splash out a grand or two, but even now the atti-tude towards money that was instilled in me by my parents is still there. Don't waste it and don't buy things you don't need.

I do hope my cricket will set me up for life financially. I've been looking into a few investment opportunities and I'm hoping to get involved in the property market, stuff like that. I'd also like to learn how to fly. I'm not stupid with my money but I do like to enjoy myself. I'm 26 years old! I like to buy the clothes I like. That doesn't always mean the most fashionable clothes, or the most expensive, but ones I feel look good on me. 7/2069141

And, as I say, the richer and better known you are the more money seems to come your way. Sometimes when I shop and buy brands I like, they look after me well, so that can be a huge saving.

I play cricket because I love it. It's my passion and my hobby and I'm lucky enough to have it as my career. Financial benefits come along when you are successful at your career and I will never forget that. The moment I stop achieving on the cricket field will be the moment the lifestyle changes for the worst and all my commercial and leisure activities are geared with that very much in mind.

I have received attention for the women in my life but I feel I am just a normal bloke with a normal attitude towards girls. I am who I am, I find it easy to talk to people and if women like me that's great. If they don't, it's not a problem. I like to have fun. I like to enjoy myself and I like to hear people laughing.

I'm a confident bloke and I have always been that way with girls but, as I said before, I am a little more wary about their motives than I was in the past. People might have got the wrong impression about me and girls. I have always wanted to settle down with the right girl and wanted to be a one-woman man. I very much wanted to meet the right girl – and now I think I have done in Jess. I think she's the one I'll spend the rest of my life with.

My friends and colleagues in the England team always reckoned that when I fell in love I would quickly get married, that I'm the sort of bloke who will fall head over heels and everything will move along within six months. I told Jess about that soon after we fell in love and we laugh about it. We'll see about marriage, but I do want to get married and I do want to have a family. I love kids. What's more, I only want to get married once. I want it to be right. To last forever. My parents have been married for 35 years and I want to be like them.

I knew there was a girl out there I would spend the rest of my life with, and I knew that one day I would meet her. I just didn't know it would happen so quickly. I wasn't in any rush but Jess came into my life and changed everything. Before her the most serious relationship I'd had was with an Australian girl called Cate. She's a great girl I was close to a few years ago. It was just unfortunate that her family were in Australia and, with me spending so much time away as a cricketer, we drifted apart. It became difficult for Cate being in England with her family so far away and me invariably not at home. At the time I thought she might be the one, but then again I never go into a relationship unless I feel there's a decent chance of it developing into something long-term. You win some, you lose some, and we split up at the end of 2004 but we remain on good terms.

Let's see what happens next for Jess and me. My life has changed immeasurably since that eventful day at the Oval so let's wait and see what the next chapter holds for Kevin Pietersen!

Adam Wheatley is a very important guy in my life. He is a former Army pilot who flew the great Ian Botham and then went into business with him. He has been my agent and friend since I first came to England to play and has been massively important to me. Let's hear what he has to say.

Adam Wheatley: *I am now the Managing Director of Mission Sports Management and I first met Kevin in Sydney when he was there playing grade cricket and I was there with Ian Botham filming a Shredded Wheat commercial. Ian and I had set up a management company and we heard all about this young lad who was making quite an impact at Notts.*

It struck me that he was raw and in need of a bit of guidance but it was difficult getting anyone interested in

*him at first because all they saw was a young county crick-
eter. It was clear that he could play, had a bit of presence,
something of an aura and quite possibly had a bit of x
factor about him, but most of the people I approached
wanted to see more than that before they got involved with
him. It was hard work for me then but not now. Now
people who turned me down three years ago say, 'What an
opportunity we missed!'*

*The one-day tour of South Africa was huge for Kevin.
You just can't begin to imagine what it was like for him
out there unless you were there. Some of the abuse I heard
him get at grounds there was pretty sick and very personal
so I can't imagine what it must have been like for Kevin
and his family. God knows how he held it all together. I
sat with his father when he hit that sensational century,
we played every ball together. To come out of that with
the figures he put on the board was amazing and it made
me realise I had someone special under my wing. The flair,
confidence, bottle and pure talent he displayed in South
Africa in the face of extreme adversity made me think this
kid is special.*

*For the start of his innings at Centurion Park I was in
a box owned by the South African equivalent of BT, being
lectured by a South African on what a bad move Kevin had
made, and where and how he should be playing his cricket.
All I could hear outside was huge applause and see the ball
flying everywhere. I cut him off mid sentence, mid lecture,
and said "sorry mate I've got to go and watch this." Kevin
was making his third Century of the series, and at the end
of the game the crowd gave him a standing ovation. He
thoroughly deserved it.*

I don't think Kevin realised how huge his innings at the Oval against Australia was until some greats of the game started calling it one of the best innings of all time. My phone hasn't stopped ringing since then with all sorts of offers and my job instantly became much more hectic but also very satisfying. I remember the day after the Oval innings Kevin's picture was on either the front or back page of every paper in the country and I was able to ring some serious people who I wanted to get Kevin involved and say to them, 'What paper have you got in front of you? Take a look at it. That's my client all over it!' That's what you dream of.

Cricketers have a short lifespan at the top and there can be a tendency to run at everything and take what's offered. But Kevin and I made sure we sat down after the Oval and decided we had to do things the right way with the right brands. The attention has been a real eye-opener for Kevin but he has got better and better at dealing with it every day.

There have been a lot of people who have criticised Kevin's lifestyle or criticised him for some of the things he has done but all I would say to them is that that criticism will only be justified if ever any commercial activity or his lifestyle affects his game and that certainly hasn't been the case up to now. Kevin is an outgoing guy. That's him. That's his character. We need people like that in sport. If the way he lives his life has a positive effect on both his own game and the publicity cricket receives then it can only be a good thing. Kevin knows exactly what got him to where he is now. Hard work. And he won't forget that. Yes, he will enjoy himself, and why not? But he knows that cricket is what he does and what has got him everything and cricket will always come first.

We are working with some great companies now and Kevin chose Barnardo's as his charity just before the innings at the Oval. It's fascinating to see him with children. In many ways he's more comfortable and at ease with them than he is with adults. I guess children know what they like, what they want, and say what they are thinking. Children want role models and heroes, and aren't interested in knocking them down.

Even though there are a lot of things happening in his life all Kevin's attention is on cricket now. I certainly won't cram up his diary. There has been the occasional rain check, like the night before his 158 at the Oval. I was a little concerned that Kevin didn't really seem to be nervous at all. Going into a game of this magnitude, particularly how the game was poised, to potentially win the Ashes was huge, and while to the outside world it was important to create that air of calm, he was giving me the distinct impression that this was just another innings. That is exactly how he approached that now famous final-day 158. I sat down with him for a brief moment in the England team hotel reception and made it pretty clear how important tomorrow could be. As he started to walk off, I remember thinking to myself: I don't think much of that went in! He was so relaxed. I shook his hand and said, 'Make history.' He smiled back at me and said, 'Cool, china.' As it transpired I had nothing to worry about.

What sort of guy is Kevin? You get everything with him. I see a very generous, respectful side to him. There is also a lot of humility, which perhaps some people haven't had a chance to see yet. There is a lot of confidence, which some people see as arrogance, but I think you need both to perform on the stage he does. Behind the cocky, cheeky aura, there is a very warm, fun-loving guy. He is totally confident in backing his own ability and, to be fair, it hasn't let him down yet. I asked him recently, after a purple patch with two very good centuries, what he thought about when the bowler was running in. He just looked at me with a wry grin and said, 'I feel sorry for the bowler!'

He has learned a lot about certain people who wanted to be associated with him and has closed ranks a little and got a bit wiser about some people's intentions, which is something he had to learn in his own time. I have a clear idea of where we want to go with Kevin and it is all based on performances on the pitch. There are some busy and frenetic times ahead and I don't want to distract him from the most important thing. The cricket. What happened at the Oval was sensational but the show goes on. It is only the start.

2

THE EARLY YEARS

'I could be a real stroppy kid,
but above all I was a bad loser.'

Kevin Pietersen

The early chapters of my life revolve around a very close family. I had a religious upbringing, and mine was a family where we backed each other up in whatever we did. It was a fantastic childhood. Mum and Dad supported us in everything. They had four boys and on any given weekend those four boys would be playing different sports at different venues and Mum and Dad would go to superhuman lengths to avoid missing any game. They would separate and Mum, for instance, would watch me while Dad would watch Bryan or Tony in their respective games, and they would switch at half time, or whatever break that particular sport had.

We would go to watch each other too. Sport was always in the family. Mum and Dad were sporty, energetic people. My dad, Jannie, played a lot of squash and first-division rugby in South Africa, while my mum, Penny, loves to exercise and played a good level of squash in Pietermaritzburg, our home town.

We are a healthy family, very health conscious, and the weather in South Africa where I grew up was a big factor in that. We were outdoors all the time. I definitely went to school mainly for my sport! I was pretty good academically and got three A levels but sport was the be all and end all as far as I was concerned. It was the same with all the boys in a sports-mad country.

There was support for all of us within our family but when we played against each other we tried to kill one another! That's where my competitiveness comes from. Everything we did was a competition. We couldn't even have a swim in the back garden without it turning into a major race. We were lucky enough to have a pretty big pool in the back garden and it was like an Olympic arena when the Pietersen boys got in there.

My brother Gregg would say to me, before we went to bed: 'We're up at 6.45 a.m. tomorrow. Let's get to the pool and race straight away. We're not even having a warm-up first.' It would be 'race you over two lengths' then three lengths or whatever. Then it would be who can do the most lengths underwater and stuff like that. We staged little triathlons and planned our routes round our neighbourhood. We would swim a certain amount of lengths, then run round a certain course and back, and then go out on our bikes.

It was just the way we were brought up. Mum and Dad encouraged the outdoor life and we were also fortunate to live in an area of green belt. We'd run and walk in the forest. Dad would be very competitive and made sure we all were, too, while Mum was a little bit more like, 'Don't let them do that to each other.' Dad wouldn't listen to that type of talk. He would encourage each of us to nail our brothers. He wanted us to play hard and to play to win.

We played all sorts of sports; which ones we played were determined by the seasons. We had four school terms in South Africa, and in the two summer ones we'd play cricket, in one other we'd play rugby and in the fourth we'd take part in athletics. That was the way it was for the whole of my sporting life and it would be the same when we had a big sporting event on.

When we had the Rugby World Cup in South Africa in 1995 we all played rugby and I distinctly remember I would support England while Bryan would be rooting for South Africa. I just liked England from a young age, particularly when the Rugby World Cup was in South Africa. You could buy these Coca-Cola tins that gave away team badges and I made sure I got the England one. I also bought an England rugby jersey and declared my hero to be Rob Andrew.

The last week of June and first week of July always turned us brothers into tennis players because that's when Wimbledon was on. We'd draw a tennis court in the garden and go and play tennis. We'd have a go at everything.

All the members of the family were very committed to each other. Dad always had a good job and worked very hard. I think he is one of those blokes who will never really retire. He just works and works and works. He is one of the directors of a civil engineering firm in Durban now and has been doing that for a good ten or 12 years. He will go to the office all day and then when he gets home he will go and work in the garden, then wash the car. He can't just sit down and watch television or anything like that. He has to be on the go. That must be where I get it from! When 8 p.m. comes along and Dad finally sits down he will go straight to sleep where he is because he has worked so hard all day.

Dad worked in Pietermaritzburg until I was about seven, then started working in Durban and commuted an hour there and back every day. Eventually we moved to Durban, but Mum, Bryan and I, the two youngest brothers, commuted the other way to Maritzburg so we were able to stay in the same school.

We had a comfortable life because of Dad's hard work but he also had a saying, 'Buy what you need, not what you want.' That's how he brought us up. So I never had anything fall at my feet. I was never spoilt. Money was never wasted and we had to work hard for everything we had, so I think that's why I have always appreciated what I had. Also, I think Dad's attitude produced something in me that makes me relish hard work too and love achieving success. I've never been given anything without having to work for it.

I thank Mum and Dad for that. Some people go through life being given everything and they can then emerge as nasty people. When they then fail at anything they don't know what to do or how to cope. I've been lucky that when I've bumped my head on certain occasions I've learnt from it. Life's not easy and you have to go through hardships at times to appreciate what you do have.

At school, everybody wore Nike trainers and when the football season came round everybody wore Patrick boots, but Mum and Dad didn't see the point of buying us the best stuff. We always had boots and trainers but never the most expensive ones. Dad said, 'You don't need to have the best. The ones I can get you do the same job.'

I can understand his point of view now but it upset me at the time. We asked again and again if we could have the best ones, the cool ones, the ones that all the kids were wearing, because things like that are important to kids, but we realised that we were banging our heads against a brick wall because Mum and Dad would never relent.

Dad was very strict. He had a cane, called an army stick. If we ever messed up or did anything wrong at school, then Dad would discipline us at home with that. It was allowed in South Africa. I would be caned for something at school and then come home to be caned by Dad too, but I can honestly say it didn't do me any harm. It grounded me and my brothers well.

We respected Dad for that. Maybe not at the time but certainly now. I respect Dad for the way he disciplined us and I think caning should still be allowed now. You should discipline kids because they get away with a lot more than they should do. I bunked off a school lesson once and got disciplined at school. Then, when I went for a bath at home, Mum noticed some marks on my backside and I told her I'd got them because I had bunked off to watch international cricket on the telly. It was the World Cup, I think, and we had all done it, all gone off to watch a big game. When Dad found out he wasn't happy at all and caned me, on top of the discipline I'd already received at school.

Dad was strict but nothing was malicious and nothing was harmful. It was all beneficial and, as I would learn, would help us in the long run. As a kid I couldn't understand Dad's methods though. When I was hit I thought it was wrong, and when I was told I couldn't have an extra sweet I didn't understand why. Yet as I got older I realised they were right.

I could be a real stroppy kid but above all I was a bad loser. I hated losing. I would break tennis and squash rackets when I lost a match against one of my brothers, and I regularly ended up having fights with my brothers when one of them had scored a try against me in rugby, or scored a goal against me playing football. We were all like that, especially when we were playing against each other.

When I was young I wasn't really a fan of the England cricket team in the way I was a fan of the England rugby team. South African cricketers Hansie Cronje and Allan Donald were my heroes. So I supported them and South Africa.

Dad is an Afrikaner and Mum is English, from Canterbury. Mum's dad was a coal miner who went to work in the mines in South Africa; she was 18 when she came out. She met Jannie while he was in the army in Pretoria doing his national service, which, thank goodness, I missed out on because it had been abolished by the time I was old enough.

While my immediate family is very close knit, we didn't see too much of my extended family, which is the only slightly disappointing aspect of my childhood. We were the only religious people in our family so maybe that was part of the reason. We didn't gel with the others because we didn't have too much in common, although I did see plenty of my grandparents.

At home Dad designated Wednesday as the day we would all speak Afrikaans, which Mum struggled with at first but learned to understand and now she can speak it. It was our second language at school and Dad felt that if we spoke it at home it would help with our schoolwork. It must have helped because I got a good grade in Afrikaans.

We were an English-speaking family, apart from Wednesdays, and we used to tease Mum about her English accent. Living with Dad, that accent changed as the years went by and, while we all felt a bit sorry for Mum having to cope with five men in the house, she is a pretty tough character. They have always had a strong marriage. I've never seen them have an up and down time. Maybe they didn't show it to us, but I have never seen Mum and Dad upset or annoyed with each other. They are really, really close, and that's the sort of marriage I want one day.

My oldest brother, Tony, is married to Penny, with two children, Michaela and Chelsea. My second oldest brother Gregg is married to Nicky and is starting a family, and then comes me and my younger brother Bryan.

Tony is a minister now and runs his own church just outside Durban, while Gregg manages an import and export company and travels all round the world. Bryan? He's a socialite! Bryan used to run a bar in Nottingham but he has now moved down to Southampton. He is the brother I'm closest to in age and see most of.

I don't speak to my other two brothers as often as I should but we are all still close. I know you should make time for family, and I speak to Mum and Dad all the time, but I am just so busy, particularly now. My brothers have their own lives but it was lovely to all be together for Christmas, for the first time since we were children, in South Africa in 2005.

You might have a stereotypical idea in your head about what

a church minister is like, but Tony is very like me. He is certainly not a quiet and studious person, he just has very strongly held beliefs. He's an outgoing character, is successful and loves what he's doing. Gregg always used to say he was going to be a millionaire and he has become very successful. Like Dad, he works all hours, and I'm delighted he has done so well, as he is for me.

South Africa is a very religious country. Christianity is widespread and most people go to church on Sundays. We would go to church on Sunday mornings and Sunday nights, where we would meet up with our best friends, the Cole Edwards family. Their son Jonathan was my age and their son Greg was Bryan's age, so we would look forward to church because it meant we could play sport with them. Their dad, Warwick, was the minister of our church. It meant church was fun. It was cool. When we arrived at church on Sunday mornings we would all discuss what sport we had played on the Saturday. We all compared notes as to how we had got on. We also played soccer with the Cole Edwards family for a team called the Savages, which, despite the rather aggressive-sounding name, was a pretty good team, at least by South African standards.

I didn't truly know the meaning of religion at this time – to me, church was fun. Church meant mixing with friends and it meant begging Mum and Dad for us to be allowed to go to church early because we could then play a game of football with the Cole Edwards family beforehand. Then home for a Sunday roast and back to church in the evening. They were good times. A very happy and settled childhood.

My parents are the two most important people in my life. They have made me the person I am. They have shaped everything in my life. We have always been very close and remain so to this day. Let's hear what they have to say about me.

Jannie Pietersen: *I have extremely happy memories of bringing up the boys. I gave 100 per cent of the time I had available to them and what a wonderful time we had. They just grew up so fast!*

You could give Kevin the biggest present in the world on his birthday but it wouldn't have the same impact as giving him a ball. When he was young I used to play squash and Kevin would sit watching me with my sweatband around his head, my wristbands on and hitting a squash ball against the wall. He had amazing hand-eye co-ordination for one so young. I just spent my weekends having every sort of ball thrown at me!

Ours was a very happy family and for a while our lives revolved round the boys' sport. I remember clearly one weekend flying to Johannesburg to watch Gregg swim and then flying down to Port Elizabeth to watch Bryan swim in different championships. Meanwhile, Penny stayed behind to watch Kevin and Tony in what they were doing. It was very important to the boys for us to be there and that sort of weekend was typical for us.

One of my principles was that the boys should try to win. They had to work extremely hard if they wanted my full support. My message was that the boys had to be self-motivated, and if they were, they would kick me into gear also.

The decision for Kevin to go to England to play his cricket was an extremely difficult one for the whole family. There were many sleepless nights. The bottom line was that Kevin had become extremely talented at cricket and was disappointed at not being properly recognised by Natal. We supported the boys 100 per cent in everything they wanted to do and this was another example of that, albeit a huge move for Kevin and for all of us.

Kevin was very good at school, so we said to him, 'We will support you in your cricket but come home if it doesn't work out.' There was a time, when he was playing league cricket in Cannock, that he was feeling homesick and wanted his family around him, so Penny and I flew over for a week to see him through that little patch. I remember we all went down to Bournemouth, spent some time with Kevin and reassured him that we were behind him, and it was just what he needed at that time. He hasn't looked back since.

Of course, when Kevin came back to South Africa to play for England we all went through an incredibly emotional time. I remember sitting in the Grandstand at the Wanderers for the first game and seeing the teams introduced ahead of the national anthems. My eyes went from left to right and I thought to myself, which side should Kevin be standing on? And then I saw exactly which side Kevin should be standing on. The England players had their arms round each other and looked like a team, while the South Africans were standing about a metre apart from each other.

That day and that series were very hard for us as parents. I had to put my head between my legs at one point at the Wanderers because of all the booing of the crowd aimed at Kevin. But it got better as the tour went on and the game at Pretoria was very emotional for us. I was sitting with my family in the crowd and at one point Gregg turned to me and said, 'The palms of my hands are soaking wet, Dad. I'm so nervous.' And when Kevin got to a hundred I just got off my chair and went over to Penny and hugged her. It was an unbelievable feeling because, right at the last, the crowds accepted Kevin and stood to him, recognising what he had achieved.

There was some fun along the way. When Kevin walked out at Cape Town with his new hairstyle I didn't recognise him at first. I said to Penny, 'That's not Kevin, is it? What's happened to his hair?' And it's true that when I heard Kevin might be getting a tattoo I said to him, 'There's no way you are doing that.' I blamed Darren Gough for influencing Kevin. I said, 'Darren, if he has that done I'm not coming after him, I'm coming after you.' It's not something I would have had done but Kevin did it and that's it. I have to accept it.

We were at Lord's for Kevin's Test debut and Penny was at the Oval for the incredible final match of the Ashes series with Bryan. After that game local TV asked me what message Kevin's success had for South Africa and I said it meant that South Africa should identify talent, protect it and recognise it. The country should build that security and protect individuals. When Kevin was here he didn't know from one week to the next whether he would be picked for the team and that was wrong. You can't achieve when you have that sort of instability.

I was at a conference in Cape Town on the last day of the Oval Test. I first got to hear of what was happening when I received a text message from Penny's sister in Pretoria which said, 'My nerves can't take much more of this but, if you can, get yourself to a TV.' Then my son Tony left a message saying, 'Dad, get to a TV.' Then I picked up a message from Penny saying, 'Where are you?'

At that point I left the conference, ran across the road to my hotel and spent the next four hours on my own, in front of the TV, watching all the drama being played out in front of me. I got to the TV when Kevin was on 85 and I watched every ball from then on until the Ashes were won. It was extremely emotional.

I'm just so grateful he gained opportunities and recognition in England.

Our trip to Buckingham Palace to accompany Kevin when he received his MBE was amazing. It's very difficult to describe it in words. I have the same birthday as the Queen and as a young boy I always wanted to meet that lady. And now I have.

The Queen did most of the talking when we met her. She knew where we were from and for five minutes she told us about her trips to Africa when her dad was King. It was clear she had travelled Africa extensively and had a passion for it. The Queen asked my son Gregg if he played cricket and he said he didn't but he had taught Kevin everything he knew! As we were driving away from Buckingham Palace I turned to Penny and said, 'That seals it.' That day proved to me, being among all those wonderful people throughout society gaining recognition for what they have achieved, that Kevin was right to make his life in England. That it was all worthwhile.

Pride doesn't come into my vocabulary. I was just incredibly grateful that day for the blessing and recognition Kevin has had. Penny's dad was a royalist and if he had been alive to see us all at Buckingham Palace that day it would have meant so much to him. It was very, very special.

Our lives have been turned upside down in the last

couple of years, culminating in that trip to Buckingham Palace. I don't think quite as much has happened so quickly to any cricketer as it has Kevin. If somebody had written this script it would have been called a fairy-tale. You couldn't make it up. Now is when it will get tough. Kevin has to keep the momentum going. All he can do is give his best and that's all you can ask for as a parent. I've never had to tell Kevin to work hard. He always has.

I don't think I would have been able to handle everything Kevin has handled by the age of 25. I'm the most conservative member of the family and I find some of the things that are going on in Kevin's life difficult to understand but I accept everything and I think, when he gets to 40, Kevin might have a good old laugh about hairdos and tattoos and other things like that. But the important thing is what happens on the field and we have all been on a marvellous journey so far.

Penny Pietersen: *All four of the boys supported each other very well when they were young. Because they were so close they were all dragged from pillar to post cheering each other on. They went through a traditional schooling, which I think gave them a great camaraderie.*

When we moved to Durban from Pietermaritzburg, Kevin and Bryan were still at school and they wanted to carry on going to the same school, because it was where their elder brothers had gone. So I drove them back to Pietermaritzburg every day so they could carry on going to Maritzburg College.

It was hectic but it was fun. When everyone spent the Christmas of 2005 back in South Africa with us I said to all of the boys, 'Can you ever remember fighting?' Yes, there were arguments when they played sport over who scored which try or who took which wicket. They wanted to kill each other then. But they never really fought. There was no jealousy or bitterness among them and they were all pleased when one of the others did well.

I can't complain about bringing up four boys. I found it easy, to be honest, but that's because the boys made it easy for me. All of them played so much sport, Kevin in particular, that we led busy lives and there wasn't time for them to hang around and have nothing to do. That's when you get problems.

Kevin has obviously been through so much already. There are times, when I look at the pressure international sportsmen are under to perform, and when everyone wants their pound of flesh, that I think maybe it would have been better to have kept him at home and made him become a banker or something like that.

But he is living the life he wanted. He was clever enough to go to varsity but he wanted to play cricket, so we set him goals and said that if he achieved them he would be able to carry on playing cricket. Each goal we set him, like playing for Natal Under-19s while he was still 17, and things like that, he achieved, so eventually we said, 'Go for it and see how far you can go.'

Kevin was always aware that I was English and we provided a very English upbringing for the boys even though they were brought up to fully respect the South African and Afrikaner cultures. We never told them British was best but they grew up as predominantly British people.

Now Kevin living in England has split the family up and, even though Kevin speaks to his brothers all the time, they don't really know the life he leads. So Gregg came with us to Buckingham Palace when Kevin received his MBE and we are going to arrange for Tony to spend a week in England, watching a Test match or something like that, so they can see how Kevin lives. Gregg went around with him, and went to a photo shoot with him, and that sort of thing keeps the family close and in close contact with each other.

All the boys were similar in ability at sport when they were young but Kevin had the greater heart for it. He was always in there to win. He would walk through a brick wall to get what he wanted but was never overbearing. I never once had to tell Kevin to go and do his homework. He would come in from school, get changed, get something to eat, do his homework and then grab a bat and ball and go out to play. He took control of his own life and did what he had to do to be a success.

Of course, it was horrible for us to hear people booing Kevin when he came to play with England in South Africa but I honestly think those people wanted to take out their frustration with the system in South Africa. I really don't think it was personal.

No one has ever ranted at me or criticised Kevin's decision to go to England. I've been in company where they don't know I'm Kevin's mother and I have heard people talking positively about him and what he has achieved. The ordinary man in the street, I think, understands why Kevin left South Africa and I am amazed at the support structure he has in this country. I saw a young guy in the *supermarket with Kevin's old hairstyle the other day and I said to him, 'You do know that Kevin has a crew cut at the moment, don't you? Will you have that done?' And he said, 'Oh no, I like my hair like this.' So I said to him, 'You know what, I do too. Keep it like that!' I don't think Kevin realised, until he came back for Christmas last year, just how highly regarded he is by the majority of people here in South Africa.*

It has been an emotional rollercoaster for us. I stood and cried throughout the whole of Kevin's innings at the Oval. I knew how important it was but I knew he could do it. I knew he had the ability and could rise to the occasion. That's a mother talking! When Brett Lee was hitting Kevin with the ball I said, 'Kevin must keep his head, he mustn't react to this, he must keep his concentration and Lee will get fed up.' And he did.

It's true that, when I was first asked about Kevin's hairstyle, I said, 'A mother will always love her son no matter what he does.' And it's absolutely true. Do you know, I hate some of the things that go with his fame. I hate with a passion some of the stuff that gets written in the papers. But Kevin and I have an agreement now. If I read or hear anything negative I phone Kevin to hear what has happened before I judge.

At first, when I saw some of the negative articles, I would ring him and rant and shout and give him a mouthful before I had heard the full story. Now I won't pre-judge what has happened.

I just think it's sad that anyone in the public eye in England seems to be damned before they have had a fair trial. People who do well at sport are the ones who build

England up and set examples for the youngsters to follow but it seems to me that the English papers want to knock them down. Everybody is human, everybody has failings and you don't have to blast every little failing all over the papers.

Can Kevin cope with all the attention? Yes and no. I think he is already a little more wary of who he mixes with now but he's 26 and he's a young guy with no responsibilities to anyone except the England Cricket Board and the British cricket-loving public. He shouldn't let people dictate to him what he can and cannot do and I don't think he will.

He knows that his family will come down on him like a hammer if he does anything wrong. We're all very open and talk a lot. At home he's not a celebrity.

Words can't express what I felt the day we went to Buckingham Palace. It was an unbelievable experience. Really, I wanted to be left alone in the palace so I could have a good look around but I'm afraid it wasn't possible! I wasn't just proud for Kevin, I was proud for every single person who was there because they all did something to be proud of and they all deserved to be there. I sat next to the mother of Clare Connor, the England women's cricket team captain, and I had a great chat with her. I was just as excited for her as I was for myself!

Kevin has always seemed to perform better on the cricket field when his family have been there and we will continue to try to be there for him wherever he plays in the world. It has been a wonderful journey so far and we will be with him all the way.

3

STANDING ON MY OWN TWO FEET

'It's nice to think, when I sit on my couch

watching him, that I had a part to play

in the development of Kevin Pietersen.'

Graham Ford

My first school was Clarendon, my second was Merchiston and my senior high school was Pietermaritzburg College, a pretty well-known establishment.

They were all fee-paying schools and all of them were strict. You always knew your place at school, respected the upper formers and you would never ever be abusive, cheeky or try to take advantage of anybody. We had to be very punctual, which was something that Mum and Dad advocated and something that is with me to this day. I can't abide lateness. I just don't think it's right. You're letting yourself down and the person you are supposed to be meeting.

Yet I had no unhappy times at school. Schooldays were happy, mainly because of sport, and I loved being young. I still do! I've always been energetic and hyperactive and busy; sports-filled schooldays suited my personality. I've never been able to sit still and I always talked a lot, which sometimes got me into trouble at school!

It helped, though, that I was able to learn things quickly. If I get told something once that's usually enough for me to take it in, and I was bright enough at school while always wanting to put sport first.

I didn't mind being at a boys-only school because it was all I knew, but what was unusual was that the first two schools I went to were for white people only, something that thankfully is now a thing of the past in South Africa. This was during the apartheid era. I'm relieved to say it didn't lead me to believe in segregation or to have an unnatural attitude towards people of different colour to myself. In fact, even though I was in a whites-only school, I had lots of friends outside of school who were black or coloured, as people were labelled in South Africa at that time.

I don't hate anybody, but this was the system that was in place as I was growing up. By the time I was getting older thankfully times were changing and the races started to mix together. It goes without saying that no one should be treated differently because of the colour of their skin, but when you're young you don't really question the system you are growing up in. I guess you are brainwashed, and when things started to change it was odd at first to see non-European faces around us. That's how unnatural the system was.

The changes that occurred in the country were huge but when it was all happening, around 1992–93, I was only 12 so the enormity of it passed me by to a large extent. I'm just glad now that things have changed for the better, not least because most of my family still live in South Africa and it is a beautiful place with an awful lot going for it.

Cricket was the number-one sport for me during the summer months but not all year round. I played for Natal Schools at rugby and squash and ran for Natal Schools at cross-country. I also swam for Natal and, of course, played cricket for my province too. I remember Dad promising me my first cricket bat when I scored my first 50 and it came, when I was eight, playing with ten-year-olds, when I was being coached by Digby Rhodes, father of Jonty, Pietermaritzburg's finest and a national hero around the time of readmission. That was when South Africa was readmitted to international sport after the worldwide boycott during the apartheid years. Off we went to King Sports and I proudly purchased my first Duncan Fearnley colt bat.

Yet, for all that, I was a late developer, partly because I had a serious accident at 12, which put me back almost a year. I was climbing on a flying fox frame, always the active one, and fell five or six metres, badly breaking my arm. I couldn't play any sport while I was out and it drove me nuts.

Not nearly as nuts, though, as when I finally was able to play again and in my first rugby game after recovering from the break a guy tackled me as I caught a high ball at full back and I snapped my arm again in exactly the same place. I was back in a cast and it was hugely frustrating.

It wasn't the first time I had suffered a broken bone. When I was five I had broken my collarbone but, much to Mum and Dad's astonishment, I was only in a sling for two weeks before I was back jumping in the swimming pool. I've always had a pretty high pain threshold and not even a broken collarbone could stop me.

This was a bit different. This time, after the second break, my arm still hadn't set properly after coming out of the cast and the doctor had to break it for me yet again and put a lot of pins in it. I thought it would never get better. But it eventually healed and now apparently it is so strong because of all the pins that went in it that I couldn't break my right arm unless I smashed it with a baseball bat!

In my final year at Maritzburg College I was such a late developer that I was still in the second cricket team but I started to excel and was only kept out of the first team because the coach, Mike Bechet, had something against me – or so it seemed to me. It's funny now because he tries to claim me as one of his successes and asks my mum for shirts and things, but I will never have any time for that man. I reckon he showed a real bias towards a guy who was two years younger than me, a guy called Matthew Cairns, who was a real teacher's pet. It was only when he emigrated to New Zealand that I finally got my chance in the first team.

Once I got in the first team, however, I started doing fantastically well, so much so that I ended up getting selected for South Africa Schools and off I went. Though I didn't get on with Bechet, I did form an excellent relationship with Graham Ford, the ex-South Africa coach and coach of Kent, who was fantastic to me and really backed me around this time.

So it was at about the age of 17 that I finally started to do well and started developing. Before then I could barely hit the ball! I was tall but I was skinny and didn't have too much strength. It was a case of getting some formation to my body.

I never knew what I wanted to do for a living when I was at school. As time went on I wanted to play cricket more and more but never knew if it would lead to a career or not. When I was 17 I decided to give it a real go and see where it would lead me and after SA Schools I went on to play for Natal B, which meant first-class cricket.

In those days I was an off-spinner and lower middle order batsman, combining games for Natal B with club games for Berea Rovers. It had only been a couple of years since I had taken up spin. When I was 13 or 14 I tried to bowl as fast as I could and would swing the ball both ways, usually telling the keeper before each ball which way I was going to swing it.

I loved my batting and fielding but, as I said before, I didn't have much strength and couldn't hit the ball very far. I couldn't hit sixes and could barely hit fours and my strength didn't really improve until I had two stints on Creatine, the muscle-building and, I hasten to add, fully legal drink. I took it while I was training during the winter with my friend Grant Rowley and we would run, bat and bowl together in addition to team practices, so it got to the stage where I was on the go all day and started to build myself up.

Everything now was geared towards cricket. I would train my backside off. I had become a decent off-spinner, good fielder and my batting was coming on. I finally had a first-team place with Natal after coming through the ranks and gradually getting more and more opportunities. I toured Western Australia with them, where I took my first five-wicket haul as an off-spinner in a match at Lilac Hill. I also had taken wickets against the touring England side of 1999/2000, and I had played club cricket, with some success, for Cannock in Staffordshire.

Every young player wants to broaden his horizons and play some club cricket overseas as he develops as a player and as a person. In my case my trip to Cannock came about through a friend who played with me in Durban for Natal. His name was Doug Watson and he had played in Cannock a couple of years earlier and felt it would be beneficial for me to do the same. They had a slot for an overseas player and the stint was arranged through a guy at the club called Paul Greenfield.

The visit to Cannock was an interesting period in my development. It was the first time I had been away from home and it was an experience that matured me as a player and as a human being, even though it wasn't always plain sailing.

It took time for me to adapt to a different environment. I didn't have my parents or my three brothers with me. In fact, I didn't have anything or anyone. There were times when I really wished my family were around because you just need someone to talk to at times and without them I didn't have that.

When I first arrived in the Staffordshire town I was immediately impressed with the facilities at the club but when they took me to my residence I found I was staying in a single room above a squash court. For me, a person who had always led an outdoor life, it was quite a shock. Totally not what I had expected. But I had to make do with that and I can honestly say I never had any real periods of self-doubt or ever questioned what I was doing there or whether I would be better off at home. Yes, as my Dad has said earlier in this book, there was a time I was feeling home-sick and my parents came over to pay me a visit and give me a lift, but it wasn't what I would call a serious setback or a threat to my time at Cannock. It was simply my family supporting one another, something we have always done.

I worked as a barman in the Cannock clubhouse and I met some very nice people there, who I keep in touch with to this day. I look back on it now and it seems a world away, what with those horrible Black Country accents I had such trouble understanding. I was very much an innocent abroad. People looked after me and I didn't have much to moan about but I did run into some trouble when I wasn't paid what I reckoned I was owed for the work I did behind the bar. I still haven't been paid that money now! As far as I'm concerned, Cannock didn't honour their agreement with me.

Also, I did have some disagreements with people at the club over the direction in which my cricket was going. At this time I was a bowler who batted but the captain of the club was a slow bowler called Laurie Potter, who had played for Leicestershire, and I didn't bowl as often as I wanted to. The good side of that, I guess, was that my batting began to take over and it went from strength to strength.

Basically, the whole thing was a kick up the backside for me. The trip made me realise that if I was going to be successful I was going to have to do it on my own. I really had to go hell for leather at what I was trying to achieve, a career in cricket. I had to do things for myself. I had to figure it all out for myself. I didn't even have a mobile phone then so it wasn't easy to ring home at difficult times.

But it was character-building. By the end of my time at Cannock I hated the place but I worked hard at my cricket when I was there. It was a productive five months, looking back now, but it was cut slightly short by me having to go back to South Africa for that tour of Western Australia with Natal. I did really well on the field and we won the league title. My experiences coping with my little room in this little town and my dispute over not getting paid what I believe was owed to me for my bar work definitely contributed to who I am and gave me a bit of something which encouraged me to stand up for myself. It helped make me more inquisitive, to ask why.

It was a very good grounding. I think it also helped me to come to terms with the different places we have to visit as international cricketers. I might not feel totally comfortable in some places and conditions may be alien but it doesn't affect my cricket when we tour difficult places. For instance, some people said I wouldn't be able to cope in Pakistan when I toured there with England because there weren't any flash restaurants or nightclubs. Well, there weren't too many of those in Cannock either and I coped. I didn't have many material things then and I can live without them now. Peripheral things have never adversely affected my cricket.

It makes me smile now when people at Cannock contact me or my agent to ask for signed shirts or stuff like that. They could have been a lot more straight and forthcoming with me during my time there.

Now I knew what I wanted to do for a living. Now I was convinced I was good enough at cricket. But then it was all snatched away from me by the decision that led to me leaving South Africa, one I passionately disagree with to this day.

Graham Ford was a very influential coach in my early development and has remained someone in the game I both respect and admire. Let's hear what he thinks of me.

Graham Ford: *I first came across Kevin at primary school. He was a real little nipper who was more into his rugby and his swimming in those days but he was an intensely competitive fellow even then. Whatever he did he wanted to be the best at it.*

Later I knew Kevin at the Natal youth academy and he always stood out as being a superbly fit individual and someone who was mature for his years, like the way he would watch the senior players and how they went about things. Lance Klusener was a player who would practise for hours on end and Kevin would watch him intently to see what he could learn. Kevin's attention to detail and dedication was pretty unusual for one so young.

When Kevin became involved with the seniors himself he would get stuck in but would also show them the necessary respect which, all in all, contributed to a pretty good attitude. I was excited by him at a young age as an off-spinner but surprisingly he didn't make the first team initially at Maritzburg College because there was another very good off-spinner there. Thankfully for Kevin, the other lad emigrated to New Zealand which gave Kevin his opportunity and he grabbed it with both hands.

Of course, he started showing just as much promise as a batsman but it was still a struggle to gain the recognition he felt he deserved, so a career in cricket must have seemed a long way off for the boy at that time. When I moved from Natal to work with the national side I kept in touch with Kevin and his father because I knew they felt doors were being closed on them and Kevin was becoming disillusioned, particularly when he was dropped from the first team after a good performance.

It was me who arranged for Kevin and Jannie to see Ali Bacher, when it became clear he was considering leaving the country. I was anxious Kevin should be encouraged and given proper opportunities because I could see him playing for South Africa. Unfortunately, Kevin and his father didn't get much encouragement from Ali so I then encouraged them to send the boy to England. It certainly was the right call for him. Kevin backed his own ability, knew where he wanted to go and made damn sure he would get there. It was the hard route to the top but it was the right one.

Yes, I know I was coaching South Africa and I was losing a potential Test player in encouraging Kevin to try his luck in England, but to me it wasn't my agenda that was important or even my country's. It was what was best for the athlete.

I hoped Ali Bacher would throw Kevin a lifeline but it wasn't to be. It was Shaun Pollock, who was captain of South Africa at that time, who urged me to ring Ali to try to help Kevin in his battle to get into the Natal side. At that stage he was a long way off Test cricket but you could see the potential was there.

Shaun's feeling was that here was a guy who bowled good spin, could strike a ball well and who was an athletic fielder, one of the best fielders in the country. He looked like someone we could develop for the future.

Shaun understood the quota system and what the United Cricket Board of South Africa were trying to achieve. He knew and I knew that Ali couldn't go out on a limb and give Kevin any sort of guarantee that he would play regularly for Natal but Shaun expressed some regret that we'd missed a trick in letting this boy go. He definitely felt that way when Kevin went back to South Africa with England and started hitting our bowlers all over the place!

Good luck to Kevin and hats off for what he has achieved. There is no animosity on my part or anyone else's I know in South African cricket. Kevin was faced with a tough decision and he's made a success of what he's done. I've never spoken to Ali Bacher about it to this day.

I thought Kevin could play for England as soon as he moved to the country. In fact, I had a bet with a friend from Natal that he would and I had to wait until Kevin returned to South Africa with England to collect my money because my friend wouldn't accept him playing against Zimbabwe as counting.

I've followed his progress all the way and it's been very exciting. It's nice to think, when I sit on my couch watching him, that I had a part to play in the development of Kevin Pietersen. I'm a bit disappointed his off-spin has taken such a back seat but he's become such a good batsman that it's probably for the best. Kevin's batting is a joy to watch and I've no doubts that with his ambition, determination, skill and hunger, he will go on to become one of the greats.

4

MAKING MY MOVE

'When Kevin comes out to bat,
people will leave the pubs to come and
watch him. That's what it's all about.'

Clive Rice

I had realised I was good enough to play cricket for a living. I had proved myself good enough to play for Natal, overcome initial selection bias against me and make a good impression against Nasser Hussain's touring England side in the winter of 1999/2000, taking wickets with my off-spin.

That was a big occasion for me. It was the biggest match of my life up until that point. Here was the England cricket team playing against my team at a time when I was trying to make my way in the game, and I did well against them. Hussain was an impressive figure. He was new to the England captaincy and was clearly trying to establish himself as the leader of his team but I felt sufficiently bold to approach him to ask for his advice at the end of the match.

Even then I knew my mother's nationality could open doors for me and I was inquisitive about the opportunities that might await in England. It was little more than curiosity at that stage but I did ask Hussain if he had any advice on how I might be able to play some cricket in England.

He thought I meant club cricket and gave me the number of his brother Mel, who played for Fives and Heronians in the Essex League. But I had bigger aspirations than that. I was thinking of county cricket perhaps, at that stage, as a non-overseas player because of my British passport. Yet there was a huge setback round the corner that I never envisaged and which forced me into the biggest decision of my life.

I was dropped from the Natal first team for political reasons. I was dropped because of the quota system that had been brought into South African cricket to positively discriminate in favour of players of colour and to fast-track the racial integration of cricket in the country. To me, every single person in this world needs to be treated exactly the same and that should have included me, as a promising 20-year-old cricketer, in the summer of 1999/2000.

As far as I was concerned I should not have been discriminated against because of something that happened years before my time. I must emphasise at this point that I am not racist. Apartheid was none of my doing and by now was – thankfully – a thing of the past. Maybe my forefathers who made those decisions in South Africa, the ones who created the abnormal society, should have been punished for what happened, but why should I? The country was moving on. Yet this was not the right way to move on.

I had started by this stage to live, eat and breathe cricket. This came along like a bombshell to ruin the progress I had been making and block the clear route to the top that I had identified for myself and which I felt was realistically attainable.

If you do well you should play on merit. That goes for any person of any colour. To me there should never be a case of someone who is not as good as you taking your place purely for political reasons. I don't see how that can do anyone any good. And that includes the person who is brought in. Surely if they know they are not in the team on merit it can only be harmful to them and the team. It can create the very divisions that you are trying to destroy.

It was heart-breaking. There had to be three non-white players in the team and one of the better ones at that time in Natal was a young off-spinning batsman like me called Ghulam Bodi. He was to take my place. I remember ringing my dad and crying down the phone to him when it happened. I also flew into a rage when they told me, flinging a water bottle across the Natal dressing room and shouting, 'I'm leaving here.' Perhaps not the wisest move but I was so angry at the time because I knew Ghulam wasn't as good as me. I had nothing against him but I didn't think it was right that he replaced me.

My dad was incredibly supportive and immediately dropped everything to be with me. We insisted on a meeting with Phil Russell, once of Derbyshire and at that time the Natal coach. Phil had taken over from Graham Ford, who I respected hugely, but unfortunately I found Phil to be a 'yes' man. He did what the hierarchy wanted him to do. He told me and Dad that he had to drop me because of the quota system, but it seemed to me that no thought had gone into it nor any consideration as to a way round it in my case. I also wondered why it had to be me. I guess if one of the better non-white players at that time hadn't been an off-spinning batsman, the course of history may have been changed.

I don't blame the player for what happened, of course I don't. It's the system. It's bullshit. And it's one that should never have been put in place because it created an artificial team and that will never do anything to encourage the racial integration of cricket in South Africa. It should have been allowed to happen naturally, but it wasn't, and I guess it's up to the South African authorities to deal with it. As for Ghulam, as far as I'm aware he has not made much of an impact in cricket, certainly not with the South African team.

It has to be said that I did have options open to me, and I'd always been aware of them. England was my mum's birthplace. I had a British passport and, as my enquiry of Nasser Hussain showed, I had often thought about playing in England, all the more so after things went well for me in Cannock. And so although it was very hard for me to take in at the time, it turned out it was the best thing that could have happened, because if it hadn't, then I wouldn't have been standing at the Oval as part of an Ashes-winning England team, and I wouldn't have been named one-day player of the year at the ICC awards dinner in 2005 and be standing on a Sydney stage in front of the best cricketers in the world.

I knew I didn't have to stay in South Africa and take this. Then Clive Rice, one of South Africa's greatest ever players and the man who had picked me for South Africa Schools, told me he wanted me to come and join Nottinghamshire, where he was now coaching. There had also been interest from Derbyshire, Warwickshire and Worcestershire; my British passport allowed me to play as a non-overseas player.

While I was at Cannock I went to Trent Bridge to have a couple of nets and Clive had become something of a father figure in the game to me. He took me under his wing. He was strict, like my dad, and told you how it was but he was also very straight with you and I liked that. There was never any room for doubt with Ricey and his personality suited me. I have always believed in telling things the way they are and if that upsets someone then too bad. Clive is the same. He had been a South African selector but he knew which way the country was going and he advised me to leave, even before the whole controversy over me being dropped by Natal erupted. He wanted me to start a new life with Nottinghamshire.

Crunch time was coming. Notts sent over a contract offer to me in the winter of 2000, which would pay me £15,000 for the following 2001 English season. That was a lot of rand for a 20-year-old, much more than I was getting at Natal.

But it wasn't as simple as that. We were talking about a huge decision here. We were talking about uprooting and emigrating to England, where I had no friends and family. But it was such a great opportunity and I was so disillusioned with my treatment at the hands of Natal that I could see no future for myself as a professional cricketer in South Africa.

I decided to talk again with Graham Ford, who was still involved in Natal cricket and who was someone I respected. He did not beat about the bush. He told me to leave. Graham said to me, 'I'd love you to stay but there's nothing for you here. Go and make a new life for yourself.' It was a persuasive argument.

Yet I was determined not to rush this huge decision and wanted to ask other people I respected what they felt. I went about canvassing as many trusted opinions as possible before I made the big leap. There was another guy called Harry Brown, who was one of my mentors, and he said go. Then I spoke to Shaun Pollock and he told me to go. And they don't come much bigger or more experienced than Shaun, who was the South African captain.

The fact was, when Natal dropped me they knew I had been in England, had talked to Clive and that Notts were interested in me. It was something I was curious to talk about, but it is a move that may well not have happened had Natal not forced the issue. When they left me out that proved to me they couldn't have thought an awful lot of me. They must have known that there was a big danger I would be lost to South African cricket but they did nothing about it, merely blamed the system. Not everybody told me to leave, some good people urged me to stay and fight for my place, told me that quality would win through at the end of the day. But all I could see was that I was good enough and that there were all these stumbling blocks placed in the way. I felt I should be rewarded for the progress I had made, not dropped for the match against Northern Transvaal at Kingsmead.

Then came the decisive meeting. I was told that Dr Ali Bacher, the most powerful man in South African cricket, wanted to see me. I have subsequently discovered that he wanted to see me only because Graham Ford had urged him to. Graham had been talking to Shaun Pollock and they were hoping that the most powerful man in South African cricket would throw me a lifeline.

This would tell me all I needed to know. Dad and I flew up to Johannesburg to see Dr Bacher and I vowed to go into that meeting with an open mind and see what the ruler of the United Cricket Board had to say about all this.

Ali Bacher, to all intents and purposes, was South African cricket. He had been a leading figure in the rebel tours that caused so much controversy during the country's wilderness years, but he was also a key figure in readmission because of his efforts to try to get South Africa welcomed back into the fold. Now he was the main man. The man who made the country's cricket tick. To me Ali Bacher was big. What he said went. He had asked to see me and I wanted to hear what he had to say.

Bacher was rude to me in that meeting, and rude to my dad. Good manners had been a backbone of my upbringing and I was taken aback by the atmosphere and tone of the meeting. There were no pleasantries, no hellos or how are yous. We simply sat down and Dr Bacher said to Dad: 'What do you do?' Not a hello Mr Pietersen, hello Kevin, welcome, or anything like that. It was like he was trying to show his authority over us straight away.

I'd never met the man before. As far as I was concerned, the least he could do was be polite. Surely he would try to persuade me that my future would be best served in the new South Africa? But nothing was coming back. Dad asked lots of questions while I stayed pretty quiet. But I was determined not to walk away from that meeting with any doubts in my mind as to what I should do for the best.

Dr Bacher said that soon the quota system would stop and that selection would go back to being on merit. So I said, 'Dr Bacher, does that mean that, say next year, if the black and coloured players are not good enough, will Natal field an all-white side?'

'No,' he said. 'They will be good enough and they will play.'

That was the big moment for me. I looked at my dad and tapped his leg. We both sort of nodded at each other. As soon as we walked out of that meeting Dad said to me, 'You're going, the quota system will never finish.' I agreed with him. We thanked Dr Bacher for his time, got back on a plane to Durban, immediately rang Clive Rice and accepted his offer to play for Notts. To qualify as a non-overseas player in county cricket I had to pull out of the Natal squad, which I did. I knew then that I would never play for them again.

This was a life-changing deal, as big as anything that would happen to me at the Oval five years later. It was never a case of going to England and seeing if things would work out, and if they didn't, go back to South Africa. We'd talked about this a lot as a family and I'd canvassed a lot of opinions. My family were fantastic, so supportive. Man, did they back me – and now not one member of my family will ever support a South African team at any time. They are England fans all the way.

I wouldn't call it an agonising decision. It was a well-thought-out decision. I thought about how I would cope on my own in a new country but I've always been a confident bloke and I was sure that, taking account of how hard I worked, I would be successful. I wanted to play international cricket and I wanted to be as successful as I possibly could be.

What would have happened had I stayed in South Africa?

Well, it's something I haven't dwelt on because the past is the past and there is no point in wondering what might have been, but I really think I wouldn't be playing cricket now because I would have been frozen out by the system. I wouldn't have put up with that and, if the England option hadn't been open to me, I would have gone off and done something else.

I had been as excited as any young sports-mad kid in South Africa when our team were readmitted to world cricket again in 1991/92. At that stage I didn't imagine that politics could possibly get in the way of my dream of emulating people like Clive Rice, who was the country's first captain on their return tour of India before Kepler Wessels took over for the World Cup of 1992.

Remember also that Hansie Cronje and Allan Donald were my heroes and it was a huge thing for me to turn my back on any hope I had of becoming like them. Back then, of course, Hansie was a national hero and it's amazing to think of the match-fixing controversy he was to become embroiled in around the time I was considering leaving South Africa. It was a scandal that rocked world cricket and went to the heart of everything that South Africans believed in. Cronje was the biggest figure in South African cricket and one of the biggest figures in the game, but he was accused and found guilty of taking money to influence matches, all so soon after South Africa's time in the wilderness had ended.

Yet that played no part in my decision. I was not disillusioned in the man I had worshipped as a child. To me it was a case of how could such a great man make such a big mistake? That's how I saw it. A human being making a mistake. Everybody makes mistakes. Hansie was in the public eye and if you are famous and make a mistake everybody knows about it. If you are not and you make a mistake then nothing is said and you are able to get on with your life. I still think Hansie Cronje was a great man and I'm never going to think any differently of him. It was a huge shock to everyone in the country when he was killed in an air accident. It was tragic.

I thought he was a fantastic captain, strong and aggressive, and that was reflected in the way he played. I loved the way he batted. I knew him a bit and played against him a couple of times. I played against him the last time he played for South Africa, the day before the match-fixing story broke. It was Natal against South Africa in a warm-up game. He batted, got 50 not out, retired, left the field and provided no clues as to the monumental thing that was about to happen. Nothing in his body language to suggest he was troubled or anything. He remains huge to me, as does Allan Donald. But no hero worship or any aspirations I once had were going to keep me in South Africa now. My mind was made up. I was off to England.

Clive Rice was a huge figure in that decision. He was a legend in South Africa, but he was the man who made my departure from the country possible. This is his view of events.

Clive Rice: *The first time I saw Kevin, when he was playing for South Africa Schools, I liked what I saw, and when I then watched him play for Natal it confirmed to me that I wasn't wrong. But it was clear that he was being held back by the South African quota system, and then I discovered he had a British passport and had scored a lot of runs in league cricket in England the previous year.*

I barely knew him but I was at Notts at the time and I approached him and said, 'I'm not even going to ask you to come over to Trent Bridge for a trial. I'm sending you a contract straight away and I guarantee I will have you playing for England in four years' time.' At Notts they thought I was mad to give this lad a job without even giving him a trial but I was adamant I'd seen someone who had something and I wanted to develop that.

I didn't have any problems in recommending to Kevin that he left South Africa, even though I knew he would be lost to our cricket. Our cricket is in complete disarray. Our under-19s even lost to Tibet. Did you know they even played cricket in Tibet? It's just embarrassing. I would recommend to any of our players that they should get out of South Africa if they can. They say they don't have quotas in our cricket now but they have targets – it's the same thing only with a different word. And it is both bad and incestuous.

It was clear straight away that Kevin was a natural athlete who could play a variety of sports and there is no question in my mind that if he hadn't left South Africa he would have been lost to cricket because he would have become disillusioned and would have played another sport to a high standard. You have to encourage people with ability, retain their interest and give them recognition. All Natal did was pick someone in Kevin's place who wasn't as good as him and the cricket authorities in my country are all still in self-destruct mode.

All I wanted to do was to make sure Kevin Pietersen's talent at cricket was not wasted. I want to be entertained when I watch cricket and it doesn't matter to me if he is playing for England, Australia or anyone else, I will watch him and support him if he can thrill cricket fans and bring people to the game. When Kevin comes out to bat people will leave the pubs to come and watch him. That's what it's all about. I don't want to watch mediocrity or be involved in a system that not only encourages it but creates it.

I didn't know Kevin as a person when I offered him a contract but it didn't matter to me what sort of lad he was. I just wanted to work with him because he could play. When I was captain of Notts, we had people in the side like Eddie Hemmings, Derek Randall and Chris Broad who could all be difficult but I didn't care as long as they were performing on the field. Bring me the devil and I will handle him as long as he can play a bit of cricket and is worth a place in my side!

Kevin made an impact instantly at Notts. He was an out-and-out match-winner from the word go. Of course he wasn't the finished article and his talent needed refining but it was a pleasure to play a part in refining it. If ever anybody in South Africa has a go at me for taking Kevin out of the country I just say to them, 'You rejected him, so don't moan.' They look for excuses now when they talk about Kevin in South Africa and try to shift the blame for him leaving. You hear a lot of rubbish when you listen to people talking about him at Natal.

He is a super-confident guy but you need that to succeed. Everybody in this life is different and you have to handle each individual differently to get the best out of them. They were jealous of him at Notts. Some people there couldn't handle a guy who was a super-confident match-winner. From my point of view, when I was coaching there, I just wanted a bit of his attitude to rub off on the other guys, but they forced me out and then, ultimately, Kevin too. With hindsight I can say now that Notts did me a favour because business has gone well since but it was the way they did it that still hacks me off. I can't accept that sort of thing.

Every now and again I still give Kevin advice and he knows if I see any little thing in his game I will text him or ring him to point it out. You get a lot of advice in this game, much of it bad, and it's a question of just taking what you can use to become a better player. I think Kevin is good at knowing what he should take on board and what he should ignore.

He listened to me from the word go and he has rapidly climbed to be one of the best five batsmen in the world. England couldn't wait to get him in their side.

I was in South Africa when he played there with England and I knew the crowds would boo him. They used to do the same to me when I played in Cape Town. Before Kevin played there for England I said to him, 'Turn the whole thing around. Say to them: "Please boo me because it will make me that much more determined to show you I can really play. Then you guys will suffer."' He did just that. The more they booed him, the better he played.

I set him targets in South Africa and it was uncanny how he reached each of those targets. I told him it was important he got a hundred quickly because it would prove to the crowds that they couldn't faze him, and he scored one straight away in Bloemfontein. Then I said it was important he scored another to show everybody that he wasn't a flash in the pan and he went out and scored the fastest century by an Englishman in a one-day international in East London. Then, before the last match at Pretoria, I told him to get a hundred and become man of the series to show them that now he was the main man. I *wanted him to emphasise to the South Africans that they had got a hiding from a South African whom they rejected. And he did it.*

Before that amazing Test at the Oval against Australia, I told Kevin he would never play on a bigger stage and to make sure he got a big hundred. He even did that.

He is determined to break my records as a player and I'll be delighted if he does. I don't think he'll break my bowling records but I'm sure he'll break my run tally of 26,000 runs and I want him to do it by a substantial margin.

He's in the top five in the world already and I want him to stay there in both Tests and one-dayers. I also want him to continue being highly entertaining because that's what people want to see. He can be like Ian Botham or Viv Richards and that can only be good for world cricket, certainly better than what is going on in South Africa or in the world game with the elevation of Bangladesh and Zimbabwe to Test status. All that does is weaken the game. If the game is not careful it will lose its audience very quickly.

I not only want to see Kevin become the best in the world but I want to see him being responsible and very focused. He's had plenty of distractions since the Oval, with lots of commercial deals and Miss Wonder Bra being around him, stuff like that. He needs to look at someone like Tiger Woods and use him as an example of how to behave. How to be totally professional. I'm sure Kevin will do that and I'm delighted to hear he has met a lovely girl who he is really happy with. And if people in South Africa are unhappy? Do you know what, that doesn't matter in the slightest. Kevin made the right decision to leave and he saw the light early. There are no limits to what he could achieve.

5

RECRIMINATIONS BUT NO REGRETS

'Kev scored a big hundred very early on during our time at Notts, at Lord's, and everyone knew straight away we had someone in our midst who was a bit special.'

Richard Logan

My move to England and Nottinghamshire was both daunting and exciting. I had been to England on holiday and to play for Cannock but never to live and now I found myself, a young man, having to fend for myself and prove myself in the environment of county cricket and ultimately international cricket.

County cricket was a whole new world to me. It is, in many ways, an exciting world, but it is also a world where mediocre cricket, cliques and a lack of ambition can be found. For me this was my first taste of a professional English dressing room, a big step up for me and a big change to what I was used to in South Africa.

People wonder what a cricket dressing room is like, what sort of characters can be found there. Well, each one is different, but one common denominator I have found, even when I had some bad times at Notts, is that the players are always laughing and joking around. There are always humorous things going on. I was to find later on in the England dressing room that someone like Andrew Flintoff would always be messing around and taking the mickey out of the likes of me and Steve Harmison. Generally, if the big characters in the dressing room are not taking the mickey out of you, you're in trouble, because it means you haven't been accepted. It can mean that they don't like you.

Being the butt of dressing-room humour can be a rite of passage, a way in which you're welcomed and an expression of affection. That's how cricketers are. Darren Gough, who will feature in my story later on, was always fantastic to have in a dressing room. I loved being around him and having him around. He was amazing. The things he used to come up with were so ridiculous and stupid but always amusing. Darren's Yorkshire accent and the way he talks were part of his charm. He was just brilliant at getting people laughing, which is so important. A happy dressing room is definitely going to help it be a successful dressing room.

There is a lot of cricket talk in the dressing room. It's where you think about the game. Of course, there are quiet, serious people who did things a bit differently and don't necessarily join in the banter. There's room for all sorts.

There is also room for a lot of outside assistance. So much of the information we take out onto a field now is computerised. It is all stored away for us to study and, hopefully, improve our game. You can see any ball from the day's play on screen, in slow motion, so you can see the position and angle of the bowler's wrist, what he is doing with the ball and his hand. So, the dressing room is a mixture of the serious and the humorous.

The England dressing room was still a long way off for me when I first arrived at Trent Bridge, despite Clive Rice telling me that he would get me to international cricket within four years. All I wanted to do, from the moment I arrived, was play for England. It was the ultimate, and it was the reason why I had uprooted and gone to live in Nottingham in the first place. I wanted it because I wanted to reach the very highest level of the game. I wanted it because I wanted to fulfil my destiny as a professional cricketer and gain the material rewards that came with that. I wanted it because whenever I do anything I want to be the best and go as far as I possibly can. I wanted it because I wanted to prove people wrong in South Africa who had stood in my path and, above all,

I wanted it because I wanted to be accepted as an Englishman in my mother's country and fulfil all my hopes and dreams in her country. It was now my country too.

I knew I had to serve a four-year qualification period before I was eligible for England but that was fine by me. In that time I was determined to learn my trade, do well for Notts and prove that I could be more than a county player. I was 21 and I had much to work on.

People might think of me as a confident character, and I am, but of course there were nerves in my new surroundings, and there were times of introspection as I came to terms with my new life. Yet the bottom line was that I never wanted to be just a county cricketer. I never wanted simply to accept what was very good money for a young man coming from South Africa, and to view playing for Notts as the limit of my ambitions.

It was an attitude that was to lead to some conflict at Notts and earn me an unwelcome reputation in some quarters as a troublemaker, a label that could have seriously hindered my international prospects at one stage. The last thing you need in this game is for people to consider you bad news, because cricket can be a small, introverted community and if you get on the wrong side it can be difficult to force your way back in.

To me it was perfectly natural to aspire to being the best I could and to show ambition in every game I played. Every game of professional cricket you play really should mean a lot, but there is so much cricket in England that it can dampen people's competitive edge. I happen to think English domestic cricket is the strongest in the world, but it could be even better if we all shared the same attitude towards seeking excellence.

There is clearly a lot of mediocrity in county cricket and a lot of players who are perhaps lucky to be earning a living from the game. To me the function of county cricket is to provide players for the England team, good players, players who have thrived at a high level and who are ready to take the next step up and compete against the likes of Australia and South Africa for Test cricket's ultimate prizes.

Yes, of course, it is important for everyone involved in any county to win things. For many players, playing for England is a step too far, so their ultimate ambition is to win the county championship or appear in a Lord's cup final. I can understand that, and when I have played for Notts, and now Hampshire, I want to win things with those counties and be part of the best side we can possibly be.

Yet county success and providing good players for England should go hand in hand. If a county aspires to excellence, is modern in its thinking and appreciates that it must serve England's cause, then winning things at county level will serve two purposes. It will justify that county's existence, if you like, and make a lot of people happy, but also provide better cricketers for the national team. Test match receipts provide an awful lot of the money county clubs need to survive, so ultimately they must appreciate that they are something of a feeder outfit for England and must never put club before country.

Hampshire is a great example of a modern, successful, flourishing club. They have built a wonderful new stadium, have done away with much of the old-fashioned thinking that has blighted England's progress and aspire both to win trophies, and to serve England's best interests by producing international players.

There are other counties who, I'm afraid, have their share of players who are never going to compete for England places, who are happy to cruise along in pursuit of their pay cheque and ultimately a benefit year, and who do nothing for the pursuit of excellence.

I arrived at Notts with the clear aim of bettering myself as a player and as a person, and learning enough to make me a contender for an England place by the time I qualified late in 2004. And the first season, 2001, went pretty well for me, if not brilliantly for Notts.

We were playing second-division championship cricket and I found it to be a level I could compete at and feel comfortable at. By this time I had become a number-six batsman who still had aspirations to be an all-rounder and who wanted to bowl as often as possible, but my off-spin was slowly becoming less of a priority, even though I was still serious in wanting to work on it.

I was working with Clive Rice, someone I respected as much as anyone in cricket, and I wasn't the only player in my position to join the county; Notts also signed the South African-born fast bowler Greg Smith who, like me, had a British passport and was eligible to play as a non-overseas player. They had also recruited a young fast bowler called Richard Logan from Northamptonshire, who was to go on to become one of my best friends and a huge ally.

Initially things went well. I scored 1,275 championship runs in my first season in English cricket, scoring at a rate of 82 runs every 100 balls. Even then my penchant for quick scoring was becoming evident. I scored four hundreds and topped the Notts first-class averages at 57.95 per innings, so it is clear that, far from being the one-day player that people tried to label me when I first emerged in the England team, I was showing at an early stage that I could play first-class cricket.

As a team we reached the semi-finals of the Benson and Hedges Cup but under-performed in the championship and could only finish seventh in the second-division table – not a great performance from a side that had been considered one of the favourites for promotion.

Yet to me it was a start. I had made progress towards my goal of being the best player I could be, and I had grown up a lot as a person by having to fend for myself off the field. Yes, there were times when I would be alone in my flat, missing home, missing my family and feeling on my own. But they were mercifully few and I saw it all as a growing-up process, and one that would lead to a better life for me. Never at any stage did I question whether I should have left South Africa or worried that I had done the right thing. Perhaps the fact that it went well for me on the field had a lot to do with that, but the fact is I'm the sort of person who makes his mind up to do something and then doesn't look back.

The next season, however, things started to go wrong for me. In June 2002 I did begin to wonder if Nottingham was the best place to be if I was to achieve my goals. It started, as far as I'm concerned, with the departure of Clive Rice from Trent Bridge. The man was a legend in Nottingham and had been one of their most successful ever captains and overseas players. I thought he was a top-notch coach and manager too, but maybe Clive ruffled too many feathers in his pursuit of excellence; maybe he was too keen to shake people out of their comfort zones.

When Clive took over at Notts he had inherited a team with a lot of those players who seemed happy to earn their money and do very little to justify it. Players who appeared happy to average 20 or 25 with the bat. When Clive took over he wanted to rid the county of that sort of player and get in people who really wanted to achieve, not settle for mediocrity. He started making significant progress but for some reason the county decided it wasn't good enough for them.

Notts sacked Clive but, to make matters worse, they did so at the same time as his father died. Ricey had gone back to South

Africa two weeks earlier to see his father, who was gravely ill, for the last time. Everybody at the club knew all about that and the sensitive family situation Clive found himself in. Yet they went ahead and sacked him any way. Clive had done so much to make the county more professional. I thought: is this really the type of club I want to be a part of? Is this the sort of environment in which I want to play my cricket?

I bitterly disagreed with Notts' decision. I had lost my father figure, the man who had brought me to England and Notts, and the man I believed in 100 per cent. His methods were my methods and I thought Notts would be a poorer club for his departure.

Clive's position was filled by former player Mick Newell, who had been working with the second team and who had not had a particularly outstanding career himself. To me, he was not up to the job. It seemed to me that he told people what they wanted to hear, not what they needed to hear, and he wasn't strong enough to deal with the disparate personalities of a dressing room and to bring the best out of them.

The day after they sacked Clive and Newell came in, I was dropped to the second team. It upset me almost as much as Ricey's departure, but I knew I had to show them and prove them wrong. I played two one-day games for the seconds, first at Yorkshire, when I was bowled by an off-spinner for something like 12 at Headingley – which proved to me that my head wasn't right, what with all that was going on with Clive. I didn't play the way I usually play against an off-spinner. They don't usually bowl me. I was struggling.

Then we went to Durham for another second-team game, where a certain Steve Harmison was coming back from injury and playing. Durham had a useful second team but I got 70 or 80-odd to win the game and I was back in the first team.

Mick Newell told me that I hadn't been playing as well as I should have been, that I was below par and that I wasn't going to play in his team on my name and reputation alone and on what I'd achieved in the past. I didn't accept his explanation and I didn't care how he attempted to justify his selection. I felt that he was just trying to push his weight around. He wanted to put me on some sort of trial.

I soon showed him that I could play, scoring four consecutive hundreds on my return to the first team before diving for a ball in the field while we were playing Glamorgan in Colwyn Bay and fracturing my leg. I was out for the rest of the season. It was a very unhappy time.

To me, it was a case of jobs for the boys. We had a decent season in the championship and eventually gained promotion to the first division, but I felt Newell had little to do with it. I had flourished before my injury and had a purple patch in which I made three career-best scores during that run of four hundreds in all cricket in ten days. That was a hugely important spell for me, only cut short by injury. I was putting the runs on the board, and while I was now doing less bowling, I was starting to become convinced that I had what it takes to become a Test batsman. I scored another three first-class hundreds earlier on in that season and again topped the Notts averages at 61.41, but the key factor for me in the team's promotion that year had been the arrival of Australian leg-spinner Stuart MacGill.

Now here was a class performer. He came to Trent Bridge in early August 2002 and promptly took 40 wickets in six matches. The guy was a world-class bowler, who had the misfortune to have been born an Australian leg-spinner at the time when fellow Australian Shane Warne was becoming the best bowler the world has even seen. How unlucky is that? If Stuey MacGill had been born in another era, or had been English, I reckon he would have won a hundred Test caps and taken four hundred Test wickets. As it is, he has always had to play second fiddle to Shane, and that's a great shame for Stuey, another player who was to become a firm friend.

Off the field things were going well for me. I was now well used to living away from my family, and I also had Cate in my life. I had met her in Sydney when I was playing a bit of grade cricket there for Sydney University, at the invitation of Stuey MacGill, and we would go on to be together for two years. But during the 2003 season, my time at Nottingham became bitter and full of recriminations. It was a time that tested my ambition to the full and earned me that troublemaker tag, which for a while seriously jeopardised my international aspirations.

That season summed up all that can be bad about English county cricket. Some players seemed more interested in themselves than the team, all they wanted to do was enough to keep their place, and there was very little spirit within the side. As captain we had Jason Gallian, who I didn't think was particularly good at the job.

The campaign began with people talking about a top-three finish in the championship first division but ended with us relegated and splits appearing within the camp. For the third successive year, my only three years in English first-class cricket, I topped the Notts averages. I managed to score another 1,488 championship runs at an average of 51.31 with four centuries. I also scored 776 runs in the one-day league, one of the best tallies in Nottinghamshire history.

I felt I had done my part, but others appeared more interested in back-biting than achievement. I always believe in speaking my mind and telling people what I think and I had no hesitation in saying publicly that I felt I was carrying the team. It got so bad that I would sometimes warm up on my own rather than be with certain team-mates. I started to look seriously into the possibility of taking legal action to release myself from the final year of my Trent Bridge contract.

It was awful that it had come to this but I was determined to stand up for what I believed in, and if that saw me as a man apart then so be it. In any case, I wasn't an isolated figure in the dressing room. Richard Logan and Stuey MacGill were close friends and it would be too simplistic to say that I didn't get on with anybody else.

Matters reached a head. I said I wanted to leave. I also let it be known that I didn't think Gallian was a very good captain. Then Bilal Shafayat rang me to tell me that Gallian, a man who was supposed to lead by example, had dumped my cricket gear over the balcony at Trent Bridge. What's more, he did it while I wasn't there. I don't think he would have had the guts to do something like that in front of me, and if he had attempted to do so I would have thumped him, no question. Yes, I probably said a few things I shouldn't have said, but then again I was just sticking up for what I believed in and trying to get the best out of myself. It was even more clear to me that I had no future at this club.

I still haven't had an apology from Jason Gallian over that incident. The funny thing was, it was his benefit year in 2005 and he had the audacity to ask me for a lot of stuff for his auctions. I was never going to give him anything. I wasn't just going to forget the past. It was a very frustrating time.

It was only selection for the England Academy that winter that rescued me from a horrible situation. I will come to this later but suffice to say that this huge development, coupled with the hardly enticing prospect of a long-drawn-out legal saga, persuaded me to see out the last year of my four-year Notts contract, the last season before I would be eligible for England.

But my respect for Newell and Gallian, and a few other members of the Notts side, had gone.

I came back from the England Academy tour of India having scored runs and with a glowing report from Rod Marsh, so to my mind I had proved to the people who mattered most, the England selectors, that I wasn't this evil beast who was incapable of getting on with anyone, in the way that certain people at Notts were trying to paint me. My time at the England Academy in Loughborough and then in India matured me as a human being and toughened me up no end. I'm sure Rod Marsh will vouch for that.

Stuey MacGill and Richard Logan, and Australian David Hussey, who had joined us as an overseas player, got me through the 2004 season. MacGill is a nice, well-rounded man who appreciates things other than cricket in his life. It is funny to me that some people in the game think of him as something of a maverick, or someone who doesn't get on with everybody. Maybe if you're slightly different, or a bit more confident or strong in your opinions, the cricket community labels you as someone they are not sure about. To me, you must always take as you find and Stuey MacGill was a top-notch man in this difficult year. It was a testing year and I came through it.

I decided to be professional about everything and just get on with it. The biggest reason I was able to get through 2004 was that we were winning. It's always much easier to deal with anything cricket throws at you if you are in a winning environment. The team was promoted, and while I perhaps didn't bat quite as well as in the previous three seasons, I played my part by scoring 965 runs at an average of 53.61.

I even intimated at one stage that I might be prepared to stay at Notts. We seemed to have put our troubles behind us and were playing as a team. We were promoted. They made me an offer, which they said would make me the highest-paid player in the team. I told them I didn't care what other people earned, but I felt I deserved more than they were offering. But it's true to say that I was seriously considering staying and had told people that.

I asked Newell what was happening to the team and he told me that we would be going with the players who got us promoted. Two or three days later I discovered that my two best friends at the club, MacGill and Logan, had been released. Whether they wanted to separate us and get rid of the people I was closest to I don't know, but that was it for me. I rang my agent and said, 'It's time to move on.' And I'm glad I did.

Notts won the title in 2005, and good luck to them. I have no jealousy or ill-feeling about that. For me the key factor in that was the captaincy of Stephen Fleming, who is one of the best leaders in the world. Someone at Notts must have shared my misgivings about Gallian as a captain because even though we were promoted in 2004 he was moved aside for Fleming to take over. That was the best thing they could have done.

I wanted pastures new. My Notts experience had made me stronger. If ever things are bad, I always reflect on having come through the testing times at Trent Bridge. There was also the not insignificant matter of me now being qualified to play for England, my ultimate dream.

I have said how much I valued the friendship of Richard Logan during those dark days. Here's what he had to say about it.

Richard Logan: *Kevin and I joined Notts at the same time and as two of the younger guys in the team we hung out together and got to know each other really well. When he first arrived from South Africa he was quite quiet and shy,* if you can believe that, and kept himself to himself, but when I got to know him it was clear that he was a fun guy once he had come out of his shell.

Kev scored a big hundred very early on during our time at Notts at Lord's and everyone knew straight away that we had someone in our midst who was a bit special. He went on to average over 50 in each of his four seasons at Trent Bridge, so he was clearly an exceptional player at that level, and it didn't surprise me at all when he went on to do so well in the one-day internationals in South Africa. I was in Australia at the time and each morning would wake up, switch on the scores and say to myself, I wonder if Kev has got another hundred? And he always had!

I think his problems at Notts were exaggerated, to be honest. It's just not right to say that he was an isolated figure in the dressing room. Okay, some people might have had issues with Kev when he first said he wanted to leave the club, but they knew that he was always professional and always scored runs for the club. Yes, he was big mates with me and Stuey MacGill but it wasn't as if he never talked to the others, and I've been back to Notts with him and we always catch up with people and have a drink. I think everybody at Notts has been pleased with how successful he's been.

Of course, we joined Hampshire at the same time but it was just luck and coincidence really. I decided to move there first and then I was delighted to hear Kev was coming too, not least because it meant I wouldn't have to bowl to him! We shared a place in Southampton when we first moved there but I didn't see much of him once he was picked for England and I don't suppose I'll be seeing too much more of him in the future now!

I was sat at home on my sofa when he played that innings at the Oval and I watched every ball. It was just awesome. There's no reason why he can't go on to become one of the greats now. People wondered whether he would be found out after his first season at Notts and of course he wasn't; people asked if he could do it for England at one-day level and of course he could. Then they doubted whether he could play at Test level but he has taken to it like a duck to water. I'm delighted for him as one of his closest friends and I know he'll be able to cope with any bad spells too. When Clive Rice left Notts Kev was going through something of a bad spell and the new coach immediately dropped him to the second team. Far from sulking, he simply scored runs for the seconds and then continued scoring runs as soon as he returned to the firsts. He can cope with anything that's thrown his way.

6

MAKING THE
ACADEMY GRADE

*'It used to annoy me when people said Kevin was
arrogant. I would say, "Give him a chance."'*

Simon Jones

I got an indication pretty early on in my time at Notts that I was being considered for the England Academy, a major stepping-stone towards an international career. David Graveney, the chairman of the England selectors, had spoken to me about England's interest during my first season in England, 2001, which was both a huge confidence boost and a massive incentive to do well at county level. It appeared that, as well as Clive Rice telling me that he would make me an England player in four years, the people who really mattered, the selectors, knew who I was and what I was about as soon as I arrived in the country.

I cannot express how important the continuing interest from England was during my four-year stay at Trent Bridge. It was official recognition of my ambitions and my commitment to the country. It meant they realised I wasn't just here to cash in at county cricket's expense before buggering off back to South Africa.

That was hugely reassuring for me. Imagine those days when I found myself dropped to the Notts second team, without my father figure in Clive Rice and a long way from my family. Yes, I knew what I was doing with my life, but you cannot overestimate my determination to play for England and the buzz I received at any mention of selector interest. At the same time, I had to put England to the back of my mind because I couldn't afford to be distracted by this huge carrot that had been dangled in front of me. It was a case of living my new life, playing as well as I could play and letting the future take care of itself.

When I was picked for the academy a year before I was eligible for England, after my troubled 2003 season, it was made clear to me that the aim of this was to nurture me, get me through the ranks and find out what sort of character I was. To find out if I had what it takes.

County cricket can be a goldfish bowl. Most people know everybody else involved in the sport, at least by reputation, and most people have an opinion of others, not always accurate and often based on hearsay or a lack of context. Clearly, while they had taken a keen interest in me, the selectors had also heard certain stories about me, about my troubles at Notts, and they wanted to see for themselves what I was like. That was fine by me. I was happy to show them the real Kevin Pietersen.

I received a phone call from Rod Marsh, the former Australian wicketkeeper who was in charge of the academy, asking me to spend six months at Loughborough with the probability of a tour to India at the end of it. It was a big moment for me.

Loughborough is a fantastic establishment. It's got everything a young cricketer could possibly need in terms of making it and becoming a more successful and improved player. As well as leading coaches, the academy has the latest technology and fantastic facilities for life as well as cricketing skills. It is a great base for learning.

Everything, it seemed to me, was catered for. We even had a newspaperman brought in to teach us how to deal with press interviews and a TV reporter to show us how to deal with television interviews. All aimed at improving press and media relations. There were computer lessons, too, because with the amount of travelling you do as an England cricketer you need to be computer literate. I was pretty clued up on computers before I went there but you'd be amazed at how many people, young people at that, don't have a clue. I was really shocked by that. Computers can play such a big role in a cricketer's career now that there isn't any excuse for a player not to use one. Not only are they vital for analysing your own game and taking a detailed look at how an opponent plays, they are also crucial for keeping in touch with your family and the world on a long tour abroad.

I think some people there expected me to be trouble. Rod Marsh and his assistants Nigel Laughton and Richard Smith sat me down at the start of it and said, 'We've heard these things about you. We don't believe them. We're going to judge you on merit. You're on the academy and we want you to make the most of it.' Of course, this was a concern. These guys wouldn't have been human if they hadn't at least wondered if what they had heard about me was true. I would probably have been the same. Yet the key was that Rod Marsh and his assistants clearly wanted to make their own minds up and were not about to prejudge me. That's all anyone can ask, really, and I think it's a decent policy in life. Take everybody as you find them and decide for yourself whether they are a good person or not.

Even Geoff Miller, another England selector, had approached me around this time and said, 'What's this we're hearing? Why are you causing trouble? Why are you saying things about people? Why don't you let your cricket do the talking?'

All I ever wanted to do was to let my cricket do the talking. I couldn't believe I had got myself into this position. This was a period of reflection for me, a time to take stock. I was concerned about what people had heard about me and I took a good long look at myself to see if I had been at fault. I thought long and hard but didn't feel that I'd done anything wrong at Notts, so I just vowed to prove the doubters wrong. Cricket is my life, it's not just a game, and this was when I realised just how important it was to me. I needed cricket as my way of life. It is my priority and my number-one goal. It rules my life. It is my hobby and my passion and I absolutely love it. I couldn't let anything spoil it. Not now. Not when I had got so close to my goal of playing Test cricket for England.

When these rumours and outside influences were threatening to affect my life and all that I'd worked towards, I needed to change people's perceptions of me. At Notts I was scoring runs but I was unhappy and things were going on around me that were affecting me. I wasn't being treated the way I felt I deserved to be treated and the strong feelings I had towards the likes of Mick Newell and Jason Gallian came across in the things I said. I vowed to clear my name and put people straight about me.

As far as I was concerned I was a good bloke who loved the banter, loved being in a cricket dressing room and loved performing. I was able to prove that I loved nothing more than working hard and nothing more than listening to coaches and learning from people who had been there and done it. That's the way I went about it, and I loved it. Yes, it was difficult, but I loved it because hard work leads to success.

I was really, really determined to make a success of the academy because I'd had such a poor end to the 2003 season and I wanted to prove I was no troublemaker. I had a positive approach and the will to learn more and improve myself. I made good friendships at Loughborough and was able to get my foot in the door of the England set-up. People would watch you, analyse you and talk about how you coped. I really needed that stability and that environment after the nonsense that had gone on in Nottingham that summer.

I quickly told them at the academy that what they might have heard was a load of rubbish. They just said, 'Let's see how it goes,' and it was brilliant from day one. I never, ever had an argument with anybody. I never, ever gave anyone a hard time or had a hard time from anyone else.

The academy was tough and testing. I didn't stay on the campus as I lived nearby in Nottingham, so I had to be up at 5 a.m. to be at the academy in time for our early starts. This was my first full English winter and I felt it. When that alarm went off I would get up in the dark hoping beyond hope that the sun would soon come up. Daylight did eventually appear, but it was gone again by 4 p.m., which I found horrible. I would leave the academy at 6 p.m. and by the time I got back to Nottingham there was little time to do anything. Anyway, after a full day at the academy I was shattered. Yet it was character-building and I got involved in things I'd never done before.

Rod Marsh was disciplined. I liked him. He also believes, like me, that the harder you work and the tougher you are, the better player you'll become. I wished he had been in charge at Notts! He was an England selector too so you obviously want to impress people like that.

The academy was where I first got to know Simon Jones well. We got on with each other right from the start and our friendship is maintained to this day. I also got on very well with Michael Lumb, and Matty Prior, who has since forced his way into the England picture. Kabir Ali was also there, as was my Notts team-mate Bilal Shafayat.

I have to say that there were also a couple of players there who were wasting their time, and everyone else's, because they didn't like the hard work, they didn't enjoy the things that were put in place. It wasn't easy being in the academy, but then Test cricket isn't easy. I tell you what, when you play Test cricket against Australia you are the only one who is out there. Your family aren't there. Your friends aren't there. You've got blokes trying to knock your head off and it's really difficult.

You just have to get out there and do it and to get to that level you have to put yourself through the hard yards. You have to get up early and you have to work hard. So I knew even then just by watching them that there were some blokes in my academy intake who wouldn't make it to the top. There is no point in naming them. It's clear who they are. They are the ones who haven't come close to England recognition since then, and I have to say that it is the ones I thought would fail who have done, and the ones I thought would succeed who have done. There have been no surprises. It was clear to me then who had the character to succeed at international level and who didn't. Take a look at the list of academy students from my year and you will see who I mean. There is not one person I worked and played with who could consider themselves unlucky not to have been given further opportunities. But I wonder if they see it that way.

Don't get me wrong. The people who didn't make it have the talent. You must have to get that far in the game. But God-given talent is not enough to get to the very top. You have to have mental strength, too, when you are playing against the best players in the world. You're on the big stage, you've got the eyes of the world on you and you have to be able to deal with that.

In county cricket you might get your scores in the paper when you've got ten people watching you, but in Test cricket you have millions of people watching you on TV as well as thousands at the ground. You have to be so on song to thrive and if you are not mentally strong then you are just never going to succeed.

I enjoyed everything about the academy, and came through it

with flying colours. I definitely turned the corner that winter in terms of how the selectors viewed me and the suitability of my character to play Test cricket. I matured a lot as a person. I realised beyond any doubt that this was the life I wanted. It was a case of me growing up, and it ended with my first representative tour, a trip to India I will never forget.

Simon Jones has become one of my biggest friends in the game. It is a friendship that was forged, to a large extent, in those tough days at the academy and on the tour to India, and one that blossomed during the Ashes series of 2005. Take it away, Simon.

Simon Jones: *The first time I met Kevin was in Colwyn Bay when we were both injured! He was playing for Notts and I was playing for Glamorgan but he damaged his leg during the match and joined me on the sidelines where we spent some time talking and having the odd night out, something we have been known to repeat occasionally over the years!*

We got on well straight away. The thing about Kevin is, he will fit in anywhere and with anybody, which is why I found it so surprising that he had been unhappy at Notts. He is a great team man and such a positive person to have around any dressing room that I couldn't imagine why anybody wouldn't get on with him.

I got to know Kevin better when we both went to the academy when we really did start to have a good laugh together. India can be a tough country to tour and we had a couple of beers together at reasonably regular intervals to keep us both sane. I was trying to get back in the England side at the time after recovering from my accident at

Brisbane while Kev was trying to prove himself ready for the international scene, so we both had plenty of incentives and much to work for over the course of that winter.

One of the first things I noticed was how keen he was to have his say in team meetings. He was pretty mature for a young cricketer, which might have had something to do with his upbringing, and he would have a confidence about him in making points while quite a few others had very little to contribute. Kevin knew what he wanted, I was quite sure of that.

It must have been difficult for him at first coming from South Africa. He must have realised that some people were questioning his motives. Maybe that's why he had a bit of trouble at times. The thing was, I could see right away that he wanted to play for England and, not only that, make his life here, and that marked him down as someone different from so many of the mercenaries who take money out of our game and put little back.

I remember having to bowl at him once at Trent Bridge. I was convinced I had got him first ball but the umpire turned it down and Kevin just laughed when he could see how frustrated I was at the decision. Of course, he went on to get 70 or 80 and I never got near to getting him out again!

What makes him such a good player? Well, he has so much time to play the ball. And the key to his whole game is his eye. I've never seen a guy hit the ball as cleanly as Kevin, apart from perhaps Freddie Flintoff. Kevin has this priceless ability to seemingly be able to hit the ball exactly where he wants to on the cricket field and I have never seen anyone hit the ball as far as him when he gets hold of it.

It used to annoy me when people said, without really knowing him, that he was arrogant. I would say, 'Give him a chance.' Kevin is a confident bloke, yes, but people can mistake confidence for arrogance and all Kev has, really, is self-belief. I can think of quite a few people who would have been better players had they possessed that sort of self-belief and confidence. Too many in our game are just happy to have a cushy job in county cricket.

We had a good time during the Ashes, a real good craic. We both like a night out at the right time and we have been on a few good ones, like the time me and Kevin ended up in an Australian bar after the Edgbaston Test. That was quite a laugh and the Aussies were excellent to us that night even though we had just won in the most extraordinary fashion.

I guess the highlight of our friendship so far came at the end of the Ashes summer when I went on holiday with Kev to Los Angeles and Las Vegas. Kevin knew someone out there who opened a few doors for us and we had a wicked time. We were around a few Hollywood types, which was a bit weird, but we never really got to properly meet anybody famous in the film industry or the celebrity world.

The only aspect of that trip I didn't enjoy was being followed out there by the press, who seemed to be waiting for us to slip up or let ourselves down. I've found that a bit hard to handle since the Ashes. The fact that some people, and I know it's only a minority, want to intrude into our private lives and make out that we are not behaving properly. That's been a big eye-opener for me.

I guess it's not quite so bad for me living in Cardiff.

People here will leave you alone a little bit more but there's a lot more scrutiny on Kevin. Everything seems to be magnified in London but Kevin is very strong and he seems to be able to take everything in his stride.

I always knew how good Kev was but I think the rest of the England players knew we really did have someone special in our midst during his Test debut at Lord's when he hit Glenn McGrath for a straight six. You could see the looks on people's faces in our dressing room. It was like 'wow' and it set the tone for the whole series.

And then what Kevin did at the Oval on the last day was truly extraordinary and I made sure I was out on the balcony when he got to a hundred so I could be the first person to applaud him.

I know I can talk to Kevin Pietersen about anything and he will be a true friend. He is someone I can trust totally and there's not too many people you can say that about. I also think he could be one of the greatest batsmen the world has ever seen and I'm delighted he's on my side. With a bit of luck I won't have to bowl to him too often again!

7

READY FOR INTERNATIONAL CRICKET

'You don't have to like him, you don't have

to want to be like him and you certainly don't

have to have your hair cut at the same place as

him, but if you judge him based solely on

what he does with a cricket bat ...'

Stuart MacGill

Cate went back to her parents in Sydney while I went to India for my first representative tour at the start of 2004. It was the first time we'd really been apart since we met but I knew that was international cricket. That was what it was all about.

I had a chance to be successful and I had an opportunity to make a career and a life out of my cricket. I love touring, I love travelling and I love playing cricket, so I knew sacrifices needed to be made if I was to achieve my goals. Better to be sitting in a hotel room in India with the England A side than to be sitting in London doing a normal job. But it is not easy on your partner – I think being involved with an international cricketer is a hard life, certainly on the level of how much time we spend away from home.

At least now the England management encourage families to join the tour. That can only be a good thing, because a happy cricketer has more of a chance of being a successful cricketer.

We went to Malaysia first to acclimatise and I failed to get into double figures in three games. Not the greatest of starts. It didn't go too much better for me when we first arrived in India, where we had been invited to compete in the Duleep Trophy, the premier first-class tournament in India.

First were some one-day games in which I failed to really feature, until Rod Marsh asked me to open the batting in a game in Bangalore. I told him I would do whatever he wanted me to do. My view was that I had to bat at some stage so it might as well be at the top of the innings. It turned out very well. I scored 131 off something like 80 balls, a pretty rapid rate of scoring by anybody's standards, and my tour was off and running.

I scored another hundred in a four-day game in Chennai against India A before scoring two hundreds in the first of our two Duleep Trophy matches, against South Zone, and a 94 in our second trophy game against East Zone in Amritsar, one of the worst places I've ever been to!

So I was pleased with my contribution, even though we lost five of our warm-up games in India and both trophy matches. My form was consistent, which was a relief. I think I was trying a little too hard at first and was struggling to score runs but then I told myself to relax. I knew the wickets were poor but I knew I could play. I was averaging something like 50 in first-class cricket and I wanted to express myself. I'd never opened in my life before and the first time I did it I scored my first hundred for an England side, so that couldn't be bad. It was great to have the freedom to play my shots. I can't see myself opening again because I'm more at home in the middle order but, then again, I think as a batsman you should be able to bat anywhere.

It's just a case of adapting to any situation you find yourself in, whatever number you bat. I faced a lot of spin in India, which was good for my education. I enjoyed batting out there. Facing top-quality spin bowling is one of the hardest challenges for any batsman. It is very different to facing quick bowling and the game becomes even more of a mental challenge, the closest thing to chess that cricket, or any sport for that matter, can provide. And there is nowhere better to learn spin than in India, where some of the greatest slow bowlers that have ever played the game come from and where the pitches give more help to spin bowling than anywhere in the world.

It was an important episode in my cricketing education. At the end of the trip Rod Marsh told me I was ready for international cricket, which was music to my ears. But I still had a year to wait before I was eligible for England.

That was not a problem for me. I had made a commitment to England and a commitment to myself to achieve my goals. Four years of hard work, blood, sweat and tears were needed to achieve that goal. But it was worth it. And during the course of it I had to make sure I could ride life's ups and downs. I had to learn as much as I could from the various coaches I worked with and gain as much experience as I could. Rod Marsh was right up there with the people I learned most from. Until this stage Graham Ford and Clive Rice had been most instrumental in my development, and now the Australian coach was up there alongside them.

I guess it's not a great surprise that I should find an Australian a very good person to work with. I've always got on well with Australians. They are my favourite people! I like working with them and I like socialising with them, and they seem more similar to me in terms of their outlook on life than anyone else I've known.

My affinity with Australians goes back, to a large extent, to my time playing grade cricket in Sydney after my second season with Notts. Stuey MacGill had arrived at Trent Bridge as an overseas player and done fantastically well, and at the end of the season he asked me what I was doing that winter.

I said I wasn't sure so he said, 'You're coming with me,' and he got me a place playing for Sydney University, Greg Matthews's club. It was my second taste of club cricket away from South Africa, after my spell at Cannock, and this was a completely different experience. I stayed in a nice area in Sydney at the top of George Street in the city, just five minutes from the university.

I was looked after really well and played some fantastic first-grade cricket. I made friends and developed my game. What Australia taught me was to value my wicket. In grade cricket you can go a month without batting. Your side bats one week and fields the next and all it needs is for bad weather to intervene on a batting week and you are going a long stretch without any time at the crease.

In county and even international cricket now there's so much of it that you are batting two or three times a week so you can make up for a failure pretty quickly. I like to remember what it was like at grade level. Think of every innings as the only one you're going to get for a while, value each journey to the crease and sell your wicket very dearly. Each innings should mean the world to any batsman, and just because I'm an attacking player doesn't mean I value my wicket any the less.

I didn't break any records in Sydney but I was top scorer for the club over the season and we won the first grade title for the first time in something like a hundred years. It's a very good standard of cricket and it's interesting that top Australian players still go back to their clubs and in most cases play for them from time to time. Even when I was in Australia playing for the ICC world team towards the end of 2005, Shane Warne paid a visit to St Kilda, his old club, and got in a game for them. It's part of their cricketing culture to stay in touch with their roots, and it's to be applauded as far as I'm concerned.

I would say grade cricket is a lot better than top English club cricket but not nearly as good as county cricket. For all my observations about the attitude of some county players, I have to say the standards of county cricket have risen substantially during my time. It's right up there with any domestic cricket, with the top five or six counties being as good as any side, other than national teams, in the world. And that's another huge plus for the English game at a time when the England team is doing so well.

Before I could think of England, however, came that final year at Notts when I just made sure I was playing as well as I could and helping to win games for the team. But my motives were a little more personal that season, for the first time in my life. The team had stuffed me around so I was a little less motivated to do well for them.

Once I had finally decided to break my ties with Notts, I had to consider which county I would be better off at. There were a few possibilities. My preference was to move south. But where would I improve as a player? Where could I challenge myself? Where could I enjoy the way the club was run? Where was the money right?

Hampshire ticked all the boxes. The club was run by Rod Bransgrove, who was a successful international businessman. He knows how to run a business and a club. And counties are businesses now, which is something a lot of them still need to grasp.

Certainly Notts needed to grasp that simple fact. Notts is run by Notts people for Notts people. And a club can get lost running itself like that. Stephen Fleming rescued Notts and if it wasn't for him they would still be in dire straits in my opinion. They certainly wouldn't have won the title in 2005 without him.

By contrast, Hampshire is a progressive club. I had a meeting with Rod Bransgrove, then others with the coaches Paul Terry and Tim Tremlett. Paul is a guy who played for England and impressed me from the first conversation I had with him. I knew straight away he was someone I could work with. He also runs his own academy in Western Australia, so he knows how to coach, run a club, run an academy and interact with human beings. I got on just as well with the others, including the bowling coach Bruce

Reid. There wasn't a bad bloke among them. They were all very warm in accepting me into their club.

Most of all, joining Hampshire meant playing with and learning from the captain, the great Shane Warne. I like to think I've got a decent cricket brain but Shane has one of the best in the world and I knew it could only benefit my cricket being around someone of his calibre. For anyone who has come to cricket recently, let me tell you a bit about Shane Warne. The man is a genius. He emerged at a time when spin bowling in general and leg-spin bowling in particular were in sharp decline and in very real danger of disappearing from this great game.

I have already said how spin bowling is the closest thing to chess in sport and it is impossible to imagine cricket without it. Shane Warne has been responsible, almost single-handedly, for its resurgence over the last 15 years, and for that our game should be truly thankful. Not only that, he is a great competitor and a great character and someone I was truly keen to play under at Hampshire.

The one negative factor was the square at the Rose Bowl, Hampshire's otherwise magnificent new stadium. It has had challenging wickets ever since they first started playing cricket there. It wasn't exactly conducive to selector-nudging big scores and a lot of people speculated whether I was being sensible in opting to play there.

I thought about that, too. I asked myself what the wicket would be like, but I remained confident I could handle it. I wanted to be able to challenge myself. I had got into a comfort zone at Notts. The wicket at the Rose Bowl, I felt, was the last reason why I should worry about joining Hampshire. I wanted to know I was at a club that was well run and one where I could approach the boss and ask him why he did certain things. I wanted to be part of a club where the facilities were fantastic and where I could make an impact as a person and develop into a well-rounded human being. I also wanted to go somewhere where I could help out and get involved in helping bring youngsters on and take people under my wing.

I hadn't met Shane before. I had played against him a couple of times for Notts and he had generally got the better of me, but I had had my moments against him too. But I knew all about him and the positive things people said about him and I couldn't think of a better captain to play under.

All in all it was the perfect move. Some people said I was just going to Hampshire for the money and could come unstuck on their wickets but I got a hundred in my third game at the Rose Bowl, so I proved that one to be wrong. Runs at Trent Bridge are certainly a lot easier to come by than those at the Rose Bowl, but I challenged myself and I came through it.

England commitments meant I didn't spend that much time at Hampshire in my debut season but I'm happy there. It's a good club with good people and I hope to repay them, in future years, for the faith they have shown in me.

Stuey MacGill, as I have said, is a world-class bowler and a good friend. Here is what he thinks of our time together.

Stuart MacGill: *I was approached by Clive Rice via email to complete the English season of 2002 as a replacement spin bowler for Nicky Boje, who was to be away on international duties. It was an exciting offer for me, as I had long wanted to test my skills in the highly scrutinised world of county cricket. As the overseas player a lot was expected of you and the playing schedule meant that you couldn't really afford to relax for one minute. I was sure* that it would improve my game, which had become a little one-dimensional at the time.

My goal was always to use these six weeks as a catapult for further seasons in county cricket (not necessarily with Notts), so I decided to do a little reading online about my opponents and my team-mates.

It was at this time that I first noticed the large numbers of foreign nationals who were taking advantage of their European heritage to play as locals. (KP was just one of them, the other stand-out at Notts being Greg Smith, who would become one of my closest friends and best bowling partners through my time in the UK.)

This has contributed in no small way to the approach team-mates and opposition players within the county system have taken to KP and players like him; perhaps looking at them as stealing local pro cricket jobs and clogging the system with players ineligible to play for England. I am sure that the only way for those players to prevent counties looking overseas is to put their heads down and work on their own games, and instead of regarding players from overseas with different personalities and approaches as enemies, look at them as helping enrich the overall cricket culture. Jealousy never got anyone a head start.

Before I made it to Notts, Clive Rice had been replaced as manager by Mick Newell, who was a part of the fabric of the club and an obvious choice as successor, having played, coached and observed most of the staff throughout their careers. I have no opinion of the sacking of Clive as it did not involve or concern me. I only witnessed the reactions of individual players on my arrival.

From the start I don't think KP gave the new regime a

fair go. I think he respected Clive for the way he had treated him, played the game and run the club, and unfortunately this tainted his last seasons at Notts. Having said that, I also think that he was treated with little or no respect for the player he was becoming, and many at the club were simply waiting for him to fail. Not a healthy working environment. I always favour telling a player early and directly what I think of him and his actions on and off the field as I believe that allows an open and honest relationship to develop. KP may not always have agreed with what I said to him, but I believe he respected my approach and think this forms the basis of our ongoing friendship.

When I arrived at Notts we were sitting in sixth place in the second division, and while I certainly contributed with the ball, it is runs that allow a wrist spinner to do his thing. My second game was against Middlesex at Trent Bridge and I cashed in big time, with my career-best figures. I remember the game, however, for KP's 254 off 252 deliveries. He barely took a risk and spoke openly about his frustrations when Middlesex started setting ultra-defensive fields. Instead of getting out trying to hit over boundary riders, he dealt with it in a mature and striking fashion, running the fieldsmen all over the ground. From that point I watched with interest as he faced new challenges and worked them out in his own way.

At this time I contacted Sydney University Cricket Club in NSW and advised them to sign him – Australian club cricket is very rarely kind to overseas players, but thought that both parties could benefit. KP scored 700+ runs in 12 games and they won the championship.

I think the end for KP at Notts became inevitable when he stopped giving hard-working, ambitious but less talented players the respect that they deserved, and they responded accordingly. Provided a player doesn't actively disrupt his team-mates' preparation or execution, and always gives his all on the field, I don't see a problem.

On the final day of the Ashes at the Oval (apart from my regret at not being able to take my place in the match) I feel that I saw a further step up in KP's game. I was sure that Australia would win the game and retain the Ashes, and just prior to lunch it certainly appeared possible. Our bowlers had momentum in their favour and in the midst of a Brett Lee barrage I remember looking at KP's face on the screen and thinking that for perhaps the first time in his career he was questioning his ability. In boxing parlance, England's Ashes were saved by the bell. During the break he regrouped, developed a plan of attack and played a great innings.

From here the only thing that can stop him from playing for as long as he wants is his love of the spotlight and of the sheer domination of bowlers. He isn't the first player, nor will he be the last, to deal with this, but if he manages to put his ego aside he can achieve many great things on a cricket field.

You don't have to like him, you don't have to want to be like him and you certainly don't have to have your hair cut at the same place as him, but if you judge him based solely on what he does with a cricket bat, then he could finish his career one day with much respect.

8

MAKING MY MARK

'KP is like a sponge, always soaking up information and never resting on his laurels. The beauty of him is that he's full of life too.'

Matt Maynard

I was sitting by the pool in Majorca in the autumn of 2004 when I received a phone call telling me I had been selected by England. David Graveney, the chairman of selectors, called to say I was going on the short one-day tour of Zimbabwe.

It had been on my mind throughout the holiday. I knew when selection was and I always made sure I had my phone on me in case the call came. When I heard that some players were going to be rested and others might not be going because they didn't want to tour Zimbabwe, I really did think I had a great chance of being picked.

When the call came it was the best feeling in the world. As soon as I had qualified for England they had picked me for the first tour I was available for. All the hard work I had put in had proved worthwhile.

I thought I would get a gig for the whole winter and, while it was a great phone call to get, Graveney did tell me I wouldn't be going on the main tour to South Africa, which I was really disappointed about. There had already been quite a debate over whether I would be going back to the land of my birth as an England player and how I would cope with the scrutiny. To me, I was ready for that and wanted to go, but I think at that point the selectors were looking to protect me.

I immediately phoned Mum and Dad to give them the news. They were thrilled to bits – it was one of the happiest moments of my life. I then had a bottle of champagne at the poolside and went out for a great celebration dinner that night.

I knew this was only the start. I knew that, while this was a great honour, I would only have made everything worthwhile if I got to the very top and became an important member of the England side, a permanent fixture. After that it would be a case of becoming one of the world's best players. The hopes and aspirations were clearly defined and had always been in my mind. This was a big stepping-stone to where I wanted to be.

It was a controversial trip. I'm from South Africa so I had a better idea than most of the team about what was going on in Zimbabwe and what to expect there. I'd been to Zimbabwe before. It wasn't an eye-opener to me to see people living in poverty on the streets because I knew the problems that country had. As for whether it was right politically for us to tour there, I had to go because this was the start of my England career, and it was up to people much better qualified than me to decide on the ethics.

First we went to Namibia, hardly a cricketing hotbed to launch an international career but it would do for me, to acclimatise. My first innings for the full England side ended horribly when I was given out, slogging, to a very bad decision. Next time I got 20-odd, which gave me a little bit of confidence, particularly as my first boundary was a nice drive through the covers, followed in the next over by a six straight back over the bowler's head. So I was starting to settle in.

That settling-in process was made easier by the 'buddy' system that operated on that trip. Each player was paired with another and the 'buddies' would exercise and practise together. My buddy was Ashley Giles and it was the start of a big friendship for me. We got on very well from the start and he made it much easier for me to feel at home. The opposition wasn't great in Namibia but it was a solid enough start and even featured some outbreaks of sledging amongst the sparse crowd aimed at me because of my southern African upbringing. Little did I know that that would be a taste of things to come.

Sledging, or mental disintegration as the Australians like to call it, is a feature of cricket that fascinates many people. It was invented by the Australians in the 1970s, and it's a technique of using crude or aggressive language to put off an opponent or try to gain some sort of psychological advantage over them.

What some people don't realise, though, is that sledging can be very humorous too. People can say some very funny things to each other in the middle of a match. It is not all swearing and unpleasantness, believe me. There's so much cricket played now around the world that people get to know each other well and there are more friendships among opponents than people realise. Yes, some people get carried away when they step over the line on to a cricket field, perhaps get a bit of 'white line fever' or just go 'bombs away' when faced by an opposing batsman, but what I always try to remember is that it's just playacting. I would always rather have a laugh and a joke with players on the field. That's what I did with Shane Warne and most of the Australians during the 2005 Ashes, and that's what I even managed to do when Andre Nel was letting me have it with both barrels during my baptism of fire in South Africa, but it doesn't mean the intensity of the battle is any the less. It's just cricket and the way cricket is, and in fact the cricket being played around the world now is so professional and of such a high standard that you don't get too many indulging in sledging.

Next stop after Namibia was Zimbabwe but we nearly didn't get there. On the eve of departure we discovered that 13 of the travelling press corps had been refused entry to the troubled country, and it became clear that if the press weren't allowed to report the tour, we could hardly be expected to play in it. As a newcomer who desperately wanted to play for England this was a big worry to me. I'd already experienced politics in my career over what happened at Natal and I didn't want politics to interfere now I was so close to where I wanted to be.

We were holed up in a hotel in Johannesburg, rather like the England World Cup squad had been in Cape Town two years earlier, while frantic meetings took place over whether we were going to go. At one stage it really did look as though we were going home. The older players were not keen to go at all, while I was champing at the bit.

I was convinced there wouldn't be any physical threat to us, knowing the country better than most, but the moral issues were a different kettle of fish entirely. To me, what we were about to find in Zimbabwe was no different to a lot of what you see in South Africa to this day. There is still a lot of progress that needs to be made in that country too. And as for any potential violence? Well, to me when your day is up your day is up and there's not a lot you can do about it. It's an attitude that probably comes from my religious background. I believe in fate and I had no reason to be afraid of Zimbabwe.

We were sitting around by the pool for what seemed like an agonising amount of time until we got word that we were going and the press were to be allowed to accompany us after all. To me it was a huge relief.

I was with a bunch of guys who I looked up to, who I had played against but didn't know that well, and who had been making a lot of progress as an England team. I had been made to feel very welcome straight away and my first impressions of the captain, coach and everyone else were hugely favourable. I could see straight away why Michael Vaughan commanded respect within the team. He is such a nice man, and was clearly a captain everyone wanted to play for.

Michael is not a dictator; the whole England team respect him for the way he is, the way he comes across and the way he goes about things. He won't tell you to do something. He'll ask you a question so that you can think about what he's suggesting and then work it out for yourself. You learn more the Michael Vaughan way. It's more of a 'why, when and what' style of leadership, as opposed to a 'do this' and 'do it my way' approach. He is not a person who will just nail you. He'll tell you if you are doing something you shouldn't do, but he'll say, 'Why did you do that?' and get you thinking about yourself. You then mull it over and take in so much more.

Vaughan gets on with everybody and is somebody everybody can approach, from the coach to the most inexperienced player in the team. He will talk to you, have dinner with you, and is totally approachable, which is a fantastic quality. He's a fantastic cricketer, too, with a cricket brain that's very special. Michael is so relaxed in everything he does, he exudes a calm authority that spreads to everyone around him. If you have a captain who's biting his nails and fretting all day, it definitely does play on your mind and can lead to problems in the team.

Once it was clear we were going to Zimbabwe, the management told us how we should deal with the difficult off-field aspects of the trip, which, to be fair, were potentially more problematic than facing a weakened Zimbabwe team.

We were to play four games. The first was in front of a decent crowd in Harare with no signs of any trouble or anybody trying to make political gain from our visit. A huge relief. It was a comfortable five-wicket win for us, with me being at the crease at the end for an unbeaten 27. The second game saw me win the man-of-the-match award for an unbeaten 77 off 76 balls in a thumping 161-run victory. I was extremely happy with that, even though I knew I wasn't facing a formidable attack. They had been the only opportunities I'd had to impress up to that point, and I knew I had to take any chance that came my way with both hands.

I didn't bat in the third match and got a first ball dismissal in the fourth, in Bulawayo, but England won both matches easily. I was pleased with my time in Zimbabwe and felt I had done all I could to impress.

It was about this time that people first started raising questions about my technique and whether I was too leg-sided a player to thrive against the very best bowling. I heard it said that I might be susceptible to lbws or the straight ball. It wasn't something that unduly worried me because I was sure they were wrong and it was just something I had to deal with.

The feedback I got from coach Duncan Fletcher was good. He never tried to change my technique and I think he was impressed with my trigger movements and forward press. The truth is, I am a leg-side player, but then so was Mark Waugh and he got thousands of runs at the very highest level. If it's a strength of your game you have to play to it rather than worry about it. I'm not interested in negatives. Really not interested.

I had also done a lot of work in Zimbabwe with batting coach Matthew Maynard and I am sure he would have told me if he felt my technique needed to be changed. I could see Matty was a very positive player in his time, one who liked to dominate bowlers, and his mentality was very similar to mine. I spent many hours practising with Maynard and still do now when I'm with England. He knows my game very well and knows when I'm playing well.

Matty came back to England with the players who had only been picked for the Zimbabwe leg of the trip, while the Test players went on to South Africa, and he told me that Duncan Fletcher had been really impressed with what I'd done. I had also had a meeting with Fletcher before I left Zimbabwe and he told me he was going to try to get me to South Africa for the one-dayers after all. That was an incredible boost to my confidence. It was a trip I desperately wanted to be on.

Sure enough, I got the call to say I would be heading to South Africa at the end of the Test series in late January. Freddie Flintoff was to miss the one-day series but I don't think I was an official replacement for him as such. Anyway, they called me up. I saw this huge opportunity in front of me to play in South Africa, the land of my birth, so soon after qualifying for England. It would be the biggest test of my life. And how! But I just wish I had played in the Test matches too.

Matt Maynard, the old Glamorgan and England batsman and now England batting coach, has been a significant figure in my England career and has been someone I have worked with very closely ever since I first played for England. Here's what he has to say.

Matt Maynard: *I first saw KP when he played against Glamorgan for Notts the season after he had been to the England Academy. Simon Jones had become friendly with KP there and told us he could play, and then KP went out and took us for a hundred, hooking and pulling Simon as if he was a medium pacer.*

Then I first worked with KP when he toured with England in Zimbabwe and it's been an absolute pleasure to deal with him. Yes, he plays some extravagant shots, but he actually has a very solid technique which involves doing the basics very well and that will stand the test of time.

He keeps the game very simple, which is what I like about him. I know other people have said it but it's true that he's not unlike Viv Richards in the way he plays. Viv would play down the right line and angle the ball to leg and KP is a bit like that, only more extravagant. Neither of them play down the wrong line in their keenness to hit the ball to leg. They play straight but manipulate the ball with their wrists.

KP is wonderful to work with. He will play with the bat in front of the pad when facing spin; he plays the swinging ball late and the seaming ball early. And he is so keen to learn. For instance, the winter we were in Pakistan and India he told me he couldn't play the paddle sweep, as opposed to the slog sweep, but we worked on it intensely for three net sessions and he was able to take it into a game. It was simply a question of working on his mindset to play the shot and he was quickly able to do it.

KP gives people the impression he's comfortable with his game but he is always working on it and wants to develop it. Graeme Hick was one of the great county players but couldn't take that into the international game. KP has made that stride already and has such a willingness to learn. He is like a sponge, always soaking up information and never resting on his laurels. The beauty of him is that he's full of life too and as long as he always puts his cricket first, which he will do, he could well go on to become one of the best batsmen in the history of our game. I rate him that highly.

As soon as Duncan Fletcher and I saw him in Zimbabwe we said to each other, 'This guy has got to play.' You want people in your side who can score you hundreds and he looks capable of scoring hundreds in any company. We knew straight away in Zimbabwe that we had to take him to South Africa, and then, when he got there, he showed incredible bravery in dealing with the hostility of the home crowds and actually turning it to his advantage.

The only shot I can't claim to have had anything to do with is his reverse slog sweep for six off Muttiah Muralitharan at Edgbaston against Sri Lanka. I don't know where that came from but it was KP at his best. We had talked about reverse sweeping in certain situations but I certainly didn't coach him that. Perhaps he was fortunate that Murali bowled him a full toss, but it was audacious and effective.

The next step for KP is working out the percentages of a shot like that and that will come with experience. He's a quick learner. We all make mistakes but he tends not to repeat his. The biggest test for him is when opponents come up against him for a second time and try to operate new plans to limit his effectiveness. I believe all teams will try to be more defensive against him, play with a sweeper from the off, give him singles and try to frustrate him into hitting one in the air.

He's got to be able to cope with that but I'm sure he will and will quickly turn the percentages back in his favour from that sort of situation. Everyone goes through testing times but because of the correctness of his game KP won't be restricted by anything as mundane as defensive tactics.

9
SOME HOMECOMING!

'Let Kevin wear jewellery. Let him have flamboyant hairstyles. What's wrong with that as long as he is producing the goods? Kids can relate to Kevin.'

Darren Gough

I had known for some time that England would be touring South Africa just after I qualified to play for them. I could not have written a better script than that. The prospect of touring there, with all that it entailed, appealed to me hugely; I had been very disappointed when I was initially left out of the trip.

I think the selectors knew what would be in store for me, that the South African public would not take kindly to someone they considered to have walked out on their country coming back to play against their team so soon after becoming eligible. The selectors knew that the South Africans, a people not known for being timid, would let me know in no uncertain terms what they thought of me. It would be quite a homecoming.

But the prospect far from fazed me. It excited me. I wanted to take Clive Rice's advice and use it as motivation; I wanted to show everyone in South Africa what they were missing. I wanted it very much and I was delighted when I got another call from chairman of selectors David Graveney to say it was going to happen. It was for the one-day leg only but it was a massive development for me. Far from being worried that the extra attention would in any way damage me, I hoped that it would be the making of my career.

I got the call in early January 2005, and I hit the gym hard and had some net sessions at Loughborough. By this time I had grown close to Darren Gough, who had been in Namibia and Zimbabwe and who was someone I had been drawn to because of similarities in our personalities. I was also fully aware, of course, that Goughy had been and still was a truly great cricketer who had achieved an awful lot with England. He was somebody I wanted to be around.

I love spending time with blokes who have been around the international scene and who have been successful. I like to watch them, listen to them and see what makes them tick. That's how I go about things because I want to learn and I want to be great like them. It's why I try to spend a lot of time around Freddie Flintoff too. He has become a colossus in the England team and in world cricket.

Goughy told me to play my natural game, back myself and enjoy myself, and that was what I was determined I was going to do, however fierce the attention on me was going to be over the course of the next few weeks.

I must confess to nerves as I arrived in Johannesburg with the one-day players to prepare for our series, while the England Test team were completing their successful series against South Africa. After I had checked in to the Sandton Sun Hotel, from where England were commuting to Centurion for the final Test, people congratulated me and told me they were right behind me. It was clear to me from the start that everyone around the team considered me to be an Englishman, to be one of them, and that was marvellous for a young player in my position to know.

I had some idea what to expect from the crowds. I knew what South African crowds could be like. They can be vocal and unforgiving. I knew it wasn't going to be pretty, but I also knew that not only were the team and management behind me, but also my friends and family, who had been incredibly supportive.

Little did I know, though, that my friendship with Gough would land me in a bit of trouble before we had even started! The boys who were playing in the Test had had an early night but

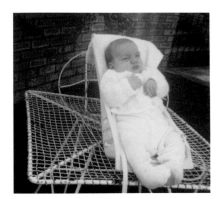

above: Me and my bro, Bryan, in the back yard. He always tried to beat me when we played cricket together as kids.

above: Jodie and I have always been pretty close. He was holding me back here though!

above: Hanging out with the lads at Maritzburg College, 1997.

above: I always preferred kicking
to anything else in rugby.

right: Me doing my
John Wayne impression.

PERM LAZER

Natal Primary Schools   **1992**   Natalse Primêre Skole

Cricket Festival   Krieketfees

PIETERMARITZBURG EAST

SITTING : D BINNS (MERCHISTON), D WANG (DRAKENSVIEW), M WHITELAW (CLARENDON),
H YOUNG (MERCHISTON), R SYMES (MERCHISTON), K PIETERSEN (MERCHISTON),
J SYMES (MERCHISTON)

STANDING : A RICHMOND (COWAN HOUSE), M HAMPSON (ESTON), B FERREIRA (MERCHISTON),
J PIENAAR (PELHAM), C MALHERBE (MERCHISTON), D BOTHA (CLARENDON),
B GREENE (CORDWALLES), C WILSON (PELHAM).

above: Playing at Hilton College.

right: Playing in the 20/20 game, Notts V Lancs.

© PHILIP BROWN

above: Being put through
our paces at RMAS.

right and below: Winning the C&G
final for Hampshire at Lords.

© PHILIP BROWN

above: Warney was a big influence in my move to Hampshire. Not sure about his hair though!

above: The Master at work. You can learn so much from Warney – he is a true legend.

left: It was all Goughie's fault.

below: Me getting my back straightened out.

left: The much talked about hairdo!

below: Part of my pre-match routine is to have a can of Red Bull. It gets me going.

© PHILIP BROWN

© PHILIP BROWN

© RYAN PIERSE/GETTY IMAGES

© PHILIP BROWN

Goughy and I, still ten days away from our first game, decided to go out in Sandton, the upmarket suburb of Johannesburg where international cricket teams stay on their visits to this part of the country. We had a good night, so good that apparently we'd been noisy when we returned to the hotel and had woken up some of the players at 2 a.m. Not the best start!

The next day we were training at Centurion Park, when Matthew Maynard told me that Duncan Fletcher wasn't happy because some of the one-day guys had been out late and had been up to some mischief. I knew he must mean Goughy and me but I tried to keep out of the way. I certainly wasn't going to admit to anything at that stage.

That was fine until Darren decided to own up. I was like, 'Don't do it, Goughy, we might get away with it!' But he told Duncan, and Duncan worked out I had been involved. I honestly hadn't thought we'd done anything wrong because there was such a long time before our first one-day international, but what I hadn't fully considered was the noise we were creating on our return and the fact that we'd woken people up who had to win a Test series for England the next day.

The social side of cricket is a very important part of the game, even in these days of enhanced professionalism. Not bad or excessive behaviour, just a night out drinking, talking, laughing and meeting new people. I'm sure a lot less drinking goes on than used to be the case in the old days, and players are a lot more sensible about their diets and professional in their preparations for the game, but at the same time there is still room for nights out, a bit of bonding and, yes, a bit of drinking. I am a fit person, in common with everyone in the England picture these days, and I work very hard on my fitness and preparation, but that won't stop me enjoying myself at the right times. Cricket is a social game and long may that continue. Better that than living like a recluse and not making any friends from the game to take on to later life.

It's just that on this occasion, as a relative new boy and with everything to prove to my coach and new team-mates, I should have been a little more sensible. Duncan took me to one side and asked me what time I had gone to bed the night before. I told him I honestly didn't know because I'd had a drink and I didn't want to lie to him. It was the truth. Better that than pretend I'd been tucked up in bed by 11 p.m. when I clearly wasn't. Even I knew that and I had been drunk! Duncan told me it wasn't on and that he had brought me over to South Africa as a reward for the promise I'd shown in Zimbabwe and that I should remember that. I mustn't let people down. It was a rap over the knuckles and it was good for me because it made me realise what was required at this level, what Duncan was about and what the team was about. A good lesson in how to behave as an international cricketer.

I put my hand up and apologised, as did Goughy, and we moved on. It didn't stop us enjoying ourselves out there. We just had to make sure we picked the right time. We're both sociable people and enjoy having fun. And we enjoyed South Africa.

Our first match was to throw me straight into the deep end. We were playing South Africa at the Wanderers in Johannesburg, the famous South African Bullring, and the most atmospheric and intimidating stadium in the country. I was nervous and my parents were nervous, but I don't think they fully knew what was about to hit me and hit them.

The night before the game, for the first time in my life, I consulted a sports psychologist, Steve Bull. I asked him what advice he could give me. I didn't know quite what to expect.

Bull kept it simple. He said to me, 'What do you do in county cricket? What do you do when you bat? What's the process? Do you watch the ball at the start of the bowler's run?' I told him I never stop watching the ball until I have either played it or left it and he said, 'Well, just do that tomorrow. Watch the ball. Don't worry about the crowd. Shut them out. Don't worry about anything.'

I vowed to do so. That Sunday afternoon in late January 2005 got off to a very emotional start when, unusually in cricket, both teams stood for the national anthems before play. My dad has already said that he looked at both teams, wondering if I was standing in the right place. I had no doubts. This was a huge moment for me. It was confirmation that I was an Englishman, standing with the England cricket team singing our national anthem. And to top it all it was in the country of my birth. I couldn't have asked for more.

There was no holding back as far as I was concerned. No self-consciousness. I stood there proud as punch and belted out 'God Save The Queen' for all my life was worth. People wondered if I would know the words. Of course I knew the words! Dad also said that when he saw both teams lined up, with us linking arms and looking every inch a team, while the South Africans looked like a disjointed bunch of individuals, he knew then that I was standing in the right place. There were never any doubts in my mind.

When we went out to field, Michael Vaughan, in the huddle on the outfield, said, 'If KP gets any abuse out here today we must all stand behind him. If they give him stick they are giving us all stick. If they say anything to him or us we must abuse them back.' It made the hairs on the back of my neck stand on end. Coming from Michael Vaughan, the England captain, it was, to me, recognition that I was part of the England team.

We made a good start and my nerves were eased considerably when I took an early catch to dismiss Herschelle Gibbs off the bowling of Matthew Hoggard. Then, and this is something I still have to ask Vaughany about, he sent me to field on the boundary in front of the noisiest section of the worst crowd in world cricket!

You might as well go in at the deep end. I tried to have some fun with the spectators but they were abusing me in the most basic way possible. They called me Judas, which is about as witty as it gets from a South African audience, and called me a racist because of leaving their country over the quota system. I just accepted their nonsense and enjoyed myself with us on top and South Africa struggling to 175 for nine from their 50 overs.

A bigger test came when it was my turn to bat. And what a moment it turned out to be. I was nervous waiting to go in, particularly as we were in a bit of trouble at 44 for three when I emerged from the Wanderers pavilion. What greeted me was the most deafening noise I have ever experienced. The level of abuse was extraordinary. I can't imagine there has ever been a reception to an incoming batsman like it in cricket history. Not that I know of, anyway. I liken it in some ways to Monty Panesar touring India, the land of his parents, with England a year later when he first broke into the side. Only it was completely different. Everyone in India was proud of Monty, made him feel welcome and made him feel special. Yes, there was pressure on him making his debut against, of all countries, India, but everyone in that country was positive towards Monty and made him feel special. What a contrast to my baptism!

The noise from the crowd was reaching a crescendo as I prepared to face my first ball from Andre Nel, one of the more aggressive members of an aggressive South African side. Watch the ball, I kept on telling myself. I felt edgy, sweaty. Not like I usually do when I bat. It was the most nerve-racking ball I have ever faced.

Nel has a real sense of drama and was playing up to the moment as he bowled me a quick delivery just outside off-stump that swung away from me. I prodded at it and just failed to get a touch. If I'd nicked that ball, the whole trip, possibly my whole England career, could have turned out very differently. Thankfully I didn't.

It was a testing time but it helped that Nel is a good friend of mine. Really, he is a big friendly giant. His bark is most definitely worse than his bite. It's all bluster and a sense of theatre with him. I just smiled at him while he abused me. Remember what I said about sledging being amusing? Nel is a great man and a very good bowler. I know he can go over the top a bit with his histrionics but he's a great competitor and a very nice human being. He certainly found a heck of a delivery to greet me first up.

Anyone can get a first-baller and it almost happened to me on this huge occasion. I never fret too much if I'm out first delivery. It can happen before you get your eye in. I am usually much more annoyed with myself if I get out in the twenties or thirties because then much of the hard work has been done and you really should kick on to a big score.

After that ball, Vaughan, the perfect batting partner in this situation, walked up to me and said, 'Kevin, just watch the ball. It's white and it's heading your way. That's all you have to do.' Luckily for me, Michael was batting beautifully at the other end and I just tapped it around after taking 11 balls to get off the mark – unusual for me!

I hit my first boundary through backward point off Nel and took a few runs from Nicky Boje as I began to relax a little and enjoy myself. The South African players were fine. They were competing in an international and were concentrating on winning rather than giving me a particularly hard time.

All except Graeme Smith, their captain. He was the only member of their side to make any snide comments to me. I had 'kevinpietersen.com' on my bat and Smith kept on asking me how much I paid myself to put that logo on my bat. Very funny, Graeme.

I'd never met Graeme Smith before but I thought he was an absolute muppet from the word go. He had not been short of a few things to say about me in the build-up to the tour. He was telling the press things like he couldn't wait to play against me and would make sure I didn't get any runs. He talked about how I'd turned my back on the country, things like that. But I had never met the man before and I hadn't done anything to upset him or force him to say things about me.

I gave it back by asking him who he thought he was. I found Graeme Smith's attitude that day and throughout the tour pretty childish, to be honest. I don't know many people in world cricket that like that man and that's sad. He's a bloke who needs the game but he hasn't got many friends in it, and I think it's a game you should play to make friendships, more than any other game, all over the world. That's what I want to take from cricket.

I could ring up any of the Australians we played against in 2005 and have a good chat with them and I could do the same with the South Africans – except Smith. He's a strange one and is a bit over the top. He got a bit of power at a young age and I don't think he knows what to do with it and how to handle himself. The bloke can bat, no question. He's a fantastic cricketer, but I reckon that his behaviour as an international captain leaves a lot to be desired.

Look at the way he speaks to people like Shaun Pollock and Jacques Kallis, great players and men who have earned the utmost respect in the game. I've heard him talk down to them, yet they've achieved a lot more than he has. They played through readmission and the hard times. I know it can't have been easy for a 22-year-old to become captain of his country, especially after all that happened with Hansie Cronje, but it's fair to say that a lot of South African people as well as players don't like Smith, and I don't think that's the way I want to be, or how I want people in the game to remember me.

I don't talk to Graeme Smith now. I think it's a waste of breath to do so because I haven't got any respect for him. Nailing people in the papers when you don't even know them is not a clever thing to do and it's not the right way to go about things. Australian players can use the press to make certain points about people but they do it cleverly and tactically and that's the way to go about things as far as I'm concerned. They don't take cheap shots.

It was great to win at the Wanderers. We had progressed to 103 for three after 25.1 overs, well on course for victory, when a huge storm came to put paid to the proceedings. We won on the Duckworth Lewis system, which was great, but it would have been nicer if the game had run its full course and we had won properly. I finished on 22 not out, but to me it felt like a lot more.

Mum and Dad were upset at how the spectators had treated me. Mum told me afterwards that she was in tears when I came out to bat and couldn't understand what was happening. They knew I would come in for some stick but didn't expect it to be as bad as it was. Neither did I. Yes, I thought some people would swear at me, but nothing like that. People who were there told me afterwards that they'd never heard anything like it on a cricket pitch. I think you could have heard the noise in Pretoria.

Yet the reception when I walked out to bat was two minutes of the biggest character-building of my life. To have all those thousands of people reacting like that and millions more in South Africa gunning for me meant that to win the game and finish unbeaten was of huge significance to me. To me, getting through that was a big indicator that I could do well at international level.

At the end Michael Vaughan was calm and my parents and brother Bryan were pretty emotional. They were happy, too, and after the game we all talked about the day back at the hotel. In a way it had made me realise, deep inside, the enormity of the decision I had made to leave South Africa and the question of national pride that it had clearly stirred up in many people. I had never thought about it in those terms before. One of the umpires that day, Ian Howell, apologised to me on behalf of South Africa and said that what I received was both disgusting and disgraceful. It was a nice gesture on his part, but I wasn't concerned afterwards. I knew it would be hard. I knew it would be tough. And I knew it would be a test of my ability. But I got through it and it stood me in great stead for what was to follow.

Darren Gough was my soulmate and my 'twin' on that tour of South Africa. I will talk about some of the other things we got up to together soon but for now let the Dazzler tell you what he made of it all.

Darren Gough: *I have never been someone who prejudges people. I like to make my own mind up about someone, so, even though I had heard some stories about how Kevin was supposed to be before I met him, I was determined not to listen until I met the man himself. And then, as soon as I met him, I thought he was great.*

It was clear he had confidence and I like people like that. I can understand why some people might think of Kevin as being a bit big-headed when they first meet him but as soon as you get to know him you realise there's a lot more to him than that.

A lot of people can mistake confidence for arrogance,

*but not me. I like someone who has a little bit about them,
and it was clear to me from the start that Kevin had a lot
about him. And as soon as I bowled to him in the nets I
could see he had all the qualities to be a top sportsman.
And I tend to be a good judge of a player. His eye and his
shot-making stood out from the first day he spent with
England in Namibia. You sometimes get people who look
the part in the nets but then can't do the business when the
pressure is on out in the middle, but it was also clear that
Kevin had the mental strength to cope with anything that
was thrown at him.*

*Duncan Fletcher knew Kevin would get stick going
back to South Africa so he encouraged me to spend time
with Kevin, to keep an eye on him and, if you like, provide
a bit of a safety blanket for him. Fletch knew that I was the
sort of character who could cope with that sort of thing
and he wanted me to help Kevin come through it. As it
turned out, Kevin loved every minute of it there!*

*We are very similar characters. We both like being the
centre of attention. We both like to enjoy ourselves off the
field, when the time is right. We quickly became very close
and started to go everywhere together.*

*What struck me straight away, too, was how know-
ledgeable KP was about his cricket. From the very first
team meeting he would say his little bit about the game
ahead, which is quite unusual for a young player. In fact,
you get a lot of senior players sitting in team meetings
saying nothing, so Kevin's input was refreshing. And I
know Duncan Fletcher was impressed by that.*

*I think Kevin's emergence was not only good for him
and English cricket but also good for Freddie Flintoff.*

People talking about KP all the time made Freddie lift himself a bit. Maybe it was a little bit of a kick up the backside for Fred and I think they have been good for each other.

Kevin's attitude was summed up perfectly for me ahead of the Ashes series in 2005 when we were talking about how he was going to play Shane Warne. A lot of people would just concentrate on keeping him out and seeing him off but Kevin said simply, 'I'm going to hit him for six.' I thought it was great to hear an English player say something like that and mean it. He has such a presence about him. You know that he could come in with your side 150 for four and, within 20 overs, the score could easily be 250 for four.

I spoke to him on the phone almost every day during the Ashes and I was proud of what he had done for himself and for English cricket. It was all summed up for me by a little passage of play during his amazing century on the last day at the Oval.

Just before lunch Brett Lee was giving him a real going over and could have got him out every ball. But KP got through to lunch, seemed to take stock, and then came out as if to say, 'I'm not having this. I'm going to take him on.' Then he just smacked Lee for six and carried on batting positively in the most high-pressure situation you can possibly imagine. That takes some doing, and if it wasn't for Kevin's innings that day the series would have been drawn and the Ashes would have been lost. Survival would have been the motto for most batsmen in those circumstances but Kevin went for it and scored one of the best and most important hundreds you will ever see.

KP has brought a bit of football-type glamour to cricket. He loves a night out, loves dressing in good clothes *and dating pop stars or models. I was the first person in cricket who, really, brought a bit of individuality to the game and I love to see it now in people like KP and others in the England team like Simon Jones. They wear their hair the way they want, wear nice clothes and jewellery and generally be themselves rather than conforming to the traditional idea of what a cricketer should look like and act like.*

Let Kevin wear jewellery. Let him have flamboyant hairstyles. Let him have a big watch. What's wrong with all of that as long as he works hard and produces the goods on the cricket field? Kids can relate to someone like Kevin much more than they could to players of the past.

The hairstyle and the tattoo can, to a large extent, be blamed on me. When we were in Cape Town with England I encouraged Kevin to have a stripe put in his hair and told him I would have two stripes put into mine. I quickly changed mine but his became something of a trademark and a talking point.

Earlier, in Johannesburg, KP had seen me have a three lions tattoo and told me he would have it done too. I thought the pain might have put him off but he saw I never flinched when I had mine done and, sure enough, he went through with it at the end of the tour. I know his dad said he would come after me if Kevin had it done but he was fine about it. I'm not sure quite what Kevin's dad thinks when he sees the hair, jewellery and tattoos but Kevin is living his own life and is living it in an individual way.

We are still close. As soon as Kevin knew he had to come home from the Pakistan tour through injury he was on the phone to me saying he wanted to come and support me on Strictly Come Dancing. *And he was there in the theatre when I won it. I think he may have even got some stick for that. Some people said he shouldn't have been seen out so soon after coming home from an England tour injured but why shouldn't he come? What do people expect injured players to do? Just sit at home moping? Watching me didn't suddenly make his injury better or worse.*

People ask me what comes next for Kevin and the answer is entirely in his own hands. The only thing that could stop Kevin Pietersen is himself. He has had a lot of things thrown his way, has earned a lot of money, has a great lifestyle and likes spending his money. You have to be a bit careful of the light because it can easily trap you. We have all been caught up in the light at times and I think he's seen that already and will make sure he knuckles down and makes sure he is not distracted. With the amount of talent he has, he has got to do that.

I have no doubts that Kevin is here to stay. He will be in the England team for at least the next five years, no question. The only problems he will have will come when he goes through a spell without scoring runs because there are people out there in the press who won't like the way he lives his life and will want to nail him. But Kevin can cope with that. English cricket should be grateful it has him and cherish him.

10

FROM TURNED BACKS TO A STANDING OVATION – THE SOUTH AFRICA STORY

'You always get branded with the South African thing. It never goes away. Some people always called me "the South African-born Allan Lamb", and it will be the same for KP.'

Allan Lamb

It was nice to wake up the next morning to see the back pages of the South African papers filled with pictures of me batting, but the last thing I felt was that I'd arrived as an England player because I'd only scored 22 runs before the rain came at Johannesburg. My feelings were simply that I wanted to play again and as soon as possible, but I must admit to feeling more emotionally than physically drained as we made our way to Bloemfontein for the second international. So drained that I slept the whole way there.

I had a nice surprise when I checked into our hotel. My brother Gregg and his wife Nicky visited me en route from Cape Town to Johannesburg. I don't always see as much of my family as I would like, so it was nice to catch up with Gregg for an hour.

Bloemfontein is the heart of Afrikaner country. My reception in Johannesburg had been bad, to say the least, so I wondered what was in store for me here. My apprehension wasn't helped by my worst net of the whole trip the day before the game. I batted like an absolute idiot with my feet going nowhere. Whether I was still uptight or nervous I don't know, but it didn't augur well. Some net bowler knocked me over three or four times and I got totally frustrated because I couldn't work out what was happening to me. I had been batting so well.

I was so concerned about this turn of events that I went to the ground early on the day of the match and had another net with Matt Maynard, which settled me a bit because it went a lot better.

When the time came for me to bat we had lost three cheap wickets so again the experience I had gained by opening the batting on the academy tour of India came in handy. Again there were boos, and this time there was a big message on the electronic scoreboard that read, 'Welcome home, Kevin Pietersen.' Maybe they were just being nice but I took it to be drenched in sarcasm.

Now I remembered the words of Clive Rice, who told me to use any stick I received to my advantage. Initially I had to build a partnership again with Michael Vaughan, which made me feel great straight away because I love batting with him. He's such a calming influence on me and we batted well together before I moved on to about 60 and started to realise that I might be able to get a hundred. It was staring me in the face.

I just had to make sure I got my head down and concentrated. What I do really remember from that innings was one of the earliest shots I hit and one that told me it could well be my day. It came against the bowling of Shaun Pollock, and you have to remember that he was a huge figure who had been a boyhood hero of mine and someone I always looked up to and admired.

Suddenly here I was lofting Shaun over square leg for six and it was an amazing moment of satisfaction and a feeling of having arrived. I was like: I've just hit Shaun Pollock for six. It was as big a moment as any in my arrival on the English cricket scene. You could even say it was the moment that changed my life.

That six gave me such a lot of confidence I knew I was in for a big day. Other things had gone my way too. I had some shaky moments. For instance, I kept on trying to hit Jacques Kallis and Andrew Hall over mid-off but, instead, kept on nicking them to third man. When that kept on happening I knew it was going to be my day and, sure enough, the big moment came when, having tried to get through the nervous nineties as quickly as I could, Makhaya Ntini bowled a ball on my legs which I hit to deep square leg for my first senior international hundred. What a moment.

It was a hell of a moment for me and one I celebrated in the most animated way, waving my bat enthusiastically to both the dressing room and my parents high up in the stand. I also kissed the England badge on my helmet, something I was criticised for afterwards by people who thought I had gone over the top. I make no apology for my feelings that day. It was a completely spontaneous reaction, one I couldn't control. I had no desire to control it. I wanted to show my feelings.

It was such a release of tension and pressure. I had scored 97 in a one-day warm-up match at the start of the tour, an innings that cemented my place in Johannesburg, but this was something different. This was very special. I was so overjoyed, so excited and every other adjective you could possibly think of. It was how I felt. I was happy for me, happy for my family, happy for my friends and everyone who had backed me up until that point. I was also happy for the selectors who had put faith in me, and for Michael Vaughan, Duncan Fletcher and the England team who had been so welcoming to me and had shown so much faith in me and given me so much encouragement.

I got so carried away, indeed, that I didn't notice a quite unusual occurrence. The whole of the home crowd had turned their backs on me. The applause was muted and instead there was just this massive gesture of indifference towards me. I didn't even notice until I saw the replays later, so ecstatic was I at what had happened.

No matter. That didn't concern me. What did please me was that we'd reached a competitive score of 270 for five in our 50 overs and I'd scored an unbeaten 108 from 96 balls. I also featured in a stand of 92 from 79 balls with Paul Collingwood that was hugely enjoyable and, I thought, probably decisive.

Yet this tour was already turning into a more than eventful one-day series and no one could have guessed at how this match would finish. Thanks to Jacques Kallis and Herschelle Gibbs, South Africa started the final six balls needing just three runs to win. It should have been simple but, incredibly, it wasn't.

Kabir Ali had to bowl that final over and it had started with Mark Boucher pulling a chest-high no-ball to the boundary. We looked dead and buried. But what character Kabir showed for a young guy making his way in the game. The next ball saw Boucher caught off another full toss in the deep by Ashley Giles, Ashwell Prince was soon run out by Ian Bell and then the game ended, with the scores level, when Geraint Jones, standing up to the pace of Kabir, stumped Andrew Hall off the last ball. A tie. Only the 20th in 2,219 one-day internationals. Amazing.

South Africa have something of a reputation as 'chokers' yet this was something else. Pandemonium broke out in our ranks while the crowd stood in stunned silence. I lifted Geraint off the floor, almost putting my back out in the process, and the guys flocked around Kabir, who had kept his nerve so well. I was man of the match and the game felt like a victory, even though it was to be the start of my habit of scoring hundreds in matches England failed to win!

We journeyed to Port Elizabeth with a very relaxed feeling in the team. We were one up with two matches gone and had got out of jail, to a large extent, in Bloemfontein. Yet it was becoming evident that there were some tired bodies in our ranks, particularly among those players who had been with the tour since Zimbabwe.

Clive Rice, such an important man in my career, made contact with me in Port Elizabeth, and came to see me for a chat on the morning of the game. Clive told me to keep on going out and showing people how good I was. He told me he knew how good I was and he wanted everyone to see it, particularly those who were giving me a hard time.

Clive's motto was: 'Don't get out. Stay unbeaten,' and it was something he always hammered into me. His argument was that you should never give your wicket away because it helps your average, your stats, and that if the opposition can't get you out you will retain your superiority over them. Don't ever throw it away, he repeated to me at the end of our conversation.

So what did I do in Port Elizabeth? Threw my wicket away to a pretty silly shot. I handed a catch to Gibbs off the bowling of Nel when I was well set on 33 from 37 balls. I was particularly annoyed because, as I've said, once you get a start like that you really should kick on, even in one-day cricket.

We had to go into the match without our captain, Vaughan, who was ill, and I think it's fair to say that none of our batsmen kicked on, with the possible exception of Vikram Solanki, and we should have got more than the 267 for eight we achieved in our 50 overs.

My day didn't improve when I missed a run-out chance which would have got rid of Smith early in his innings, and he went on to score a match-winning 105, the first hundred by a South African captain in a one-day international.

We really should have been able to defend that total under the Port Elizabeth lights and my frustration was summed up when I caught Kallis and turned to the crowd to give them a defiant fist salute. It was the first time I had reacted to abuse from the crowd in three matches. Steve Bucknor, the umpire, came up to me and said, 'It's hard enough for you over here, don't make it any harder for yourself.' Fair enough. I told him I was just having a bit of fun and we had a laugh about it.

Maybe I was making things a little harder for myself, but it was just an instinctive thing, like my celebrations in Bloemfontein. It can become difficult being nailed by the crowd in every game. Your instinct is to have a little go back, even if I did not intend it to be malicious. I'd already batted in that game and copped flak again for the third match running, so I just thought it was my turn to get my own back in a small way. South Africa had the last laugh, however, on a disappointing night for us.

As we flew to Cape Town for the fourth international I turned to Darren Gough, who was sitting next to me, and said, 'My hair's too long. I want to do something with it.' And he replied, 'Why don't you do something stupid with it?' Little did I know that that brief exchange would lead to a hairstyle that would cause so much comment and attention over the next few months.

We checked into the Cullinan Hotel, where the England World Cup side had been holed up during their ill-fated campaign two years earlier, and I went to the hairdresser's there. I'd never done anything out of the ordinary with my hair before but I thought, why not? Let's do something a bit different. Goughy, of course, insisted on coming in to the hairdresser's with me to make sure I went through with it, even though he had no intention of doing anything daft to his own hair. To be fair, he looked stupid enough as it was with his hair shaved on both sides. I think Darren's intention was to make me look as silly as him!

Gough said, 'Why don't you put a line through it?' So I decided to go for it but the lady who did it for me had never done anything like that before and I think she was more nervous than I was. I said to her, 'It had better look good, I'm on TV tomorrow,' which probably didn't do much for her confidence. I got some funny looks on my way back to my room afterwards and, to be honest, when I got there I wasn't best pleased.

It was more orangey red than the blonde line that was to become something of a trademark for me in the summer of 2005 so, in effect, it was half a job. I guess you'd call it the skunk look. It was interesting, that's for sure. Some of the boys in our team thought it looked good, others laughed, but nobody questioned it or asked me what on earth I was doing. It was something I did and it was taken by everybody in good spirits. I really don't think hair is a big deal. It really shouldn't be an issue. Yes, I know I bring a bit more attention on myself having my hair styled in different ways but, come on, your hair is not going to make you bat any better or worse. And it doesn't seem to have done my batting any harm.

It certainly didn't do me any harm in South Africa because on that trip I went from strength to strength. One thing I must say at this point is that I don't think it does cricket any harm to have a cooler image among young people than it has in the past. There are so many things that young people can get into, so many distractions and so much competition for their time that cricket cannot afford to be thought of as an old-fashioned pursuit or something stuck in the dark ages.

I saw on a website the other day an item about how many people had copied my hairstyle. And that must mean they are showing at least a little bit of interest in cricket. It's both surprising and nice, really. If it helps make cricket be a little more fashionable and it helps make cricketers seem a little less boring to the public then it can only be a good thing as far as I'm concerned.

Cricket doesn't have to be traditional and it doesn't have to be middle-class. For cricket to become even more popular than it did in the summer of 2005 the game needs personalities and it needs characters, and I don't see anything wrong in a modern hairstyle and a modern lifestyle as long as it doesn't interfere with your game and your training.

In my case the way I look and my lifestyle has never interfered with my personality, never interfered with my training and never interfered with the way I play or my mental toughness. It's just a haircut. Duncan Fletcher is fine about it. Jimmy Anderson was the first England cricketer to have a hairstyle similar to mine and other players have shown streaks of individuality with earrings and things like that.

Duncan has a laugh about it, actually. He will call me skunk or raccoon and generally make fun at my expense, which the boys enjoy and is good for team spirit.

In Cape Town, Herschelle Gibbs batted beautifully. He's a sensational player, has been since he was very young. This was the game where South Africa moved Gibbs down to number four to accommodate AB de Villiers at the top of the order and it certainly worked for them on this occasion.

Gibbs got himself a hundred and South Africa scored 291 for five in their 50 overs, but we really should have reached that target. It was the first time I had played at Newlands and it truly was a beautiful venue, just as good as it looked on the television. It was also hot as hell but that didn't excuse our poor batting as we collapsed to 183 all out. I scored 75, so at least I had contributed, but it was a bad day for us and we had now gone 2–1 down in the series.

It had been a long tour and fatigue was setting in. The boys had achieved their major goal of winning the Test series and were in the middle of a long one-day series of seven matches. The workload was taking its toll but it was important to us that we did our utmost to make sure the tour didn't end with a whimper.

East London, in the Eastern Cape province, is not nearly as picturesque a place as Cape Town, but it was the venue for an amazing fifth one-day international, particularly for me. Heavy rain had left the ground saturated overnight and led to the unusual scenes of big patches of sand on the outfield to make sure it wasn't dangerous to field on.

It wasn't the best day for our bowlers and Justin Kemp got after them in some style, hitting 80 of the most emphatically struck runs I have ever seen off 50 balls. Smith again showed that he is a good batsman despite his personality limitations with another hundred, very much in a supporting role, and South Africa piled up an emphatic 311 for seven, the highest ever on this ground.

Vaughany made a very good start for us but by the time I came in to join him we had our backs to the wall and it was clear all I could do was go out there and try to smack it as far as I possibly could.

I could have been stumped on 16 but after that chance was missed, everything seemed to go off the middle of the bat. I'm never scared to get out but on this occasion I knew I had absolutely nothing to lose as we were chasing a huge target. I knew the bowlers, I was in good form and I had the licence to go and have a smack. If ever I was going to have a good old slog, this was the game, and I ended up scoring a hundred off 69 balls, the fastest ever by an Englishman in a one-day international and the 10th fastest of all time.

In one-day cricket the key to a good innings is manipulating the field, but I do have plans for each bowler. The ball normally stops swinging around the 12th over in one-day cricket so then you just have to manipulate the field and watch out for the variations of the bowlers.

I scored a lot of my runs in East London on the on-side but, again, that is natural in one-day cricket because invariably the ball doesn't move off the straight so it's easier to play across the line and manoeuvre the ball. Essentially, one-day cricket is about scoring runs off every ball and it doesn't really matter how you get them. Since this innings people have commented on my whip shot to leg, but it's one that I see as an essential part of my one-day armoury. It's effective. Every ball on or outside off-stump I can hit through midwicket with that shot and there's usually at least two runs in it, hopefully more. When you play through the on-side like that you force the opposition to react and that can open up gaps on the off-side, again manipulating the field.

East London, though, was more about a good old heave-ho, one that unfortunately left us just short of what would have been an amazing victory. Before the last ball, Goughy, who was by then batting with me, said, 'Look, we can't win the game, but you can get your hundred, so try to do it.' That meant scoring a six off the last ball but even though the game was lost I decided to go for it. Andre Nel presented me with a full toss and I duly hit it for my fourth six of the innings.

It was great but there were mixed feelings, essentially negative ones because we had lost again and now couldn't win the series. The realisation that, however fast the hundred was, it had come in a losing cause, took away any elation I felt in an instant. I hate losing and to score a hundred in a losing cause never leaves me with a smile on my face. Scoring one run and being part of a winning team leaves you with a much better feeling than scoring a hundred and losing, believe me.

The next game was, in many ways, the biggest I was going to face. It was to be played in Durban, at my old 'home' ground of Kingsmead, close to where I was born and grew up in Pietermaritzburg, and I have to confess to feeling wary about what sort of reception I was going to get.

As it turned out I had nothing to worry about. My 'home-coming' started as soon as we arrived in Durban when Goughy emerged with some balloons he'd purchased from somewhere with 'welcome home' on them, which he duly tied round my wrist. Then there was an amazing welcome from the staff of the team hotel, who sang to us and played music as we checked in.

It was wonderfully kind and yet it didn't feel like going home. By this time I was looking at South Africa from a totally different perspective. Staying at nice hotels, being looked after and being surrounded by security guards gave me a different experience of South Africa and made me feel more and more like a visitor.

It was a homecoming of sorts but I had never felt more English, being with the boys and being a part of the team. I wondered what sort of reception was in store for me at Kingsmead, the ground where I took my first tentative steps towards a professional career, and the ground where it ended, so abruptly and with such acrimony, when I was dropped by Natal because of the quota system.

Unfortunately, because of more bad weather, I was never to discover whether I would have been booed on my way to the wicket in Durban. It was the only game in which I didn't bat on the whole trip. But I was fielding at cover point or on the boundary during South Africa's innings and the response I got from there was very good.

Some people who went to my college were sitting just behind me and I had a good craic with them. It was the first time I had enjoyed fielding on the boundary in South Africa. Nobody from Natal Cricket said much to me. I was polite and friendly towards anyone I spoke to and got on with my job.

I was there to play cricket for England, not to be a politician or cause any hassle. And this was one ground where I dearly wanted to bat for England. I was the next man in when the rains came as we were attempting to chase an adjusted target of 213 from 48 overs. So I was left frustrated. But maybe it was meant to be. Maybe someone didn't want me to bat in Durban in case I was disappointed, either by the reaction to me or by not getting many runs. As it was, the no result meant that South Africa, 3–1 with one to play, had won the series.

I tended to go out with Goughy and a couple of the guys for a few drinks after each game, mainly to unwind, particularly as I was so tense and uptight most of the time and emotions were running high. After day-night games you are usually wide awake, so there is not much point going to bed before about 2.30 a.m. unless you just want to lie there awake. The adrenalin was pumping throughout that trip and generally I was only getting around four or five hours' sleep a night.

So we would tend to nip out to a club, and I was usually well received, but Durban was the only place where our security guard, Faisal, insisted I didn't go out. He was worried somebody might have a go at me in my home town and he didn't want to have to get me out of any awkward incidents. We compromised in the end and went to a quiet bar rather than a club, but even then Faisal arranged for six security guards to come with us!

We were soon back where it all started at the Sandton Sun Hotel for our last game at Centurion. I thought that as I had done OK up to that point, I might have started to win the crowd round, but when we were in the field I copped some of the worst stick I had received on the whole trip. And that was as we were warming up! I think some of the local guys had gone to the ground for the Sunday morning start direct from their Saturday night out, and a big crowd of them sat on the banks at Centurion Park, shouting and swearing at me.

My walk to the wicket, with us again in trouble, was just the same. This time we really were struggling at 68 for six but together with Ashley Giles I pulled it round and we got up to 240, at least respectable. This, meanwhile, was probably the best of my three hundreds on this tour because I had to start very cautiously, reaching 50 off 80 balls, but then accelerating, hitting six leg-side sixes and a second 50 in 24 balls.

Those, however, are just the bare facts. What made this hundred different from the others, and what made it particularly special, was that, as I reached three figures, the South African crowd, at last, rose to me. They gave me a standing ovation.

It was almost as if they were saying, 'We have given this bloke stick all tour, not least today, but he has shown character and come through it. Let's recognise that.' It was one of the most emotional moments of my life. I don't think there is anything else in life that can take you to the place where that innings took me.

As the crowd finally accepted me, my head was a whirl of emotions. I thought about the decision I had taken to leave the country, everything that had been said and written about it, the sacrifices, and I was just dumbstruck, hearing the ovation and acknowledging the people.

I was grateful to the people of South Africa. I think I would have got a similar response on any other South African ground by that stage. It was the end of the tour, we had lost the series, and people were being magnanimous towards me. It was, before the Oval at least, the highlight of my career.

We lost the match and the series 4–1 but hopefully some pluses had come out of the one-day leg of the tour for England, and it couldn't be forgotten that the Test series had been won, so there was a good party in Sandton that night. I was handing out lots of Valentine's roses to the ladies, just as Goughy and I did in a club in Cape Town, and to this day I don't know where we got them from. They just seemed to appear in our hands. We were also drinking lots of the local champagne, and I gave thanks to the selectors for giving me the chance to show that I was mentally strong enough to play cricket for England in South Africa.

It was a tour I hadn't even been selected for originally, but one that I will remember for the rest of my life, whatever happens in the rest of my career. We had been playing against a South Africa side who had good balance in their team with experience and flamboyance and were led well by Graeme Smith, even though he wasn't the nicest individual. Hopefully, despite the scoreline, we had made progress too. And there was one little bit of business I had to take care of before I left South Africa.

Allan Lamb is someone who knows what I went through by coming to England from South Africa because he did exactly the same and went on to become a major Test batsman. You can even still see him in that 'Beefy and Lamby' TV commercial with Ian Botham! Let's hear if his story is similar to mine.

Allan Lamb: *I have an idea what it's like being Kevin Pietersen. I went through the same thing. I guess it was slightly different for me coming from South Africa to play for England because at that time South Africa was isolated from international cricket and I still encountered some difficult times as a person perceived to be South African representing the England cricket team. I would get called a racist in Australia and New Zealand but never, funnily enough, in India or Pakistan.*

You always get branded with the South African thing. It never goes away. Some people always called me 'the South African-born Allan Lamb', and it will be the same for KP.

I'm sure 99 per cent of the English cricket-loving public have accepted him completely. He has every right to be here. He has an English mother and a British passport. He made his decision and he is acting perfectly within the rules.

I was called a mercenary and told to go back to South Africa by some people in the media when I started playing for England in 1982 but, I tell you what, I'm still here! Kevin will be the same. I have noticed even now some media people still describing him as a South African and I guess he's got to live with that because you can't beat the media. They are too powerful.

All I will say is that as an Englishman I am delighted that KP is on our side, and, even though I don't know him too well, I have enjoyed meeting him and been hugely impressed by him as a batsman.

The only guy I have ever seen play like KP is Viv Richards and it is a hell of a big call on my part to compare the pair of them. But there are striking similarities and I sincerely hope KP goes on to achieve as much as the great Viv did.

The big test for Kevin will come when he has a bad patch. There will be lots of people telling him to change his game or do things differently. Remember Graeme Hick when he first came into international cricket in 1991? People analysed his technique and encouraged him to change the game that had got him there in the first place. What happened? He became a confused and ulti-mately lesser player. I firmly believe, from what I have seen, that KP has the strength of character not to let that happen to him. Don't let them confuse you, Kevin – that's what I say.

KP likes to dominate the bowling, which is always a good sign. There is also that little bit of arrogance, just like Viv, and it is clear that KP thinks about his game and is a quick learner. Centre stage is where he wants to perform and he has made it known that he wants to be number one. Good luck to him.

Kevin Pietersen is tall, powerful and can hit more shots than anyone else. His armoury is fantastic and the world is at his feet. People will work out how he plays the more they see of him, and I'm sure the Aussies will have a few new plans when they meet again in the winter of 2006 but he can deal with that. I look forward to watching him develop even further with a keen interest and relish. As a fellow Englishman.

11

KEEPING MY LITTLE
SECRET HIDDEN FROM DAD

'You had better tell Goughy to sort his

bad knee out and get in some sprinting

practice, because I will be after him.'

Jannie Pietersen

There was a postscript to my South African tour. When we arrived in Johannesburg at the start of the one-day leg, Darren Gough had decided to have a three lions tattoo on his forearm. I told the press I was considering having it done too, which Mum and Dad picked up on straight away. They rang me and said, 'What do you think you're doing?' I told them I was only messing around and Dad said, 'You had better be joking.' He wasn't happy about the prospect of his son having a big tattoo at all.

'If you have that done,' Dad went on, 'you had better tell Goughy to sort his bad knee out and get in some sprinting prac-tice, because I will be after him for putting the idea in your head.' I laughed and told Goughy who said, 'Bring it on.'

Then, after the final one-dayer in Centurion, I was really tempted to follow Goughy's example and get it done. By this time it had turned into a bit of a saga with the press asking, 'Are you going to do it?' and 'When are you going to do it?'

As I have said, we had quite a party after that final game and after my second, third, fourth, fifth and sixth drinks I was getting more and more into the idea of displaying my commitment to my country in a very visual way. Goughy, meanwhile, kept on saying, 'Bet you don't do it.' The evening ended with me insisting I would.

So I got up at 9 a.m., after two hours' sleep, and went down to the tattoo shop in the Sandton mall where Goughy had had his tattoo done. It wasn't open, so after a return to my room for a little doze, I went back and told the guy what I wanted to have done.

He proceeded to do as I asked and, mid-tattoo, I rang Goughy and said, 'Listen to this,' placing my mobile phone next to the needle so he could hear it. He still didn't believe it, asked where I was and then spluttered, 'Are you in some bird's room?' Darren hadn't even been well, missing the last one-dayer through illness, but within two minutes he had collected his senses and joined me in the tattoo parlour, where he said, 'Hats off to you. I didn't think you were going to get it done.'

If I say I'm going to do something, I'm going to do it! And in this case I liked the idea of an England tattoo – I just had to pluck up the courage to tell Mum and Dad.

In the end, I didn't tell them myself. A couple of the press guys had heard I finally had had the tattoo done and were keen on a picture, but I was determined to delay the moment that Dad found out as long as possible. So I denied I'd had it done, kept it well covered on the journey home and vowed to keep it out of the press for as long as possible. I'd forgotten all about it when, during a one-day international against Bangladesh early in the 2005 season, I sat on the balcony with a vest on and the TV cameras picked up on my tattoo. It had been hidden for four months! It didn't take long for Mum and Dad to pick up on it. That night I had a message on my phone from Mum saying, 'What is that on your arm? Dad says he is not happy and is after Goughy!'

Thank goodness I was in England and they were in South Africa. In the end Mum and Dad accepted it. They know that when I want to do something, I'll do it. I like it – and I added a second tattoo later that summer when I played Test cricket for England. The second one, which I had done underneath the three lions, is simply DCXXVI – 626 in Roman numerals and my

England Test number. I became the 626th player to play Test cricket for England when I made my debut against Australia at Lord's, and I decided to commemorate it in this way.

Test cricket is much more traditional than the one-day game and has been around for much longer so I thought the Roman numerals were a nice way to celebrate the significant landmark. I had the second tattoo done in Selfridges in Oxford Street in the middle of the 2005 summer, after the Edgbaston Test, and it only took about 15 minutes, much quicker than the original.

Is that the end of my body art? Well, I certainly don't think I'll go as far as someone like David Beckham and have tattoos all over my body, but I would consider having the names of my wife and children tattooed on me when the time comes.

I basically think any tattoo should be personal. The three lions and my one-day number are personal to me, as is my Test number. No one else can have them done, unless they just want my personal numbers on them! Also, the names of my family would be personal and unique to me. I would never want to get anything that someone else might have done. No Chinese writing, no football badge or anything like that. But I look forward to the time when my wife's and children's names are displayed on me.

12

PART OF A NEW FAMILY

*'Even when we were kids Kevin wanted
to be the best batsman in the world.'*

Bryan Pietersen

After the South African tour I had a feeling of satisfaction and pride. The figures did make good reading for me. In six innings in South Africa I had scored 454 runs from 430 balls at an average of 151.33. Not bad for starters! I felt I had done well at my job and now I was being recognised a lot more in the street and getting a lot more recognition within English cricket.

My main concern was not to make a huge deal out of this. I always try to keep things simple and I wanted to keep any success I had in perspective. The last thing I needed was to get carried away by it all or for people within the game to get carried away and think that I had arrived.

It was a case of going home, moving to Southampton for the start of my Hampshire career and making a new start. I was relishing the idea of a new club and a new beginning, a fresh challenge with Hampshire. It was also good that my younger brother Bryan was preparing to move to Southampton with me, as he had done when I first went to Nottingham. He is probably my closest relative and I have shared more time and experiences with him than any other person.

I had gone to Australia for a week's holiday after South Africa and ended up hurting my foot running on the beach, which put me back in my preparations for the new season, one that was undoubtedly huge for me.

Hampshire were delighted that I had made an impression in

South Africa and started saying to me, in good humour, 'Will we be seeing much of you this summer after all?' and 'We got you on the cheap signing you up before South Africa!'

I quickly felt at home at Hampshire and the dressing room seemed a much better place after all that had gone on at Notts. I also quickly realised that Shane Warne was every bit as good a captain as I had been led to believe and I felt straight away that it was a great privilege to play under him. Shaun Udal was an excellent vice-captain, too, and positive thoughts applied to everyone at the club, down to the people who served the food and ran the bar. I couldn't have asked for a nicer welcome. It's a great club to be a part of.

It was clear to me straight away that Shane had taught Shaun Udal, his deputy, a lot in terms of how to captain the club. I think it revitalised Shaun's career playing under Shane. Udal, or Shaggy as he has always been known, apparently because of a youthful likeness to the Scooby Doo character, was an experienced and successful off-spin bowler who had given tremendous service to the county, but when Shane came along Shaggy proved that an old dog can indeed learn new tricks. In the winter of 2005, at the age of 36, Shaun Udal made his Test debut for England in Pakistan, and gave a lot of credit to Shane for the influence he had on him.

I think Shane taught Shaggy, and indeed anyone who came under his wing at Hampshire, a lot of positive things about how the game should be played and the way a captain should lead his team and speak to people. It's just a reflection of how good Shane Warne is and how people follow his lead and the way he goes about his business. You can see it in Shaggy's captaincy now. I saw it when I played in the Cheltenham and Gloucester Trophy final for Hampshire against Warwickshire, one of the few big matches I was able to play for my new county in what became an extremely hectic year.

Shaggy encouraged everybody, was totally positive, and I could just imagine Shane Warne saying exactly the same things if he was in charge. That sort of attitude rubs off on people and brings out the best in them. Certain people can lift others, and it helps if you are playing under someone who is hugely respected and one of the greats of the game like Shane.

Hampshire is an international club. Rod Bransgrove is very well connected in worldwide business interests. He knows how to run a business and he knows how to run a county cricket club. It's a club that cares about the people within it, and that adds up to a total that is even greater than its individual parts.

It is a county where time is taken to speak to the players about family matters, about how you're feeling; a club that provides a support system for when you are away and even includes the little things that mean so much, like congratulatory texts from chairman, coach and captain if you have done well for England abroad. Even the sponsors all feel part of what we are trying to achieve, and that makes one big family, who all pull in the same direction and want to make a success of things.

It is a club where no one has a different attitude towards you if you score a duck as opposed to a hundred. That was emphasised to me when I made a bit of a slow start to my Hampshire career in those early days of the 2005 summer. I wasn't happy with my contributions and was itching to do well for the club, but there was never any pressure from the people who matter at the county. They were incredibly supportive when I failed to get a big score. That means a lot to a player. It means that your bosses and colleagues are not just interested in your performances, they're interested in you as a person, in your welfare.

It was completely different to anything I had experienced at Nottinghamshire. They were not like that at all at Trent Bridge. For instance, they weren't like it in their attitude towards Richard Logan. They weren't like it in their attitude towards Stuey MacGill. And they weren't like it in their attitude towards Clive Rice. All good people who could have enhanced the club if they had been allowed to stay longer.

I loved it at Hampshire from the start, yet there indeed was a chance they wouldn't see much of me during my debut summer because all the talk now was whether I was ready to play Test cricket for England after what happened in South Africa.

I was optimistic of making my Test debut in the biggest of summers, with Australia coming to town for the Ashes, but then again I wasn't. I thought I was good enough but England had been very successful and I couldn't see an obvious vacancy. I missed the start of the season with that foot injury and then when I did start playing I might have put a bit of extra pressure on myself because I kept on getting out in stupid ways. That didn't help.

Meanwhile, a debate was going on as to whether England should stick with the class and experience of Graham Thorpe in the middle order or plump for me. It seemed to come down to that straight choice as far as most people were concerned, even though I wondered if there was any other option, any other way that I could get into the team.

Thorpe was a legend as far as I was concerned, one of the great batsmen of the last generation, and it seemed a big call to replace him with me.

Before the Ashes, England had a two-match Test series against Bangladesh and then a triangular one-day series and another three-match one-day series against Australia, so there was plenty of cricket to come before the hugely anticipated first Ashes Test in July. Yet I couldn't help thinking that the team picked for the first Test against Bangladesh would probably be the one that went into the Ashes because, with due respect to Bangladesh, the batsmen picked would almost certainly fill their boots with runs.

The big question people were asking was whether my technique would stand up to Test cricket. The more high profile you become, the more people look at you and analyse you, and there was so much talk that I decided to have a close look at my technique on DVD to see whether the doubters had a point. I have always had faith in my ability but if anybody offers me any constructive criticism I like to take it on board, think about what they are saying and see whether they are right and if I can learn anything or put any defects straight.

When I looked at how I was playing at the start of the 2005 season it's fair to say my feet weren't moving at all, so I endeavoured to stand as still at the crease as I could and then get my feet moving, and things started to click after that. I scored a hundred for Hampshire at Canterbury and then another hundred in my third innings at the Rose Bowl, a big one for me because I wanted to prove I could make runs at my new home ground, but it all came just a little too late for selection against Bangladesh. David Graveney rang me to say I had just missed out.

The truth was I had not done well enough at that stage in county cricket to justify selection. I have always been philosophical towards setbacks like this. Selection for England doesn't come easy and you have to put figures on the board. I was always confident I would get my chance eventually and that when it came I would take it. I was humble on the phone to Grav and vowed to score as many runs as possible in the build-up to the one-day series.

So I was analysing my technique at this time but I also thought to myself, my record is better in four-day cricket than one-day cricket, so maybe I don't have too much to worry about. You don't have to manipulate the ball as much in first-class cricket. There are more gaps in the field. I don't have to walk in front of my stumps. I can play more proper cricket shots and pursue my normal positive, attacking, confident game. That's the way I looked at it. I thought, after I had carefully considered the matter, that it was a bit simplistic of people who had not seen too much of my batting to assume that I played the same way in first-class cricket as I did in the one-day game. I concluded that I didn't have to change my technique just because some people didn't think it looked totally orthodox. Mark Waugh again came to mind. He scored the bulk of his runs through square leg and midwicket. Why couldn't I if that was a strength of my game?

So I got on with the business of establishing myself at Hampshire and scoring runs for them while England cruised to a monumental innings and 261-run victory over Bangladesh in the first Test. It was a similar story in the second Test, as the gulf between the established Test teams and the minnows like Bangladesh and Zimbabwe was sorely exposed. All our batsmen gained runs, as I expected them to, and Thorpe barely got a chance to bat. When he did get to the crease, at Durham in his 100th Test, he scored an unbeaten 66 which, coupled with Ian Bell's big century, seemed to close the door on any potential batting vacancies in the England Test line-up for the time being. I couldn't worry about that for now. Before that came my first one-day international cricket in England. And the opposition did not come much bigger than Australia.

My younger brother Bryan has been the biggest constant in my life. While the rest of my immediate family remain in South Africa, he has made his life in England with me. Here he shares some of his experiences.

Bryan Pietersen: *Being the youngest of four brothers can work both ways. I was often beaten up by my older brothers, but they also looked after me. None more so than Kevin.*

All my brothers are caring but Kevin is particularly kind-hearted. I know I can ring him at any time, even if he is in the middle of a Test match, and he will always be there for me. We're the youngest of the four and as such have always spent a lot of time together, from the early days when we played courtyard cricket at our house in Pietermaritzburg. We have always had similar interests.

Kevin was an awesome sportsman, even as a youngster.

We were all pretty competitive and committed but he always stood out. He was brilliant at hockey, rugby and particularly squash. He just worked so hard at being perfect in every sport and was so committed it wasn't true.

So much so that he didn't have much interest in anything other than sport when we were kids. I wouldn't say he was a nerd, but he didn't really want to go out much. All he wanted to do was play sport as much as he could and would even rush through meal times so he could be outside getting more practice.

Even though he was a provincial rugby player, it was cricket that Kevin was best at. We would have some amazing games. He would nominate the player he was going to be when we played and invariably he would shout out, 'I'm Brian Lara,' while I would bowl at him pretending to be Shane Warne. Kevin would even try to assume the characteristics and batting styles of the player, even the left-handed ones like Lara. Even then I think he wanted to be the best batsman in the world. He was so focused. And I'm so proud of the boy that he is well on the way to achieving that.

It was a massive decision for Kevin to leave South Africa to come to England. I was the most upset of anyone when he left because I felt I was losing a brother who had always been there for me. When he was homesick in the early days it was hard for me too because I felt helpless. Yet we all knew it was something he had to do to be a success and the whole family was always totally supportive.

Eventually I came over to live with Kevin in Nottingham and then I moved to Southampton too when he went down there, and now I live round the corner from him in London. We tend not to leave each other alone!

I always knew Kevin had talent but I could never have imagined him living the life he leads now. Fame hasn't *changed him a bit. He's still the brother he has always been. To me, it has made him an even better person. He never feels he's superior to anyone and certainly hasn't let money go to his head. He still remembers the little things that once meant so much to us all.*

Kevin is not only a role model for a lot of aspiring kids but he's also a role model for me. I'm trying to follow in his footsteps now and learn from him. If only I had had his focus when I was young maybe I would have already followed him into cricket but I'm hoping it's not too late.

I want to achieve what Kevin has done. Yes, I'm a little bit jealous of him to be honest but mainly proud. I'm having trials at the moment with Worcestershire and Essex and it's going really well. I'm just giving it a good shot in the hope that even now at 23 I might be able to make it as a professional cricketer.

I'm a number-four batsman like Kevin but I bowl a bit of medium pace rather than his piddly off-spin! Playing against big bro would be a dream come true and playing alongside him would be even better. The ultimate. It would be like going back in time to when we were small. And I tell you, if we ever did come up against each other in cricket it would be so competitive, live or die! We would try to kill each other! But we would remain as close as brothers can be.

13

IF THIS IS WHAT TEST CRICKET IS LIKE, BRING IT ON!

'KP is a rare talent. South Africa's loss is England's gain. At the time not too many people were trying very hard to stop him leaving the country, but now they would love to have him back! Well, I think they left it just a little bit too late.'

Ian Botham

I went into the summer of one-day cricket backing myself and my methods. I thought, why should I change? If you have got yourself to a high level playing the way you play, why should you meddle with it? If it ain't broke, don't fix it.

I listened on TV to Ian Healy talking about Adam Gilchrist during an Australian match around this time and he said that Gilly was a true champion because he came into any situation and played his natural game, was never fazed by anything. Adam Gilchrist plays the same way whether his side are 80 for five or 400 for five, and to have the confidence and ability to do that is the sign of a great player. I want to be a great player. I want to be a champion. And if I want to be among the best, I feel I must try to emulate the way Gilly plays and play my natural game whatever the circumstances. It's a quality I feel I have.

Yes, my natural game might not always work, but I'm not scared of failure or getting out. You are going to get out at some point so you have to make runs while you are out there and, while I believe playing my natural game is imperative, I also am acutely aware of the importance of playing situation cricket. If you can marry your natural game to the needs of the situation, then you really are getting somewhere, in my book. And I think with experience comes a certain know-how. The more I play the more I will mature and be able to adapt my natural game to the needs of the situation.

My game developed over the four years I spent qualifying to play for England. If I'd been thrown in when I first came to England, at the age of 21, I might not have been able to cope, but I have worked my game out and feel comfortable with it. I always want to improve and ask questions of myself but the bottom line is you have to back yourself to be able to play.

Our contests against Australia got off to the best imaginable start in the first Twenty20 match played between the countries. It was staged at the Rose Bowl and was a fantastic day for Hampshire, who showed that they could stage top cricket at their new ground and stage it well. What a shame that the Rose Bowl is still being overlooked for Test cricket and has not been awarded an Ashes Test 2009, as was hoped. It will come. It is a venue that is made for international cricket, and we got a glimpse of its potential and the interest of the Hampshire people on that memorable day when Twenty20 cricket and the Australians came to town.

We had talked about playing Australia and decided that from the word go we would get in their faces and refuse to be bullied. Their dominance over the years has been characterised by their ability to bully their opponents, stamp their authority over them. Duncan Fletcher and Michael Vaughan decided that would not happen to us. They told us we would not put up with it.

It was my first game against Australia and I stood there at practice looking at the likes of Ricky Ponting, Brett Lee and Glenn McGrath. I wouldn't say I was in awe of them. I was just looking at them and thinking: how can we beat these blokes?

Undoubtedly, it would be by having the self-belief and mental toughness to take them on and get at them. We wanted to knock them off their pedestals by playing positively. We made 179 in front of a wonderful, loud, enthusiastic crowd with me scoring 36. Yet that was nothing compared to the excitement when Australia batted.

Darren Gough and Jonathan Lewis, as well as the other England bowlers, just ran through Australia with a brand of aggressive, positive cricket that proved overwhelmingly too good for our opponents. Freddie Flintoff also struck a meaningful blow by hitting Brett Lee on the shoulder, an injury that would cause him to miss the first weekend of 50-over cricket, another psychological step forward for us. This result would also, I would discover later, set the tone for the entire summer.

Goughy was bowling as well as I'd ever seen him. At one stage he was on a hat-trick and bowled a fierce bouncer with the hat-trick ball, a sign of his aggressive intent being above the desire to reach any personal landmark. He was like a bat out of hell. The Aussies, barely credibly, were 31 for seven at one stage and eventually 79 all out. Amazing. I took three catches and was voted the Sky viewers' man of the match, another confidence boost for me.

It was only a Twenty20 game and Vaughan was quick to try to play down its significance afterwards, but I think we all knew that we had put down a marker for the summer. We had shown Australia we meant business. I'm convinced that, after that game, the Australian attitude was: 'Gee, they are up for it this summer. They are good enough and there are players in their team who can stand up to us.' That was the crux of the matter. A formidable England team had stood up, from the word go, against one of the best teams ever to play the game. The Twenty20 game had set the tone, and as the summer went on was to gain even more significance, in my opinion. The Ashes build-up had begun.

Excitement at what was ahead was now starting to build as we approached the first weekend of the triangular one-day series. We thought it was game on but I'm not sure we felt we could win the Ashes. Yet. What a weekend, though, that first one turned out to be. Again, with hindsight, a very significant weekend in the course of an incredible summer.

First there was an even bigger surprise than Australia being bowled out for 79 in the Twenty20 game. In their first international, they lost against Bangladesh in Cardiff the day before we were due to play them in Bristol. It must be one of the biggest upsets in one-day international history. We certainly couldn't believe what we were hearing as we practised at Bristol for the next day's game.

Now, we had to make the most of this. We were starting to think we could give Australia a real run for their money, and I thought that if we could be competitive there was a chance we could not only win the one-day series but we could win the Ashes. Now we had to believe in our abilities, back each other and work hard for each other to fight for our country and bring cricket in England alive.

Bristol is a small ground – but Australia still managed to cause problems for themselves by turning up at the wrong entrance – with a great atmosphere, and it was packed on a very hot Sunday for our first 50-over match against the Aussies. Australia started off pretty well until Paul Collingwood took one of the best catches I've ever seen to dismiss Matt Hayden and we came alive.

When I came in to bat that day we needed around 150 to win and it was a testing challenge. As soon as I came in Damien Martyn shouted at me, 'You can do it in Twenty20 cricket, let's see if you can do it now in the big stuff.' That stuck in my mind and made me graft that little bit harder in what was my first big innings against the best team in the world.

I knuckled down, knocked it around for a while and, when we started losing wickets at key times, I thought it was time to have a go. They have small boundaries at Bristol and I knew that nine or ten an over was far from impossible there because there is always a good chance of a couple of boundaries an over. I managed to hit a few shots until the key moment when Jon Lewis came in and played a very mature little innings in his first one-day international. He did a good job while I slaughtered them at the other end. It was an amazing feeling.

I remember a couple of shots off Jason Gillespie in particular, but my favourite hit of the innings was a six I struck out of the ground over cow corner off Brad Hogg. It was the shot that got me going in an innings that enabled me to pass my first massive test against Australia. I finished on 91 not out, we had beaten Australia, and when I sat next to Michael Vaughan in the press conference afterwards he said I had shown 'a little bit of genius'. I couldn't believe what was happening to me.

Collingwood was the key man with an amazing individual display in our next match against Bangladesh at Trent Bridge, the day when Mum and Dad finally found out about my tattoo! After an undefeated 112 in our massive 391 for four, with Andrew Strauss striking 152, Colly then took six for 31, the best one-day figures by an England bowler. Colly was in good company. Viv Richards is the only other cricketer to have managed a century and a five-wicket haul in a one-day international.

Australia started to find their feet in the day-night game we played at Durham when they beat us by 57 runs after we had made a very poor start with the bat. Even in defeat, though, we managed to score a few psychological points and have a good laugh in the process, when Darren Gough decided to have a bit of fun at the expense of Aussie all-rounder Shane Watson. The papers had been full of stories of the Aussies being haunted by ghosts at their Lumley Castle hotel overlooking the ground, an opportunity Goughy found too hard to resist. When Watson, who apparently had not been too keen to be alone in his 'haunted' room, came into bat, Darren crept behind him before saying 'boo' in true Scooby-Doo style. I'm not sure poor Shane knew how to react. He tried to suppress a grin but also looked a bit embarrassed at being spooked by Goughy!

Bangladesh were duly despatched by both us and them, and we had a very lively little encounter with Australia at Edgbaston when Simon Jones accidentally struck Matt Hayden with a full toss and for a moment players were squaring up to each other. It may not have been the most savoury scene but the important aspect of it from an England point of view was how quickly all our players rallied around Simon. It was a case of 'you take one of us on, you take all of us on', and Hayden was left in no doubt that he wasn't going to be allowed to push one of our bowlers around. That game was eventually rained off but we were taking psychological strength from each match.

Finally, we got ready for an England *v* Australia final at Lord's in the first truly significant match between the sides in the summer. We put Australia in and bowled them out for 196, a good effort in the field and one that should have set us up for a comfortable victory. But unfortunately we slipped to 33 for five, with me being among the casualties.

Thankfully Collingwood, again proving what a good cricketer he is, and Geraint Jones led the fight-back and lifted us to the stage where we needed 19 off the last two overs to win. That came down to three needed off Glenn McGrath's last delivery and my good friends Ashley Giles and Darren Gough scrambled two and the match was tied, so soon after we had tied a match in Bloemfontein. And they say lightning never strikes twice! The NatWest Trophy and the series was shared – not the worst result for us.

The players of both sides and, I think, the cricket-watching public were ready for the Ashes now. There had been a lot of good one-day cricket, a lot of good incident, but everybody seemed to be ready for the main event.

First, though, was the NatWest Challenge and three more games against Australia, this time with the added innovation of 'super-subs' being introduced on a trial basis. This was a gimmick brought in by the ICC to enable people to replace any of their players, football-style, at any point during the match. I always had my reservations about this because it was a bit artificial; it did not prove a success and was abandoned in 2006.

We made a great start to this little series at Headingley by inflicting on Australia their heaviest one-day defeat, by nine wickets, with Marcus Trescothick scoring a century after Collingwood had again been among the wickets. We lost the last two one-day matches of the summer, though, raising questions as to whether Australia were now finding their feet. Gilchrist, in particular, looked to have found his with a big century at the Oval in the final game, and people were loudly asking whether we had missed our chance by not catching the Aussies cold.

I always try to be consistent and the middle of the one-day series was quite disappointing for me. The public were keen to see me and Freddie bat together but it didn't work out in that series. Freddie and I are good mates and enjoy spending time with each other. I was looking forward to batting with him, after he had missed the one-day series in South Africa, and he was looking forward to batting with me. I think the whole cricketing world was looking forward to it, certainly the England fans, but although it didn't happen in the one-day section of the summer I'm hoping we can get together a lot over the next few years in England's cause.

I'd always thought, ever since the side was picked for the Bangladesh Tests, that I wouldn't start the Ashes series because I didn't think the selectors would make any changes for the first Test at Lord's. But the one-dayers gave me another opportunity to prove I was ready to play Test cricket.

That quest started very well at the Rose Bowl and at Bristol, and even though I then had a couple of failures, I was determined to remain positive against the Aussie bowling because I was convinced that would be the right way to go in the Test series. My technique still seemed to be a talking point but I was confident it would stand up to the test. Some people still seemed to think I would be too leg-sided to play in Test cricket, that top bowlers would somehow find me out. I didn't agree. We would see.

Yet the last one-day innings I played that summer, in the final match at the Oval, which saw Australia clinch the NatWest Challenge, was hugely significant, I feel, in my selection for the first Test.

The Aussies were certainly keen to turn up the pressure on me. During that Oval game they were saying to me, 'This is what Test cricket is like. Can you handle it?' It seemed to me they were trying to target me, trying to destabilise me before the Ashes came around. My reaction was: well, if they're right and this is what Test cricket is like, then I want to be a part of it. I'm enjoying this.

I put a lot of pressure on myself at the Oval. We were up against it and I said to myself, this is the innings that could get you into the team for Lord's. There was talk that Thorpey was having trouble with his back and it had also emerged that he was going to coach in New South Wales the following winter, effectively ruling him out of the England picture at the end of the summer.

So the scene had changed a bit since the Bangladesh Tests. All that was going through my head. I really grafted for my 73 at the Oval, and I firmly believe that if I'd scored nothing that day I wouldn't have been picked for the first Test. It was the most significant innings I would play all summer even if, again, it was in a losing cause. How sweet it was at Bristol to play a big innings in a winning cause for England!

After the Oval I had no doubt that for the first time I was ready for Test cricket. I even told the press so that evening. Why lie or deal in platitudes? I don't like to beat about the bush and I like to speak what I believe to be the truth. So when I was asked the question in the post-match press conference, I told everyone that I was ready. I felt, leaving the Oval that night shortly before the first Test, that I was good enough for Test cricket. I had put my name down for selection and now I had to wait and see if the selectors agreed.

Ian Botham is still the biggest name in cricket. The man is a legend. Beefy still has the aura about him and is a man everyone in the game still listens to and respects. I am also proud to be a part of his management company and am delighted he has taken time to tell us what he thinks of me for this book.

> **Ian Botham:** *I think everybody who saw KP when he first turned up on the scene knew he would be good. The thing that impressed me most about him first up was that he was a guy who realised he was not going to get a fair chance in his own country and decided to do something about it. He was clearly good enough but because of the political correctness of the selectors in South Africa his dreams were about to be shattered, and it took a real gutsy person to pack his bags, come to England and set his heart on playing for us.*
>
> *To do that and to have the determination to do that tells us that here is someone a bit different and someone*

who has achieved what he has achieved by grafting and doing it the hard way. I think he has fitted in tremendously well very quickly with Team England and the way he plays excites me.

In many ways KP is an unusual player. He has his own style of play but it is a very effective style. You won't find a lot of the shots he plays in the textbook but that is not a problem to me because he brings individuality to the game and is mightily effective in the way he plays it.

You can't coach someone to play like KP and nor should you. The lad has such a natural talent that you have to let him get on with it. He is a special player, an enormous presence in the England team, and the world really is his oyster. If he makes the most of his talent and the opportunities he has worked so hard to gain, then there is no limit to what he can do. There is definitely a lot more to come from KP and I expect him to go from strength to strength.

It is still early days. In the short time that he has been around he has played two or three of the most memorable innings you will ever see, but he has to keep on producing the goods and appreciate that the hard work, in many ways, has only just begun.

The important thing is that we all leave him alone to get on with batting the way he does it. It's all very well criticising him for getting out to a loose shot but you have to take the rough with the smooth. We can't expect him to be this amazing strokemaker who can win matches on his own without accepting that there will be the odd lapse and the odd soft dismissal.

I don't have a problem with anything concerning his lifestyle. I tell you what, all cricket lovers in England care *about is what happens in the middle and nobody will mind KP having a good night out or wearing lots of jewellery as long as he is playing the way he did at the Oval against Australia.*

KP is a rare talent. South Africa's loss is England's gain. I know a lot of people in South Africa who are saying, 'How did this happen? How on earth did we lose this boy?' At the time not too many people were trying very hard to stop him leaving the country, but now they would love to have him back! Well, I think they left it just a little bit too late.

14

FIRST BLOOD
TO AUSTRALIA

'When Brett Lee was flying in, Kevin and I came
together in mid-pitch for a chat. But he said,
"Sorry, China. Can't talk now. Too pumped."
For a debutant Kevin had some match.'

Geraint Jones

I had just fallen asleep in my apartment in Southampton, around 9 p.m., when I got the best of the phone calls that David Graveney has made to me. He said, 'I've got good news for you. You've been picked for the first Test.'

Even though I thought I was ready, it still took me by surprise. Deep down I thought they would have gone for Graham Thorpe's experience for the first Test and, of course, he was also the man in possession and this England selection panel are rightly keen on continuity. But I had done enough in their eyes and that was good enough for me. Graveney went on to confirm to the press that my name had dominated early-season selection meetings but that, as I suspected, it wasn't until my innings at the Oval that the selectors were convinced I was ready for Test cricket. It was a tight call but I was in.

Richard Logan, who I shared a place with in Southampton, was with me and he couldn't have been happier for me. I rang Mum and Dad straight away and they were absolutely thrilled. It was 11 p.m. in South Africa by then and I woke them up, but it was clear they were not going to get any sleep after hearing my news. Nor did I!

I had to travel to Lord's in the morning to do a press conference and when I got there and the team was read out the realisation hit me that I had been picked for the first Test of England's Ashes summer. Nothing could take the smile off my face. It was the most sensational feeling and the most sensational phone call of my life.

Then it was a case of focusing on the job ahead the following week. Everybody wanted the Ashes to start by now. The countdown had been going on in the papers for ages and the days left were down to single figures.

I was told that I'd been selected because I'd done well being positive, and there was no need for me to change my game. Play the situation, as I had been doing, but play naturally, positively and confidently. It was music to my ears.

The build-up was very relaxed because I had been with the boys the week before and knew them all pretty well. One of the biggest pluses of the new England is that you never feel like an outsider coming into the team for the first time now. The advent a few years ago of central contracts, which means that top players are first and foremost international players and secondly county players, has encouraged team spirit and a sense of belonging in the England set-up.

There were no new faces to meet, and the summer was rolling on, which was ideal because the last thing I needed to do as a debutant was dwell on the enormity of the match ahead. It wasn't a case of 'I must do this differently or that'. It was the same focus we had had for the one-dayers, the same approach.

The Aussies, meanwhile, were trying to take strength from the way they finished the NatWest Challenge with two wins. Adam Gilchrist talked about how 'stories have been made up about us, pictures of us carrying handbags have been in the papers and people have been laughing at us. Now it's important to forget all that stuff because the Ashes are round the corner.'

He had touched on the many ways we had scored psychological points up to that juncture, but Gilchrist's argument was a valid one. To all intents and purposes the summer started now.

When the big day, Thursday 21 July 2005, dawned I can

honestly say I was more excited than nervous. I'm lucky I don't make mountains out of molehills. There were some nerves, of course, but there was much pride when Graveney handed me my Test cap before the match, especially as my parents had flown over for the Test and were going to be there at Lord's, watching.

There is a certain routine you go through before any game, but in this case any anxiety or nerves could only be heightened by the enormity of the occasion. The sense of anticipation among everybody was truly amazing. On the day of play you get to the ground around 9 a.m. and breakfast is laid out for you. Then you have to find your place in the dressing room, in this case the historic home dressing room at Lord's, and take ten to 15 minutes sorting out all your kit and getting ready to take to the field. At Lord's you can't help gazing at the honours boards, where every England batsman who has scored a Test century there and every England bowler who has taken five wickets in an innings or ten in a match is listed. It is every Englishman's dream to see his name up on those boards.

The dressing room on the morning of a match is full of activity. The bowlers and the keeper get their ankles and fingers taped to cope with the demands of the day ahead. Everyone these days tends to see the doctor to get their pills for the day. Throughout 2005 I was taking painkillers and anti-inflammatories for my bad back, so it was a case of going to the doctor and saying, 'Can I have my cocktail please?' Then, in true Tom Cruise style, he makes it up for you.

After about 20 minutes the pills kick in and you get yourself sorted. Then it's time for warm-ups, and if it's the first day of a Test the big question is, 'Are we batting or bowling?' Now, probably around 10 a.m., you start putting your whites on and getting prepared, both physically and mentally. We are looked after very well but it's our responsibility to have all the right gear ready and to make sure all our clothes are pristine. We are talking five days' worth of clothes here, not just a shirt and shorts for a football match, and you also have to ensure all your washing is done so you look smart enough to represent England. Conversations would also have been had with your sponsors, and in my case I'm very fortunate that in Woodworm I have a company who will get me anything I need within 24 hours.

On the field you have to be ready for business. Yes, you have laughs and mess about occasionally, but it's generally pretty intense out there. You have to have worked out your fielding positions and how you're going to approach each batsman, with plans having been made for each member of the opposing team.

When you are in the field you must watch the captain all the time. I like to be running around as much as possible. Always remember to encourage your team-mates and always expect the ball to be coming towards you. It's amazing how time flies when you are out in the middle!

The Aussies had earlier tried to crank up the pressure on us in their own inimitable way. Glenn McGrath had said that the only result he could see was 5–0 to Australia. Michael Vaughan, meanwhile, had turned our relative inexperience against Australia into a positive, saying we would not be carrying any baggage in the contest. So many of England's best players over the last 20 years had never been able to taste success against Australia, and our captain's argument was that, as so few of us had played them before, we couldn't go into the series with any hang-ups.

Michael was absolutely right when he said we didn't fear playing Australia but were looking forward to the challenge. And I couldn't help remembering the last Ashes series. I was playing grade cricket in Sydney when England were last there and all I could think of was how England had got crucified at the hands of the Australians. They copped it all day, every day on chat shows, on adverts, on everything. I hoped the English press would do the same to Australia should we get on top. Again, we wanted to get in the Aussies' faces straight away, like we did in the Twenty20 match. Our team talks revolved round the need to play positive cricket and not be intimidated.

Ricky Ponting won the toss for Australia and elected to bat under cloudy skies on that much-anticipated first morning. As we left our changing room and made our way towards the field we experienced something I'd never seen before. Outside the door of our dressing room a guard of honour had formed that stretched all the way down the stairs. As we passed through it the noise was unbelievable. It built up and up so that when we entered the Long Room the place erupted.

Now, MCC members are renowned for being restrained, sometimes to the point of inertia, but they were cheering, clapping and shouting. It was an incredible feeling walking through the Long Room to the loudest roar I had ever heard. It was just amazing. We felt the support was so strong. The MCC members thought we had a real chance this time and they wanted to let us know it.

Far from intimidating us, this reception inspired us. I felt ten feet tall walking out on to Lord's that day, and I'm sure that wasn't just because I was a debutant. All the lads felt the same. Vaughan, meanwhile, wanted to guard against us becoming nervous after such a welcome and reminded us what we needed to focus on.

Steve Harmison bowled the first ball of the most eagerly awaited Test series in years, and I reckon the attention and the eyes of the nation were on us from that point until the momentous day at the Oval.

We were not that unhappy when Australia decided to bat because conditions looked far from easy. And Harmison could not have got us off to a better start, with an over that set the tone for the whole series. With his second ball Harmy smashed one into Justin Langer's right arm just above the elbow. He went on to hit Matt Hayden and Ricky Ponting early on too. It might not sound like cricket to please the traditionalists but it was vital we showed them we meant business. Duncan Fletcher had called it 'getting in their space' and Vaughany wanted us to show anger.

Our approach even extended to us keeping our distance when Ponting needed treatment after being struck on the helmet by Harmy. Nobody wanted to see a player hurt and we were later accused of breaking the sport's convention, which says you should always make sure someone who has been hit is OK, but we wanted to show Australia that they wouldn't be getting any sympathy from us.

Soon I was to experience an anxious moment when I dropped Ponting in the gully, and little did I know then that my catching, before then such a safe part of my game, would become one of the issues of the summer. For now I was just relieved when he was quickly dismissed by Harmison.

It was all going like a dream. One of the biggest moments in the field for me came when Simon Jones dismissed Damien Martyn with his first ball of the match. It was an emotional moment for Simon, who had suffered a horrific knee injury the last time he had played against Australia, in Brisbane on the last Ashes tour.

Jones is another guy I have become very close to. I had spent time with him at the academy as he made his comeback from an injury that could so easily have finished his career. He had been back in the England team for a while by now but that was the moment when his frustrations at what had happened last time were well and truly put behind him.

At lunch Australia were 97 for five. Unreal. It is very unusual, though, for Australia to capitulate completely and they dragged themselves up to 175 for six, with the highlight of the afternoon session being Flintoff's dismissal of the dangerman Gilchrist and his roaring celebration, which showed just how crucial it was to get Gilly early.

Australia's fightback was shortlived. Harmison returned to take the last four wickets, I dropped another hard chance, this time Brett Lee, and the Aussies were all out for 190, with Steve getting his name on the famous Lord's honours board for his five-wicket haul. The atmosphere was electric.

The drama, though, was far from over. In the press conference that was held the morning I was selected for England, David Graveney had to field a question from Sky TV's Tim Abraham which basically suggested that Graham Thorpe would be a better option than me if England were struggling at 50 for three on the first day at Lord's.

Grav had pointed out that we had been in trouble in some of the one-dayers in South Africa when I had come to the crease and that I'd coped well enough, and he was confident that I would be fine should it happen in a Test. Little did he know, however, that I would be batting on my first day in Test cricket with England 21 for five! True, it wasn't a fantastic Lord's wicket but we were reduced to that ignominious position by one of the truly great spells of bowling from Glenn McGrath. And what a situation to find oneself in on debut!

My technique had been questioned and before I went in to bat I felt apprehension. There was a feeling of the unknown. Much had been said as to whether I was up to this, and now I was about to find out. I wondered what was in store for me, but once I got into the middle I was fine.

What better stage, I thought, to play cricket on? Against the best team in the world on the first day of an Ashes series. People had talked about me being weak on the off-side but that afternoon was the biggest test of technique and temperament that I could ever face. And I came through it.

I got myself a 50 as we hauled ourselves up somewhere close to the Aussies' total of 155 all out. To my way of thinking, if I could get a half-century against these boys on debut, then that could only augur well for the senior batsmen in our side for the rest of the series.

On that first day at Lord's I scored 29 runs off 70 or 80 balls in really testing circumstances. That to me showed that the temperament was there, the mental strength was there and, yes, the technique was there. John Buchanan, the Australian coach, had suggested I was a slow starter but I came through that first day. I began to show glimpses of the more positive me on the second day when I hit McGrath into the middle tier of the Pavilion – how I enjoyed that – and started to have the first of my tussles with the great Shane Warne.

I have already said how much I admire Shane, and by the time of the Lord's Test he had become a friend as well as my county captain. It helped that we were mates. It relaxed me out there and helped me be positive against him. I knew I needed to be quick on my feet and knew Warney would be trying his hardest to get me out. I really enjoyed facing him.

Just after I had completed my 50, I struck Shane into the second tier of the Grandstand. The next ball he offered me the chance to do it again, but this time I didn't hit it quite as cleanly and was caught by a diving Damien Martyn just inside the rope. I was a bit disappointed to get out having reached 57. Yes, it was fantastic to get a 50 on my debut, but I knew I could have got a few more and got us a little closer to their total. I do set myself very high standards. I don't ever want to settle for just being OK. I winked at Shane when I hit him for six but he just patted me on the bum and said, 'Well batted.' Then he got me out next ball. You're always learning.

People wondered if my friendship with Shane would help or hinder me. I hadn't studied him too closely in the Hampshire nets because he didn't do too much bowling there but I had watched him very closely during Hampshire games. And the thing was, I quickly realised that his bowling for Hampshire was nothing like his bowling for Australia. The man is an absolute genius, never more so than when he is bowling for his country. If he bowled the way he does in Test cricket in county cricket he would take 120 or 130 wickets every season. But I guess it's impossible for him to maintain those standards all the time.

Shane Warne is one of the greatest sportsmen who ever lived, in my opinion, and he deserves every ounce of success he has achieved. One of the saddest things, from a mate's point of view, is that Shane's name is not on the Lord's honours board for taking five wickets in a Test innings there. If anyone deserves it, he does. And he came so close to finally achieving that landmark in 2005.

In fact, Shane had a go at me for not keeping Simon Jones away from the bowling of McGrath at the end of the Lord's match when Shane had four wickets in the innings. As it turned out, McGrath cleaned up Simon, with a certain Shane Warne taking the slip catch, and I was left unbeaten on 64 at the other end as we lost by 239 runs.

I told Shane on that occasion that I fancied scoring runs off him at the other end, which was why Simon was facing McGrath, and we did talk quite a bit in the middle. Warney would bowl to me, go back to the non-striker's end, rub his hands in the dirt, look up at me and say something. I could see they were showing my face up on the big screen and I was trying desperately not to laugh. Sometimes I had to turn my back on Shane to make sure I didn't giggle.

It made me feel calm having Shane there, and I think our relationship eased any tension there might have been between the teams. Sportsmanship became a big part of the series and I think our committed but friendly clashes in the first Test set the tone for that. He certainly wanted to get me out and our friendship didn't reduce his competitive edge one little bit. From the first ball he bowled at me he wanted to get me out, and the first ball he bowled at me in the second innings at Lord's was one of the best I have ever received. It was an absolute peach.

I touched the ball after that for four and as I ran down the wicket I said to Shane, 'Where the hell did that previous ball come from? You're supposed to be my mate.' He just said, 'I want to get you out.' Warney wanted to get me out badly and I was determined not only to stop him getting me out but also to be positive against him and score runs against him.

The most successful batsmen against Shane over the years have been the ones who have gone after him. People like Brian Lara, and Sachin Tendulkar and some of the other Indian batsmen. The best way to defend against Shane is to attack him. It worked, to a large extent, for me in the first Test, and it was fantastic being around all these wonderful cricketers.

Not so wonderful, though, was the result. I had got something right in the field early in Australia's second innings when I ran out Justin Langer from point, but then had my worst moment in my baffling summer of dropped catches when Michael Clarke, on 21, drove the ball firmly, knee-high, to me at extra cover off Simon Jones. This was the easiest of the three catches to come my way in this match but inexplicably it went down, and Clarke went on to score another 70 runs in a partnership of 155 with Martyn that took Australia out of our reach.

It was a catch I should have taken ten times out of ten. There are no reasons why I dropped it and the others, no excuses. If the ball touches my hand I should catch it, that's the standard I set myself. My hands have always been safe in the past, just ask my coaches, and I have no real explanation as to why this happened.

I don't drop many balls but sod's law decreed that I would drop these three chances at Lord's, and another three as the series went on. It started to prey on my mind but it never once made me scared of fielding or worried about catches coming my way.

I love fielding and I love jumping and diving. I hated the fact I dropped those catches and I hated it when the Aussie fielders called me cymbals. Duncan Fletcher later said that maybe I wasn't totally balanced when the ball was coming towards me and, watching a few replays, maybe it's fair to say I wasn't as still as I should have been at the point of delivery. I've been working on that ever since.

I had been practising hard at catching and it wasn't as if I wasn't trying hard. I am as determined to be the best in the field as I am with the bat, and I'm sure it had nothing to do with concentration lapses or having too much energy.

As the series went on I would will the ball to come my way and then it would but I would drop it. I just don't know. Hopefully that summer was a one-off and I won't become renowned as a person who drops catches again.

My reprieve of Clarke helped Australia get to 384 and we were all out for 180, with my only consolation being that I had become only the eighth England player to score two half-centuries on Test debut.

Myself, Geraint Jones and our bowling coach Troy Cooley were the only members of our side to go in the Australian dressing room afterwards. My main intention was to congratulate Warney. They were having a great time in there because they had won a Test at Lord's, and I made sure I spoke to a few of the other players as well as Shane because I wanted to pick their brains. They were the best. And they had shown it again by beating us convincingly even after we'd got off to such a good start.

They were complimentary towards me but it's easy to do that after you've won, and it didn't mean too much to me because we'd lost the Test. Some of the guys went home but I went out with Shane and Stuart MacGill, who was also in the Australian party, and had a really good night.

People might find it odd that I should go out with the opposition but it is pretty common practice in cricket. All we did was go to a nice bar and club and just talk and have a few drinks, the way mates do. We talked a bit about the game that had just finished but you tend not to talk in such great detail, particularly as there were still four Ashes Tests left. You also try to forget about what has just happened and catch up on old friendships, asking how mutual friends are and basically getting into perspective what has just happened on the cricket field. There are other things in life and you have to remember not to get too bogged down in what is happening to you. You have to realise there is a big world out there that doesn't necessarily revolve round the Ashes, so I think it does you good to let your hair down and relax in those circumstances. Shane, Stuey and I had a good evening.

There was no point in licking our wounds. We just had to accept we had been beaten and make sure it didn't happen again.

This was no time for Australia to be thinking: 'Same old England. We're going to beat them easily again.'

And I now knew exactly what Test cricket was like. It had gone pretty well for me personally but not so good for the team and that hurt. But above all I loved it. I loved the whole experience and I wanted more, lots more.

I felt at home, but it would be interesting to hear whether my team-mates thought I looked at home. Here is wicketkeeper Geraint Jones.

Geraint Jones: *I wasn't surprised at how quickly Kevin made himself at home at Test level because of what I'd seen him do in South Africa. What did surprise me was how he scored his runs. He is an amazing front-foot player, but in the first innings at Lord's he played the short stuff so well, too. I could see he was really up for it. At one stage, when Brett Lee was flying in at him, we came together in mid-pitch for a chat at the end of an over and he just said, 'Sorry, China. Can't talk now. Too pumped.' For a debutant, Kevin had some match.*

15

THE GREATEST MATCH OF ALL

'He is a belligerent individual. He is cocky and confident. I love it, so long as he produces runs.'

Geoffrey Boycott

I t has been called the greatest Test of all time. Our match against
Australia at Edgbaston had everything. From pre-match injury
drama to incredulity at the toss and then some of the most amazing cricket. And it all came with us desperate to hit back after our
embarrassment at Lord's.

The build-up to the second Test was dominated by what we all
thought was extremely harsh criticism of my buddy, Ashley Giles.
Gilo is no Shane Warne and he knows it, but, then, who is? What
Ashley also knows is that he's invaluable to the side. He bowls
well, bats well and fields well and is a vital member of the England
team. He has become one of my closest friends in the England side
and that goes back to him being my designated 'buddy' on the trip
to Zimbabwe.

I felt for him in the aftermath of Lord's because, while we all
felt bitterly disappointed at our defeat, the last thing we needed
was for the press and public to indulge in a huge inquest after
just one game, particularly as a lot of the flak was flying unfairly
at Gilo.

What was particularly disappointing is that much of the flak
seemed to be coming from ex-players who should have known
better. They were people who perhaps had not achieved as much
as they would have liked in their own careers, or some who could
have no idea what it was like playing against this incredible
Australian side.

It goes without saying that the boys were firmly behind Ashley, a point emphasised by Michael Vaughan when he talked to us ahead of the game. He told us we had to erase from our thoughts what happened at Lord's. He reminded us that there were still four games to go and that we were still in the series. But he felt we hadn't got into the Australians' faces enough at Lord's, as we said we would do, and that we had to be positive, enjoy ourselves and get right back at them.

We had a scare when the captain was struck on the elbow by my promising young Hampshire colleague Chris Tremlett in the nets two days before the match. For a while we feared the worst, but X-rays revealed no break and Vaughany was back among us and ready to play.

Which is more than could be said for Glenn McGrath. At 9.15 a.m. on the morning of the game, the Australians were playing tag rugby to warm up when McGrath went to retrieve the ball. In doing so he stepped on a stray cricket ball on the outfield and damaged his ankle. One of the world's greatest bowlers was out of the match.

It was said later that we had taken no notice of this development and had just prepared as usual for the Test, but of course it must have an impact on you when you discover that McGrath is unable to play. For one thing it meant the Australian bowling had to be affected, because no McGrath meant less discipline in their attack. It meant more four balls for us to hit. And it meant that Australia had to try to find someone else who could bowl 20 overs for 40 runs. The likelihood, and we knew it, was that anyone else who came in was more likely to bowl 20 overs for 80 runs.

We knew we had to be positive, particularly now Glenn was out and had been replaced by Michael Kasprowicz. And we knew we had to be positive against Shane. What we didn't know was

left: Winning the Trent Bridge Test to go 2–1 Up.

below: The faces say it all. I don't think a six off McGrath was in the script.

right: The crowd enjoying another six.

© PHILIP BROWN

above: Brett asking for one.

© PHILIP BROWN

above: Hayden fumbles one

above: 'The catch' Warney put down.

left: Me nearly getting one! Brett Lee was pretty hostile after lunch at the Oval.

below: A really great sportsman. Shane Warne told me to enjoy the moment.

above: Celebrating a crucial wicket. A moment I'll never forget.

left: Freddie had played so well. We were so proud of him.

above: The moment we had all worked so hard for.

right: Finally, I had the Ashes in my hand. Such a good feeling!

below: The celebrations were immense. Freddie just taking a 5 minute snooze. Vaughney's sunglasses were a must!

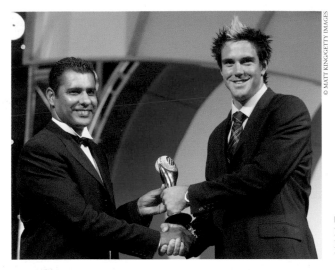

left: Receiving the I.C.C One Day Player Of The Year award.

above: A very proud moment.

above: My Mum and Dad were so excited to meet the Queen.

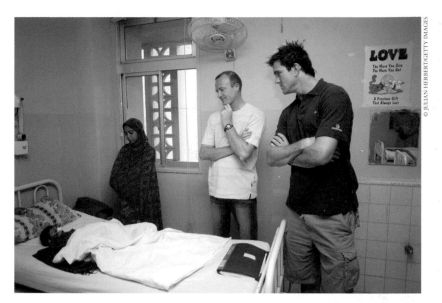

above: Me and Shaggy visiting a hospice for children in Islamabad on a day off from cricket in Pakistan, 2005.

right: The Urban Cricket launch, 2006. It was great to have Jess along for the day. She bats pretty well for a singer!

above: Just checking the ball wasn't coming my way.

left: Celebrating my ton at Edgbaston. The bat ended up in Row F!

that Ricky Ponting would hand us the opportunity to be positive sooner than we thought when he won the toss and, incredibly, asked us to bat.

We felt it had to be a batting first pitch. It's certainly what I understand Michael would have done had he won the toss. And if you look at it from an Australian perspective the decision seemed even simpler because they had just lost their best pace bowler but still had the greatest spinner of all time available to them to use against us in the fourth innings. But, for whatever reason, Ricky invited us to bat and we were more than happy to accept. What followed was one of the most spectacular days of cricket in living memory and one that completely changed the tone of the series.

Marcus Trescothick and Andrew Strauss immediately went on the offensive. It was the most positive statement of intent after our captain and coach had told us to go after the Australians. And without McGrath there was far too much loose stuff from the Australian attack. Even Shane found himself on the receiving end, with Marcus hitting him back over his head for six in his first over.

Only Andrew was out in the first session but that failed to stop our momentum, with Marcus amazingly taking 18 off the final over before lunch, bowled by Brett Lee. Unfortunately Marcus fell ten runs short of what would have been a well-deserved maiden Test century, and Ian Bell and the captain went soon after.

That meant, however, that I was to be joined by Andrew Flintoff for the first meaningful partnership between us. It was brilliant. There was no need to look at the scoreboard. It moved along very nicely. All I had to do was watch and admire the fantastic strokeplay of Freddie.

Freddie had waited a long time for his first Ashes Test and when it came, at Lord's, it had been a disappointment for him. Now he was keen to make up for that. All I wanted to do initially was rotate the strike and leave it to Freddie because he seemed to be in great nick and then it was a question of me getting into the swing of things too.

There was never any suggestion of us trying to out-hit each other. That is never going to happen despite what some people may think. It was just a pleasure to be at the other end with Freddie Flintoff playing the way he can and I was delighted to see him batting like that, with such freedom, to get back in the runs.

Some of the shots Flintoff played that day were unbelievable, particularly one off Lee, which was one of the best shots I've ever seen. He's a great cricketer and the best all-rounder in the world. It was spectacular batting, with 157 runs coming in the afternoon session from 27 overs, and we had some good laughs in the middle.

After Freddie went I attempted to step up the pace and got another 50 to become only the sixth England batsman to begin my Test career with three half-centuries. When I went there was a danger, after such a dramatic day, that we'd fall a little short of where we needed to be, but some big hitting from Simon Jones and Steve Harmison took us up to 407 all out, all in one day. Amazing. It was only the second time since the Second World War that England had scored 400 on the first day of a Test, and their highest first-day total since 1938!

I thought it was a job well done and, above all, a statement of intent, but not everybody was happy. Some commentators felt we had missed an opportunity to get 500 and really put Australia out of the game, a fact I was reminded of as I drove back to our hotel at the end of the day's play and saw Geoff Boycott and Tony Greig attempting to flag down a taxi.

I stopped and told them to jump in. I was particularly keen to meet Greig because our careers had followed such similar paths, but I barely got the chance to introduce myself. That's because neither Tony nor I could get a word in. Geoffrey dominated the conversation. He was telling me how stupid I was in not making sure I got my first Test hundred. He said, 'Don't throw those opportunities away,' but I thought I'd batted well with the tail and tried to point out that there would inevitably be times when I died by the sword because I lived by it.

I tried to tell him how important it was for us to be positive after what had happened at Lord's and that I had to have a go when I was in with Matthew Hoggard, but he insisted it wouldn't have happened in his day because he would have made sure his partners stayed with him while he got to three figures.

I didn't regret giving him a lift because I will always take criticism of my cricket on board – not so much the criticism of my jewellery that I was to get later from Boycott – but I must admit I have never been so happy to see a hotel entrance in my life. Boy, was I willing that journey to come to an end and the hotel to come into view.

And Geoffrey made me drop him right outside the main door before waving me on as if I was a taxi!

No, Boycott was fine. I get on fine with him. He has his views and makes everybody aware of them but he's one of the greats and that's his prerogative. Unfortunately, my chat with Tony Greig, in which I want to ask him about how he arrived in England as a young cricketer from South Africa, will have to wait for another day.

The newspapers the next day were full of my batting with Freddie and I was hoping it would have an effect on the Aussies' batting. We knew we had to capitalise on our cricket of the day before and we flew at Australia from the word go. Justin Langer was hit on the head by Harmison before Hoggard got Matt Hayden out with a perfectly executed plan first ball.

Then it was time for Giles to show how misplaced all the criticism of him was. By the close of the second day Ashley had taken three big wickets and Australia had slipped to 308 all out, giving us a valuable first-innings lead of 99. One of the best moments of the match, and the entire series, came when Gilo took his first wicket, that of Ponting, to huge roars of acclaim from his home crowd and to our delight. At that moment, both players and supporters left no one in any doubt what they think of Ashley.

Trescothick and Strauss walked out to one of the biggest ovations I've ever heard at the start of our second innings, but we always knew it was going to be difficult second time round to put the match out of Australia's reach.

Even more so, on the third morning, when Brett Lee produced a spell of three wickets in nine deliveries to change the course of the match. I might have been his fourth wicket, possibly getting a faint touch on my first ball, but that didn't make my disappointment any easier to take when, after hitting Shane for two sixes, I was given out sweeping Shane when Rudi Koertzen decided I had made contact with bat or glove before Adam Gilchrist took the catch. Replays suggested I hadn't but these things happen and you have to take the rough with the smooth.

Soon we were in bigger trouble when we subsided to 75 for six, a lead of just 174, and Fred damaged his shoulder. Surely we were not going to suffer more agony at the hands of Australia after such a great start to the match? No, we were not, thanks to an awesome display from Flintoff. He imposed himself on Australia and the match.

At one point Freddie put Brett Lee onto the pavilion roof, and then he added 51 off 49 deliveries for the last wicket with Simon Jones that effectively put us back in charge. When Freddie was out, for the most hard-hit 73 imaginable, the crowd rose to him and, for the first but not last time in this series, the great Shane Warne ran after an English batsman on his way back to the crease and said, 'Well done.' Another fine gesture from a man who had just taken another six English wickets.

It left Australia with a target of 282 but that was reduced to 235 with the minimum of fuss and the nerves were starting to jangle. Until Freddie again stepped forward. He then produced one of the greatest overs in Ashes cricket, dismissing Langer and Ponting in the most aggressive and skilful manner possible. Michael Vaughan would later say that that was the moment when he first started to believe that we could win the Ashes.

It was the start of another momentous afternoon that would see Australia slip to 140 for seven and Vaughan claim the extra half hour. We couldn't finish it off that night, but when Harmison trapped Michael Clarke with a slower ball just before the close, Australia were 175 for eight, still 102 behind, and the match looked all over bar the shouting. But was it?

I really thought we would just clean up on the Sunday morning and level the series but Shane and Brett Lee batted sensationally and slowly, agonisingly for us, managed to start ticking off the required runs.

It was heart-wrenching stuff. I couldn't believe what was unfolding in front of me. When you are involved in the action you feel in control but I felt helpless in the outfield as the game ebbed and flowed and totally drained all of us involved.

The tension grew and grew and the Aussie supporters were counting the runs down. I was thinking, what on earth is going on here? Then Shane trod on his stumps, which was crucial, and we had to show more of the togetherness, determination and sheer will to win that has characterised our cricket over the last couple of years.

It was also crucial the captain held his nerve, and he did so even when the target got smaller and smaller. The target was down to 20 when Flintoff hit Lee on the hand. Then the batsman got an inside edge to the boundary and scampered a single.

With 15 needed, Kasprowicz cut Flintoff down to third man where Simon Jones, who has the safest of hands, spilled the chance. I really thought then that it was all over. I'm not one to talk too much about dropped chances but when the ball was in the air travelling towards Jones I jumped up and thought, that's it. Then when it went down I also thought, that's it. Only this time I meant Australia would win. I thought to myself: are we actually going to lose this after all we've done to win?

As Australia's target fell into single figures the enormity of what a loss would do to us became apparent. How could we possibly recover from this? The Ashes would surely be gone. Four were needed to win. Lee sent a ball flying towards the boundary but Jones was there to field it and keep Australia down to a single.

Two balls later, with our last throw of the dice, Harmy bowled a ball that reared up off the dead pitch and hit Kasprowicz round his glove. The ball went down the leg side where Geraint Jones took a neat catch. Cue craziness. The feeling of relief, happiness and joy was unreal. It was the greatest of feelings. Those sporting highs, those moments, nothing else can take you there. It's a unique thing and something that I'm really grateful for in my career.

The number of days I've had like that already in my career are amazing. And I've only just started! Long may it continue because they are the best days of your life. I'm not stupid enough to think there will never be bad times, bad tours or bad runs of form, but it will always be that little bit easier to handle because of the highs we have all experienced as a team.

Then followed one of the images of the series when Freddie

consoled Brett Lee, who had done so much to give Australia the most improbable of victories, and the mother and father of all celebrations.

A few of us went on a pub crawl in Broad Street, where I was introduced to Guinness. I'm not a beer man at all generally but I was that night. Simon Jones and I were the last to return to the hotel, but not before we had ended up in an Aussie bar, which was great fun. Aussies are good people and I get on really well with them. They win well and they lose well, although they do tend to whinge a bit too!

We had some fun with a few of them that night and I ended up wearing a headband, sunglasses and generally acting like a complete idiot. We had been annihilated at Lord's and now we had triumphed in the most amazing of Tests. What could possibly come next?

Edgbaston was where I added the title of Geoffrey Boycott's taxi driver to my CV! Boycott is one of the most outspoken critics in the game, but, as a great former opening batsman, is one that I always listen to, to see if I can learn from him. He has infuriated me, such as when he criticised my lifestyle before the Oval Test, but he has also made some valid points about my batting. Here's what Geoffrey thinks of me.

Geoffrey Boycott: *I certainly didn't have anything against Kevin Pietersen's selection for the Ashes before the series because I like his mental strength, but what I didn't want to see was England being too gung-ho in the early stages.*

I always thought he was one of the best young prospects in English cricket and, while I agree that he should not change his batting style, he should have a good look at the way he gets out and he has got to start playing straighter in Test cricket.

He is not very good at defending because his game is based on confrontation. Some people can play long, defensive innings but it's not a strategy that works for most people. It's important to know what your strength is, and Pietersen played to his at the Oval in particular.

Full marks to the lad because he's done terrifically well. I had been saying before the Oval against Australia that he hadn't made a major contribution to England for five innings but when it mattered he came good. He is a belligerent individual. He is cocky and confident. There is a touch of arrogance about him. I love it, so long as he produces runs.

All the great players have had self-confidence and self-belief. They have all been full of themselves. But the point is that they have delivered. Up until the Oval, Pietersen had the persona but not the runs.

16

THE AUSSIES' GREAT ESCAPE

'Look at the Australians. Look at how they're celebrating a draw. When did they last do that?'

Michael Vaughan

We had just one day to recover from the emotion and sheer mental toil of Edgbaston before we were on our way to Manchester for the third Test. Back-to-back Tests are a necessity these days because of packed international itineraries, and they are great for spectators but they are certainly draining for players. Still, after Edgbaston I for one didn't want to wait long before we got stuck into the Aussies again. It was a case of 'bring it on'.

We were as positive as it is possible to be going into Old Trafford. We'd beaten Australia in a Test match, in itself something of a rarity for recent England teams. After being humiliated at Lord's we had hit back and won despite almost throwing it away. We showed a collective strength of character to win an absolute thriller and the confidence that gave us was massive.

We knew then that this Australian team could be beaten, and we knew for the first time that we could win the Ashes. The consequences of defeat at Edgbaston were just too harsh to contemplate but we didn't have to worry about that any longer.

It also became clear that our efforts were now being watched by a significantly wider audience than usual. Cricket was everywhere. Freddie was on all the front pages. People who had previously shown no interest in the game were suddenly becoming alive to it, and those who had always loved it began to think that maybe, after all the years of struggle, England finally had a chance of beating Australia.

Our first concern upon arrival at Old Trafford was the pitch. Manchester has a reputation for taking spin and, of course, we needed no reminding that this was the venue where Shane Warne introduced himself to the English public with the 'ball of the century' to Mike Gatting in 1993. But on first inspection the surface looked hard and abrasive, perfect for the reverse swing of Simon Jones and Andrew Flintoff.

Injury news seemed to be in our favour too. Not only was Glenn McGrath still struggling with his ankle problem, but now Brett Lee was diagnosed as having a knee infection. We could not afford to worry about them, simply concentrate on our own affairs, and our captain Michael Vaughan was particularly keen to get a score on the board after so far in the series failing to reproduce his outstanding batting, such a feature of England's last tour to Australia. We all knew that it wouldn't be long before he would make the Australian bowlers pay.

As it turned out both McGrath and Lee were fit to play but we were in such a positive mood that it wouldn't have mattered if Australia had been able to call upon Lillee and Thomson. Michael won the toss and there was a big shout of yes in the dressing room because we so wanted to bat. We had no hesitation in taking first strike.

And the captain made the most of taking first dig. He scored the century that we all thought was just around the corner with some world-class shot-making, and the first day was also notable for Shane Warne taking his 600th Test wicket. Warney had nicknamed me 'Six hundred' when I first started playing for Hampshire because he said I was going to be his landmark victim, but as it turned out Marcus Trescothick had that honour, and it is an honour when you think about it, because Shane is the greatest there's ever been. The Old Trafford crowd stood to Shane and he thoroughly deserved every plaudit that came his way.

The rest of us didn't quite give Vaughan the support he deserved. I decided to take on the new ball towards the close but was caught on the boundary, hooking, by sub-fielder Brad Hodge. What was it the Australians would be saying later about us using good fielders as substitutes? Anyway, I was upset with myself because this was one occasion where perhaps I hadn't played the situation properly. It's such a fine line. I always look to be positive and want to play to my strengths but it doesn't look great when I get out like this at a time when perhaps I should have been a little more circumspect until the following morning.

It all comes down to experience, and the most important thing is retaining my belief that I can take on the best bowlers. If that ball had flown for six, like so many in the series, I would have been applauded. And it wasn't far away from the boundary. It's a question of the situation, the shot selection and the percentages all being right but on this occasion it didn't work out for me, my disappointment being compounded when nightwatchman Matthew Hoggard was out to the final ball and suddenly we were 341 for five after dominating for most of the day.

The other particularly pleasing performance in our innings, after Michael's 166, was a 50 for Ian Bell. Amazingly, some people were questioning his place after Lord's but thankfully knee-jerk reactions are a thing of the past in English cricket and the selectors continued to back his obvious class. This was where Belly repaid them.

We got up to 444 and then our guys bowled exceptionally well, mainly Simon Jones with his reverse swing, and a quite fantastic delivery from Ashley Giles. All the attention had been on Shane and his 600 Test wickets but here our spinner Gilo produced a ball as good as anything the great man has mustered to bowl Damien Martyn, pitching outside leg and flicking the top of off-stump. It was a lovely moment. Not so lovely was my fourth dropped catch of the series, a hard one low to my left off Adam Gilchrist. Still can't explain it.

At one stage we really did look as though we would get the Aussies to follow on but bad weather on the third day hindered us and we weren't as sharp in the field as perhaps we might have been. When the fourth day dawned we were determined to make up for lost time, not least Simon who took the last three Aussie wickets quickly to reduce them to 302 all out, a lead of 142 for us and a commanding position.

Jones, meanwhile, had taken six for 53, his best Test figures, and ones he could enjoy all the more because of the adversity he came through after that horrible injury in Brisbane. When you have been through all that Simon has, thinking his career was over before battling back to the top, success means so much more and I was delighted for him. But I was also sad for Shane who had batted really well for his 90 and deserved his century. Like the absence of his name from the Lord's honours board, Shane seems destined not to score a Test century and it would be a great shame if he never got there. His batting has certainly come on in leaps and bounds in recent years to the point where he can be considered as an all-rounder in my book.

Now it was a question of trying to score runs quickly and efficiently and then see if we still had enough time to force a victory, despite the time lost to the weather.

Marcus Trescothick and Andrew Strauss got us off to another very good start before Straussy took charge in the final session, despite having a patched-up ear after being hit by Brett Lee.

Andrew had encountered problems against Shane earlier in the series, and Warne had played on those, but he had clearly worked out how to play against the great leg-spinner and went on to his sixth Test century and first against the Aussies. It's brilliant when a class batsman can work out a plan to combat a great bowler who has troubled him and then see it work. Ian Bell, meanwhile, scored his second 50 of the match before Geraint Jones finished our innings with a flourish by scoring 27 from 12 balls. Me? Unfortunately I got a first-baller, a delivery I didn't even see from Glenn McGrath. Yet I was less upset than I was in the first innings. That is the sort of thing that can happen to anyone and I just lost the slower ball in the air and couldn't get my bat down in time before it thudded into my pads and I was on my way.

The most important thing was that Vaughany's perfectly timed declaration after Geraint had hit McGrath for six back over his head towards the close of the fourth day left Australia 423 to win, a target that history will tell you is virtually impossible to reach in the final innings of a Test match. From our point of view it was a question of whether we could take ten wickets in the time remaining and go 2–1 up in the series.

The final morning of the third Test brought scenes as extraordinary as any in this extraordinary series. Lancashire had offered final-day admission at £10, and £5 for children, so I thought there might be a decent enough crowd. What I didn't expect was that people would start queuing at 3 a.m. and the gates would be closed by 8.30 a.m.

When we arrived at the ground some people thought there must have been a bomb scare or something and the crowd had had to be evacuated because there were thousands of people on the streets and it was difficult to battle our way through them to get to the ground on time for warm-ups. A ten-minute drive was taking longer than an hour. It later transpired that around 20,000 had turned up that day and were not able to get in the ground, as well as the 23,000 who made it. More were told in the city centre not to bother as they started to make their journey to the cricket. The last time anything remotely similar to this had happened was the final day of the 2000 series against West Indies at the Oval, when a mere 5,000 were turned away. The attendance at an Old Trafford Test had broken 100,000 for the first time. When we did our warm-ups, a full house was already there, cheering our every move. Truly amazing.

I had other things on my mind, too. By this time I was having a lot of trouble with my back, and I had to take a large number of painkillers to get through that day. It is an injury to my ninth vertebra that has hindered me for some time now and one that I was to aggravate on tour later that year in Pakistan. It is some-thing I just have to deal with but it certainly was not serious enough to even remotely threaten my place in the field that day.

When play finally started the roof almost came off after the first ball. Hoggard produced the perfect delivery with his first ball of the day to dismiss Justin Langer, but any thoughts we might have had that Australia would subside meekly were destined to be dashed.

Matt Hayden and Ricky Ponting proved particularly difficult nuts to crack. Hayden was edging balls everywhere but they just wouldn't go to a fielder. Eventually it needed the intervention of Freddie, whose image on boards and masks was everywhere at Old Trafford, to prove again that he was not just the local hero but also a national one by comprehensively bowling Hayden.

Just two wickets down at lunch and plenty of drama to follow. Throughout the afternoon session we would take wickets at key times but then Australia, as the champions they are, dug in and started to build another partnership that threatened to take the match away from us.

Ponting is one of the best batsmen in the world and how he started to prove it now. The guy is clearly a world-class performer and was under a lot of pressure all summer as it became clear that, for once, this Ashes series was not going to be the easy stroll for Australia that it had all too often been before.

Now he lost three partners before tea as Australia slipped to 182 for five and we became clear favourites to win, but still Ricky wouldn't succumb to our bowlers.

The old ball was reverse-swinging again, a key factor in our success all summer because the Australians, and the dangerman Adam Gilchrist in particular, just couldn't seem to deal with that. They had obviously encountered reverse-swing before but such was the skill with which it was applied by Jones and Flintoff in particular that the Aussies had little answer to it all summer.

But Ponting found a willing ally in Michael Clarke and for a while even the remote possibility of an Australian win began to look slightly less fanciful. That was never in our minds though. For us there were only two possible outcomes, and the one that saw Australia escaping with a draw, we felt, was still the most unlikely, particularly when Simon Jones produced an absolute jaffa of a delivery to bowl Clarke with an unplayable reverse in-swinger. Australia were now 263 for six and in walked Jason Gillespie, who was having a dismal tour with the ball, ahead of Shane Warne seemingly to block out our bowlers. Australia had given up on victory and were going for the draw! Even that was a boost to us, particularly when Gillespie lasted just five balls before falling to Hoggard.

Now it really was game on. Ponting had reached a truly awesome century by now and had been joined by his vice-captain, Warne. The final 15 overs began with Australia 314 for seven. Suddenly Warne hit one towards me at short midwicket. I dived and was certain I would collect it but it popped out. Agony. Why on earth was this happening to me? I still couldn't believe it, but you really do have to put dropped catches out of your mind and concentrate on the next ball, otherwise you will be in trouble. We were to receive another blow when Simon then had to go off with severe cramp. Our most potent bowler of the match wasn't there for the finale and we still had three wickets to take.

Our hopes soared when Geraint took a superb reflect catch off Andrew Strauss's thigh to dismiss Warne, and Fred celebrated with an acrobatic caterpillar movement more at home on the dance floor than a cricket field. Substitute fielder Stephen Peters almost ran out Brett Lee before what I thought must be the crucial moment. Steve Harmison dismissed Ponting to a gloved leg-side catch to end seven hours of determined resistance from the Australian captain. Now it was 354 for nine and we were on the brink of a 2–1 series lead.

We had 24 balls to wrap up the match and Lee had been joined at the crease by McGrath, a renowned number 11. Surely we would do it? But Jones was off the field and Flintoff and Harmison had given everything to the cause. Could they keep on going, at the end of incredible back-to-back Test matches, to claim that last vital wicket? Fred had a huge lbw shout against Lee turned down and then Harmy just couldn't break through in the final over. More agony. Australia had escaped.

It wasn't a great match for me individually but it was another Test that had everything. Top-quality hundreds, a 600th wicket for Shane Warne, an agonisingly close finish and a draw. Any American taking an interest in what was going on in an English summer probably couldn't understand the fact that there had been no winner after five days but all English and Australian people did. The match had everything else.

And, again, came another significant moment. The Australians were celebrating immediately afterwards as if they had won the Ashes. The scenes of joy on their balcony were unbridled. Michael Vaughan called us into a huddle on the outfield before we left the field and said, 'Look at the Australians. Look at how they're celebrating a draw. When did that last happen to them? When did they last do that?'

Of course, afterwards the Aussies tried to seize the psychological high ground by saying that they had been lifted by that great escape and now expected us to be demoralised. Something along the lines of, 'England have had their chance but couldn't take it. Now normal service will be resumed.'

But we knew different. Our captain, immediately the game ended, articulated what we all felt deep down and which we all needed to hear. We had emerged the stronger team from another epic battle and we would be in the ascendancy when we travelled to Trent Bridge for the fourth Test. I left Old Trafford believing more strongly than ever before that we were going to win the Ashes.

17

HISTORY WITHIN REACH

*'People started throwing pens at me to see if
I would drop them. They thought it was funny.'*

Kevin Pietersen

This incredible journey moved on to Trent Bridge. After Edgbaston and Old Trafford it seemed to me that no way could there be another close finish. Surely we were due a quiet Test match after all the tension, drama and excitement. But this match was just as amazing as the last two and it is only now, one year on, that I can truly take on board what happened to all of us in the summer of 2005.

For the third Test running the pre-match injury news had centred on Glenn McGrath. He had made a rapid and unexpected recovery to play at Old Trafford but now he was doubtful with an elbow injury, one he showed no signs of while warming up for Trent Bridge in a tour match at Northampton.

Maybe playing at Old Trafford had forced him to place too much pressure on other parts of his body in order to protect his damaged ankle. Whatever, the great fast bowler was out again and, as we did at Edgbaston, we would be looking to take advantage. Shaun Tait, a young fast bowler who had had a short and unsuccessful spell at Durham, had already been picked to replace the out-of-sorts Jason Gillespie, so Michael Kasprowicz again deputised for McGrath.

We, however, had no such problems and were unchanged for the fourth successive match, virtually unheard of in England. In fact, the only other England side to go unchanged throughout a whole Ashes series was Arthur Shrewsbury's side in 1884/85, so another piece of history was within reach. Consistency of selection and an improvement in the treatment of and avoidance of injuries has certainly played a big part in the success of this England team.

There was a lot of rain around in the days leading up to the fourth Test but we were still confident that it would be a bat-first pitch and Vaughany duly won the toss and elected to bat, any worries about what the weather might have done to the pitch being quickly dispelled by Marcus Trescothick and Andrew Strauss racing to their seventh century stand in 18 Tests at five an over!

The momentum was continued by Vaughan but by the time I joined the captain we had slipped to 146 for three amid interruptions for the weather, and I had a couple of slices of luck early on when Kasprowicz missed a return catch I offered to him and Hayden almost ran me out.

Which made it more disappointing that I didn't go on and get a big score. I had done the hard work and, having missed out at Old Trafford, badly wanted to contribute to the cause, but, whether it was a technical problem or not, I was out for 45. I'd done well in the first Test and got another 50 at Edgbaston and it was about time, as far as I was concerned, that I put three figures on the board.

That was my concern at that time. But thankfully it was not an issue at Trent Bridge because the indomitable Andrew Flintoff put those three figures on the board instead, at the best possible time for the team.

Freddie had given everything on the final day at Old Trafford, bowling 25 overs at the end of back-to-back Tests that would test anyone's stamina. He had decided to get away for a couple of days in France before the fourth Test and now, in a partnership of 177 with Geraint Jones, he put us into the sort of position from which we really could push for a 2–1 lead.

It was great, too, for Geraint, who had had his ups and downs throughout the series and had to live with the almost constant refrain of some people questioning his place in the side. Not in the England team, they don't. He is a valuable member of our side. Jones's 85 showed that he is a batsman of true Test class and we got up to 477, our highest total in a Trent Bridge Test for 67 years.

It was said in the build-up to Trent Bridge that this was where Matthew Hoggard would come into his own. More of a conventional than reverse-swing bowler, Hoggy had made some vital contributions in the series up to that point and continued to be a crucial member of our attack, but hadn't claimed the really big haul that his partners in crime, Flintoff, Harmison and Jones, had done.

It could not have made it any easier for him that people were expecting Hoggy to step up to the plate just because Trent Bridge usually assists swing. It is not as simple as that. Swing can be a baffling cricketing phenomenon and sometimes even the leading practitioners of it can have days when it just won't happen, for whatever atmospheric reason.

Hoggard, though, lived up to every expectation anyone could have had for him at one of his favourite venues, taking out Langer, Hayden and Martyn in a final session of the second day that ended with Australia 99 for five.

The good work was continued the next day when we made Australia follow on for the first time in 17 years and 191 Tests against any opposition. It was magical stuff. Simon Jones was again in his element and Andrew Strauss pulled off a catch to rival Paul Collingwood's in the one-dayer at Bristol when he dived at second slip to somehow catch Adam Gilchrist. It looked as though we would have a first innings lead of over 300 but Brett Lee smacked 47 off 44 balls, including two huge sixes off Steve Harmison. As it was, Australia were 218 all out and Simon had taken his second five-wicket haul of the summer, including four for 22 in 32 deliveries on that third morning.

Vaughany called us all together towards the end of the Australian innings and asked what we thought about making Australia follow on. Once it became clear that our bowlers felt fresh there was really no doubt in the captain's mind, but the one problem was that Simon was now starting to feel pain in his ankle.

As it turned out, Jones managed to bowl just four overs in the Aussies' second innings and had to leave the field. It was a huge blow for Simon and for us, and it would later lead to him not only missing the final Test but also the tour of Pakistan that winter. His absence, furthermore, was to lead unwittingly to the one big controversy in a summer noted for its sportsmanship.

The other bowlers, as usual, performed heroics in Simon's absence, and the Aussies were making a better fist of their reply until Ricky Ponting was called for a quick single by Damien Martyn but was beaten by a direct hit from Simon's fielding substitute, Gary Pratt of Durham.

Ponting was clearly agitated even before the third umpire gave him out but what happened next took us completely by surprise. We were all together, waiting for the verdict and preparing to have a drink, when Ricky started effing and blinding at us. We had absolutely no idea what he was on about. It was astonishing.

When he finally stormed off, the Australian captain then started venting his anger at our coach Duncan Fletcher, who had been, it later transpired, making some toast in the dressing room but had wandered on to the balcony to see what all the fuss was about.

It later transpired that Ponting was angry at our use of substitute fielders. He reckoned that we were allowing bowlers to take breaks and replacing them with agile fielders. What he didn't seem to take into account was that Simon Jones was in hospital at the time so we could hardly be accused of giving him a break when he wasn't injured. Not only had we not broken any rules but, as far as we were concerned, we were acting completely within the spirit of the game.

The Aussies started talking about only designated 12th men from the existing squad being allowed on to the field, and how a bowler should replace another bowler, stuff like that. But they had conveniently forgotten that I was caught by Brad Hodge, one of the best fielders in their squad and certainly not the designated 12th man as far as I was aware, at Old Trafford in the third Test.

If we had a decent fielder as our substitute, then so what? Are we supposed to have a donkey in reserve? That wouldn't be the smartest move. To me it was a revealing moment. We knew the pressure had been mounting on Ponting ever since he won the toss and inserted us at Edgbaston. This was evidence that the pressure was getting to him, and I really hope it didn't sour in people's minds the splendid relationship the series was played in.

It didn't as far as the players were concerned and, really, it was all a storm in a teacup. Simon Katich was another batsman who lost his rag when he was out in that innings as we moved smoothly towards a winning position. Meanwhile, my latest dropped catch of the series, to give Kasprowicz a reprieve, left me dumbstruck.

Six drops in all during the series. Something I hope and trust will never be repeated. I had it all, with people in restaurants throwing pens at me to see if I would drop them, and a few other 'jokes'. They thought it was funny. As I have said, I have never had a problem with catching in the past and I sincerely hope I never will again. Duncan highlighted the need to be completely balanced as the ball comes towards me, and I have taken that on board. Others have suggested that maybe I was just too excited by the whole Ashes experience. Rather than have a theory, I just feel it was one of those things and won't happen again.

The Aussies refused to go quietly in their second innings but when they were dismissed for 387, we were left with just 129 to secure a win that would ensure that we could not lose the series.

It would have been nice to think we could just knock those runs off for the loss of two or three wickets and then celebrate, but in this series? Not a chance. It was to prove the most nerve-racking of chases. In the dressing room we vowed to play the ball and not the situation. We were determined not to do anything we wouldn't normally do, but that didn't stop Trescothick racing away at the start.

Tres was stopped in his tracks by Warne and I suppose the first ripple of apprehension went through us when our vice-captain was dismissed by Shane's first ball. Next over Vaughan went to Warne too and suddenly he had taken two wickets for no runs in seven balls. We were 36 for two.

When Andrew got out to a disputed catch, again off Shane's bowling, I came in to join Ian Bell and any nerves I was feeling, and there were a few, weren't helped when Bell was out in the next over to leave us 57 for four.

We were not even halfway to our target. This was serious. But I took a lot of confidence from the fact that Shane bowled round the wicket to me as soon as I came in. We were only chasing 129 and to me this was a negative tactic. I know Shane feels he can bowl anyone round their legs but I don't think he can get me out that way. I just don't feel it's possible.

Out came Fred to join me and on this occasion we very much had to play the situation and not get carried away. For 45 minutes it went well. As I have said, when you are in the middle you feel in control, especially when you have got Freddie Flintoff up the other end. I was sure we were going to see England home, particularly when we reached 100 for four with just 29 needed.

But then I went for a drive off Brett Lee, a ball I thought I could hit to the boundary, but instead I edged it to Gilchrist and it looked bad, like I had chased a wide ball I didn't need to play. I felt devastated. Helpless. When I got back to the dressing room I just didn't know what to do with myself. All I could do was start chewing one of my wristbands on the dressing-room balcony. It was the most nervous I can ever remember feeling at a cricket ground.

Especially when Fred was out to an absolute beauty from Lee. Emotions in the dressing room then were running wild and I'm sure we would all have burst into tears if we had lost this game. At 111 for six, there was a lot still to do.

Geraint Jones tried to hit Shane over the top but only succeeded in picking out Kasprowicz and, with 13 needed, Matthew Hoggard walked out to join Ashley Giles. The dressing room was at fever pitch. Simon Jones was preparing to go out and bat on one leg and Strauss was preparing to run for him. I was still chewing away at my wristband and Fred decided to relieve the tension by punching Strauss repeatedly on the leg. Steve Harmison was due to be next in but didn't appear to be in any fit mental state to get out there. Chaos.

Every one of those last 13 runs was greeted as though it was the winning one, especially the two no-balls signalled by umpire Steve Bucknor when Lee overstepped the front crease. Then with eight needed came another of those many moments from this summer that will stay with me forever.

Matthew Hoggard cover-drove Brett Lee for four. He really did. Hoggy had been working really hard on his batting and had become a difficult man to get out and a reliable nightwatchman. But he was rarely an expansive strokemaker. That shot brought absolute ecstasy to the dressing room together with the realisation that now only four were needed.

A couple more singles meant that Gilo was on strike to Warne and two more runs were needed. Shane was at the very peak of his powers and I think both Ashley and Hoggy felt more comfortable against the pace of Lee, such was the genius of Warney. A rare full toss from Shane seemed to be the moment we had been waiting for but Ash hit it at Simon Katich's boot. Next ball almost bowled Gilo. This was unbearable.

Then it happened. Warne over-pitched on leg-stump and Gilo stroked it past the infield. The ball was racing towards the boundary but our heroes scampered two just in case. Pandemonium again on the balcony. We even had a lap of honour at the end, such was our joy and the reaction of the crowd.

Freddie was man of the match and deservedly so, but most of my feelings were with Giles. He had really been through the mill at Lord's. He had come back strongly at Edgbaston and he had bowled the ball of this century so far at Old Trafford. Now he had scored the winning runs amid high drama at Trent Bridge. Wonderful. Subsequently I have sat and watched the DVD of Trent Bridge with Ashley to live through it all again. You have to savour these moments, enjoy them and use them to give you motivation to repeat it all again another day. Special memories. But the most special, for me, was still to come.

18

AS GOOD AS IT GETS

'KP's hair doesn't bug me.

You've got to have the odd nutter.'

Duncan Fletcher

It was one of the biggest events, it seemed to me, in the history of British sport. The build-up to the final Ashes Test at the Oval left no one in any doubts as to how much the destiny of the famous little urn meant to everyone in the country.

Millions of people seemed to be interested, everyone wanted a ticket for the game and it seemed as though everything had come down to this moment, like it was a one-off Test with the biggest prize in cricket up for grabs.

The Aussies seemed to think so too. They were talking up how everything was coming down to this game, and how as Australia had been in this situation many times before their greater experience of winning would tell in the end. We would see about that.

I tried to stay as relaxed as possible on the eve of the match. I spent much of the day with Shane Warne, which I guess was quite unusual for two opponents on the eve of such a big game. But I thought that was a good thing. I thought it was civilised and commendable that we could come together to do something for charity with the outcome of the Ashes just about to be decided. Shane made the odd comment when we did a couple of television interviews, talking about the game ahead and other generalities, the usual stuff, trying to turn up the psychological heat before the match, but that didn't bother me in the least.

We both knew the importance of what was round the corner and neither of us needed to be told what was in store. We had come together mainly for a company called BGC, an American organisation that was particularly badly affected by the 11 September atrocity in New York. Their two floors in one of the World Trade Center buildings were directly struck by an aircraft and they lost a lot of staff, so every year on 11 September every penny they take on the trading floor goes to the families of the victims.

We were recruited to raise awareness of that as 11 September fell during the Oval Test, and in doing that their chief executive gave us both 50,000 dollars to donate to our favourite charities. Shane put his to the Shane Warne Foundation, while this was the day I decided to adopt Barnardo's as my chosen charity. I love children and it seemed the perfect choice for me. Indeed, I was to receive a phone call from my agent, Adam Wheatley, on the night before the final day's play at the Oval to say that BGC had rung him pledging 500 dollars for each run I scored the next day to Barnardo's. I didn't think much of it at the time but as it turned out, my innings was to provide a tidy little sum for a very worthwhile charity.

I had taken a fair bit of stick in the lead-up to the decisive game over my sponsorship from a London jeweller. As part of the sponsorship deal, the jeweller had pledged to give me a neck chain with '100' made out of diamonds on it if I made a century and that had received a bit of publicity. I was also presented with a pair of earrings worth £50,000 to wear during the game. I didn't see the problem with that myself, but both Geoff Boycott and Mike Gatting found cause to have a go at me over it. Fair enough. They both achieved a lot in the game and I guess they are entitled to say what they like, but it did upset me a little bit because I thought it was irrelevant to my batting. I thought it would be stupid to turn down something like that if I was offered it. Having nice jewellery does not affect my cover drive.

It was my first series and it was an incredibly demanding one but I was still averaging 40 before the Oval even though I hadn't got as many runs as I would have liked since Lord's. I knew, though, that I wouldn't have properly arrived as a Test batsman until I scored a century.

There was good and bad news on the fitness front. Ian Bell had collapsed at the crease while batting in the Cheltenham and Gloucester Trophy final at Lord's for Warwickshire against my Hampshire side, a game I'm pleased to say we won, but it turned out to be nothing more serious than cramp and he was fine. The news was not so good, however, on Simon Jones and he had to miss the game with that ankle injury forcing us into our first and only change of the series. In the end Paul Collingwood was preferred to Jimmy Anderson for that last place.

At breakfast on the first morning of the match the mood was fairly subdued among the team. In a team meeting the previous night Vaughany had said to us, 'This is what we have prepared for. This is what we have waited for. Enjoy it.'

Mind you, it was tough to treat it as just another game. Goodwill messages came from, among others, Tony Blair and David Beckham, and it seemed that everyone had an opinion as to how the game would go and what we should do to win. Meanwhile, the whole country was being urged to sing 'Jerusalem', which had by now become firmly established as our official theme song.

McGrath was back for Australia but could do little to prevent Marcus Trescothick and Andrew Strauss again giving us a positive platform after Michael had again won an important toss. Positive, that is, until Shane Warne entered the match. Ricky Ponting had thrown him the ball after just an hour and the great man was at his absolute best, quickly taking three wickets to reduce us to 104 for three.

I'm afraid Shane made it four wickets when he bowled me as I tried to hit a ball to mid-wicket. I looked back at my stumps in disbelief that I had been bowled for 14. Again I had got a bit of a start and had not taken advantage of it – the cardinal sin.

Yet whenever the team was in need that summer someone would respond, and now Strauss and Flintoff added 143, with Strauss reaching his seventh Test century in his 19th Test, a hell of a start to a Test career. Fred, meanwhile, cantered to 50 and at 274 for four we were in good shape. By the close of the first day, though, we had slipped to 319 for seven and Shane had taken five wickets in an innings yet again. It was his ninth five-wicket haul against England and his 31st in all.

We failed to make 400 but 373 wasn't too bad, at least not until Justin Langer and Matthew Hayden made their best start of the series. They had cruised to 112 without loss when the umpires offered them the light and, surprisingly for a team who had to win, they accepted it. Time for another first: the crowd cheering as the players went off for bad light! However much the spectators had paid for their tickets and however much they wanted to see good cricket, the need for an England win or draw was more important and they were happy for any time to be lost.

A bit of rain delayed the start on the Saturday but Langer moved on to his century and Australia moved on to a strong position. Hayden also moved to three figures at a time when his place was being called into question, and the day closed with Australia at 277 for two, still 96 behind us but with enough time to put us under pressure.

It had been, certainly with the way this series was going, a relatively quiet couple of days, but the series exploded into life again on the penultimate day. And it did so in the form of Freddie Flintoff. Freddie had started getting some bowling rhythm on the

Saturday night and now he carried on until just before tea with one of the great bowling performances.

In 18 overs Freddie took four more Australian wickets as Hayden, Martyn, Clarke and Warne all fell to him. Somehow, from 323 for three, Australia subsided to 367 all out and we had the most unlikely of narrow first-innings leads. It was the final colossal performance from our talisman.

And unexpected though it was to get a first-innings lead, it still left us with a day and a half to make sure we achieved the draw that would win us the Ashes.

The weather was still on our side. Clouds were rolling in. England fans were putting up umbrellas to try to con the umpires into thinking it was raining. Aussie spectators, meanwhile, stripped to the waist in the crowd as if they were basking in the sun at Sydney. Even the Aussie players entered into the spirit of the occasion, all wearing sunglasses to try to reduce the glare when they came out for one aborted session.

We moved to 34 for one with 59.4 overs lost to the weather. Now the equation was simple. The greatest Test series of them all was going down to the wire and we had to make sure we would bat all day to achieve our holy grail. I slept well, as I invariably do, and then played the innings that would change my life, as I charted at the very start of this book. We were 335 all out and there was only time for Australia to reach four for no wicket in reply. The match was drawn and the Ashes were ours. I had been the leading man on the final day, an absolute dream.

The umpires wanted to end the series in a ceremonial way but made a bit of a song and dance over it all, being very precise and almost officious over the rules, until the big moment finally came. When the bails were lifted off the stumps and we were finally able to celebrate, there were hugs, kisses, cigars, beer, champagne, wine, cigarettes and Ashes winners' caps and T-shirts all round. There was a carnival in our dressing room. People were hugging and shouting and whooping and laughing and almost crying with the joy of it all.

The boys were so happy and there was such a release from the pressure and tension that you could touch it. We came out, received the Ashes to wild applause and then started walking round the boundary amid scenes that will be with me for the rest of my life.

The supporters seemed to be even more relieved than we were. As I have said, when you are playing you are in control, but when you are watching you're not. And I can't imagine how tough it must have been watching that series, particularly on the last day. I wouldn't have been able to do it. If I had been a fan, I'd have been pacing around all day rather than have to watch that.

At the time, I didn't realise how winning the Ashes and scoring a century on the last day would change my life, but it has. At the time I was just relishing walking round the Oval and savouring the moment. It wasn't a case of me thinking I played a massive innings, and I didn't fully appreciate what was to come.

We celebrated in the changing room for ages afterwards. I went into the Australian room and chatted to Shane and Stuey MacGill. They were fine. I felt sorry for Stuey because, as usual, he wasn't able to get a game because of the presence of the great Warne, but I didn't want to dwell on their disappointment too much because of the absolute elation and joy that we were experiencing.

That evening was humungous, as was much of the following week. All the stress not just in our lives but also in our families' lives had been lifted. We just went out and enjoyed ourselves and I think everyone deserved it. The whole country seemed to agree with that. I think it might be the only known case of a national sporting team being allowed the mother and father of all celebrations without anyone thinking we were out of order. We could stagger out of a club every night for a week and nobody would mind. Quite right too.

I got about three hours' sleep the night we won the Ashes, which was about three hours more than some players. I went to a club called Kabaret with Simon Jones and a few others and when I got back to our hotel near Tower Bridge around 2.30 a.m. some of the guys were still in the bar. Freddie and his mates stayed there all night. There were reports of bar bills running into thousands but I didn't seem to have paid a penny towards any of the many drinks I'd had.

We had to jump straight on to our open-top bus the next morning. We didn't really have a say over what was going on in terms of the celebrations but I was happy to go with the flow. I know the England and Wales Cricket Board attracted some criticism for putting provisional plans to have a parade in place a week earlier, but to be fair to them there has to be a certain amount of organisation involved in something like that. You can't just rock up, rip the top off a double-decker and set off. These things have to be planned, even if it was interpreted as counting our chickens before they'd hatched or tempting fate.

The most important thing from my point of view was that my mum was on the bus to share the experience with me. I rang her that morning and told her to get over to the team hotel as soon as she could, but I didn't tell her what was happening until she arrived. It was a day she'll never forget either. I just wish Dad could have been there too, but unfortunately he couldn't get over from South Africa because of business.

In fact, Mum probably remembers an awful lot more about the day than I do. After the night before we weren't exactly at our best that day and I wish, to be honest, we could have that open-top bus parade again, only this time sober. Then I could have taken it all in. I wish I had more memories of that day.

When I think of it now I wish I'd had a camcorder with me, I wish I'd had a digital camera with me, but I know that if I had had anything like that I'd have probably lost it. In fact, if my head hadn't been screwed on I'd have probably lost that too.

Normally I can only drink alcohol at night. I'm not one for lunchtime drinking or anything like that. Yet this day I started drinking as soon as I got up again after my three hours' sleep. It's certainly the only time in my life I've had alcohol for breakfast. It was bizarre. And it tasted horrible, but it had to be done and I got through it. First there was a reception before I staggered on to the bus with a big jug of beer, and I almost never drink beer, for the ride.

Everything passed me by in a blur. Not just because of the alcohol but because of the adrenalin and the release of pressure and everything that went with it. Midway through the journey I was bursting to go to the toilet so they had to stop the bus for me while I traipsed into a Starbucks. The staff didn't know what was going on but they cleared a path for me, I went to the toilet and then jumped back on the bus outside.

There were thousands more people than I expected. People were packed ten deep on every street. Some were hanging off buildings; how they got there I'll never know. Mum kept on pointing things out to me as we went along. We couldn't believe some of the things we were seeing.

After a sing-song at Trafalgar Square it was off to 10 Downing Street for a reception with the Prime Minister and his wife. It was the first time I'd met them. When we got there they only had water and orange juice and the boys weren't very happy about that. A couple of them said, 'We're not drinking this,' and soon afterwards a couple of cases of wine appeared from somewhere and the drinking continued.

I'm not very good at remembering faces and I don't know much about politics. I had a chat with Cherie Blair but it's true that I turned to Ashley Giles afterwards and said, 'Who is she?' I had no idea. Afterwards I said that I couldn't remember speaking to the Prime Minister but that wasn't strictly true. I did remember having a very nice chat with him but I didn't want to tell people what had been said, or what was in Downing Street, because it seemed a bit intrusive. It just seemed easier to say that I couldn't remember.

Tony Blair was very happy for us, as indeed was the whole country. Our magical tour ended with a stop at Lord's and another reception. Then the partying continued for at least a week. I never wanted it to stop!

I have made it perfectly clear about what I think of our captain Michael Vaughan and coach Duncan Fletcher. It is their triumph, as captain and coach, more than anybody's. Let's allow them and my colleague Steve Harmison to have the final words on the Ashes.

Michael Vaughan: *In this team, whatever the situation, there is always someone who comes along and puts up his hand. Kevin Pietersen has a bit of genius about him to play like he did at the Oval. It was an extraordinary effort. The guy is so positive. He is a show pony, no doubt about it. I think people are going to have to be careful of him in that when he does badly they're going to blame his hair and blame his earrings. But that's unfair because that's the way he is whether he's doing well or badly and I don't think it affects his game. He's very dedicated when it comes to practise* *and when it comes to cricket. I do believe people have misjudged him slightly. They see the white flash and think he must take himself very seriously indeed. The point is that to wear something like that on your head you have to have a sense of humour. If you took yourself too seriously you wouldn't dare.*

Steve Harmison: *You've got to have something about you. You've got to have balls, that big-up character about you. You don't walk around with something like that and go into your shell. That's his character. He's larger than life, he likes the attention and being in the public eye. But at the end of the day if you can't back it up you're just setting yourself up for a fall, and the one thing Kev hasn't done so far is fall. He's been magnificent. Throughout the whole of the South African one-dayers, he really impressed me. Because I must admit, seeing Kev come into the side, I was thinking: is he going to be able to do this? He's been a bully in county cricket for a long time and how is he going to attune to the demands and the disciplines of international cricket? How is he going to cope against South Africa, his home nation, when there's bound to be flak flying around? But I was so impressed by what I saw out there and how he handled himself that I thought, we've got to play him. He has worked hard and he has been the life and soul in our dressing room. And he has stood up to everything that South Africa and now Australia have thrown at him. He was awesome at the Oval.*

Duncan Fletcher: *KP's hair doesn't bug me. Jimmy Anderson used to have something similar and I liked that too. People say Kevin is not the archetypal kind of Duncan Fletcher player but they have the wrong impression. I've always said cricket teams need characters, otherwise it could be a very boring game. You've got to have the odd nutter. All I'll say is, if you've got a good attitude, you're positive and you work at your game, you can do what you like. As long as he gets results, works at his game when there's practice on and doesn't let his team-mates down or bring distractions, well, what more can you ask?*

19

GLITZ, GLAMOUR, THEN GRIND

'I still don' t know what happened in my head.

I just went to the wicket and danced on it.'

Shahid Afridi

It was very flattering, after the Ashes, to be selected for the one-day World XI to play Australia in the ICC's Super Series in Melbourne. Coming so soon after my introduction to the England team it was quite a compliment, and it was awesome to play alongside so many superstars.

In particular, I became good mates with Brian Lara. It was the first time I'd properly met him and we got on well from the start. We are similar characters. Brian works hard, plays hard and enjoys himself, like me.

The trip to Australia came straight after the Ashes and the matches turned out to be like benefit games, really. From a player's point of view, it was difficult to bring the best players in the world together and expect them to gel as a team within a week. The ICC tried it, they tried to make it a special occasion, and it was enjoyable but I'm not sure the concept has a long-term future. It just wasn't the same as playing for your country, however seriously we all took the matches, and it was no surprise, really, that Australia had the better of the games both in one-day cricket and also the Test that followed. It certainly seemed to matter to Australia. After losing the Ashes they were looking for a boost and these games provided it.

I love Australia. I always have a fantastic time there and this particular visit was made complete when I received two awards at the ICC's gala awards dinner. I thought I had a pretty good chance in the emerging player of the year category but to win not just that award but also the one-day player of the year title in my first year of international cricket was a complete shock. And a very pleasant one.

The glamour and glitz of Australia was to be quickly replaced by the very different environment of Pakistan for our first tour of the winter. It could not have been a bigger contrast to the Ashes, and it could not have been a more difficult place to get back to work after the joy and the celebrations of the summer.

Yes, we had celebrated long and hard after beating Australia and we were entitled to do that, but everybody's minds were very much back on the job by the time we left for Pakistan in October 2005. There was no question of us being complacent or arrogant. We want to be the best side in the world and we knew that we had to keep on winning if this was to be achieved. Beating Australia to win the Ashes took us close to that but the hard work, really, had only just begun.

The subcontinent is a very hard place to play cricket and Pakistan are particularly strong at home. We knew that, in many ways, it would be even harder to win there than the Ashes, but we knew that the last England team to play there, in 2000, had emerged victorious and we wanted to do the same.

For me, though, there was still the problem of the long-standing injury I had to the ninth vertebra in my back, which had hindered me throughout the Ashes series, particularly on the last day at Old Trafford when I had to take painkillers just to get through the match. It was something I never mentioned in public during the summer but it was a problem that was still troubling me, so much so that it was to cut short my tour of Pakistan after two of the five one-day internationals, but not before we had been beaten in the three-Test series and I had registered my second Test century.

The cricket in Pakistan was different to any I'd played before, even in India. A lot of us didn't have any experience of the place and perhaps that was a factor in our eventual defeat, but the cricket was amazing and the local people were very friendly to us. They clearly love their cricket. We were one of the first western teams to tour the country for some time because of security concerns, but there were never any worries on that score from my point of view. The Pakistani people treat their cricketers as Gods and there's no way that anybody would ever do anything to harm them or the game. And the security we were given was comprehensive to say the least – usually being surrounded by armed guards, just in case.

To be honest, Pakistan is not a place I'd rush back to. We were usually confined to our hotels and, while they were fantastic and everything we needed was catered for, I became restless. I am a person who likes to get out and about, likes to do things, and night after night of DVDs or PlayStation started to get a little dull.

But the Pakistan tour helped me in terms of the development of my game and taught me that, however positively I want to play the game, I must be patient at the crease at times too. Really, we lost the series in the first Test in Multan, when we lost the match on the last day after dominating the first four.

I guess it was a lesson to us. Perhaps our batting was too frenetic on that last day as we chased 198 to win on a largely blameless pitch. But it is that fine line again. We are a positive side and it is positive cricket that has brought us our success. As I have said, you just have to marry that with the needs of the situation you find yourself in at times and, really, one of us should have taken us to that small target in Multan. As it was, we fell 23 runs short and I was out for 19, having been out for five in the first innings.

We had to go into the match without our captain. While batting in a warm-up match in Lahore, Michael had had a recurrence of the knee problems that affected him earlier in his career. Marcus Trescothick stepped up in his place.

What a match Tres had. He scored 193, captained us really well, and should have been rewarded with a Test victory. But I'm afraid we couldn't quite do it for him. When you consider that Marcus had also learnt during the match that his father-in-law had been badly hurt in an accident at home, a worry that he kept from us, his efforts in that game were particularly outstanding.

My low scores in the first Test had been a continuation of a poor start to the trip but that didn't overly concern me. I don't get too fussed about scores in warm-up games and, even though I failed twice in Multan, I felt in good nick and was confident that a big score was round the corner. It came in Faisalabad in the second Test.

I was very pleased with my second Test hundred, in my seventh Test, in a high-scoring draw on a flat pitch in Faisalabad. I knew I was in decent form and that a score would come. I always retained my self-belief on that tour.

The one disappointing aspect of that innings was that I was out immediately after reaching three figures, pulling Shoaib Akhtar, who was to be a big influence on Pakistan's success in that series. Interesting character, Shoaib. He had been part of the ICC world squad in Australia but we had barely seen him, he just didn't seem to turn up most of the time, and I think he was under pressure to perform against us to prove he was still committed to the game. He responded in sensational style and there are few better fast bowlers in the world when they are firing than him. His slower ball, very hard to detect, was one of the most notable features of the trip. He runs in and you are expecting a ball at

95 miles per hour, then it seems to be heading for your face, then it dips and, if you're not careful, either bowls you or traps you right in front of your stumps.

Shoaib did not celebrate in quite the conventional way when he got me out. Instead he ran around flapping his wings like a chicken, a sight that bemused most of the crowd. I knew what he was saying, though. When we were in Melbourne one day during the ICC match, Makhaya Ntini of South Africa had said that he thought I walked like a chicken, just banter really, and everybody had had a good laugh. Now Shoaib was saying that he agreed with Ntini. It was nothing malicious or abusive, just a bit of fun. Mind you, I can't see it myself!

I have said that there were no security worries on that trip but the only time our safety remotely became an issue was during this second Test when, while we were batting, there was a sudden and huge explosion. It was one of the loudest bangs I'd ever heard and for a moment we all wondered if we were going to be on the first plane out of Pakistan. As it turned out the explosion came from a Pepsi gas cylinder, something that gave them a lot of publicity, and caused immense relief in the dressing room when it was revealed to be the cause of the bang.

While the explosion was being investigated, all eyes were on the section of the crowd where the bang came from. All, that is, except Shahid Afridi. While everyone else expressed concern at what might be happening, the Pakistan all-rounder decided to use the distraction to try to scuff up the pitch. Pakistan had already scored 462 in their first innings and he decided to use foul means to try to bring a bit of life back into the surface as we began our reply.

Now that was not on. As soon as it became clear what Shahid was doing, I took it upon myself to tell him in no uncertain terms that he was out of order. It was no surprise to us when he was subsequently suspended for the third Test and the first two one-day internationals. That sort of behaviour has no place in cricket.

The second Test was drawn and we went to Lahore for the third still in with a chance of squaring the series, but we had our worst game of the tour. We could only score 288 on a good batting wicket, which was put in proper context when Pakistan replied with 636. Unfortunately we could only score 248 in our second innings, with me scoring 34 and one in the Test, and we lost by an innings and 100 runs to lose the series 2–0.

I played in the first two one-day internationals but by the second one it was clear to me that I couldn't carry on. Even a cortisone injection wasn't enough to enable me to get through. With another big tour of India coming the following February, the only option available to me was to go home, rest, get treatment and get fit again.

But I hate missing matches, and not even being able to return home in time to watch my old mate Darren Gough carve out a new life for himself by winning *Strictly Come Dancing* on BBC Television could compensate for leaving the team three matches early. England lost the one-day series too but at least ended the tour on a positive note by winning the final international in Rawalpindi, after we had also won the first one in Lahore, with me scoring 56.

The tour was quite a contrast to the summer. It is not easy to win in Pakistan but it was very disappointing that we didn't play anywhere near as well as we could. I guess it was such a contrast from the highs of the summer that we were always on a hiding to nothing, but we all know that we can't stop working if we are to become the best side in the world. Pakistan was a reminder to us that we have some way to go yet.

Shahid Afridi was guilty of one of the most blatant bits of games-manship I have ever seen when he scuffed up the pitch in Faisalabad. Here's what he has to say about the incident.

Shahid Afridi: *It is one of the biggest regrets of my life. Kevin is a good guy and I must give him a call soon to explain what I did and apologise to him. I remember when Kevin told me what I had done had been caught on camera. I just said, 'Really, are you sure?' But I knew it was a problem.*

I'm aware the cameras will always be on me now but I can assure you there will be no repeat of what I did against England. As a professional cricketer I don't need to do this sort of thing.

If you ask anyone about my reputation they will tell you I never did these things before, never in my life. But some-thing just came into my mind. I don't know why. It was a real batting track and I knew the match would be a draw. I still don't know what happened in my head. I just went to the wicket and danced on it. Afterwards I felt very guilty.

The match referee called me in and said, 'Look at the TV and tell me what happened.' I didn't look at it. Just said, 'Yeah, guilty. Straight up. I'm sorry, do whatever you want.'

20

BURNING THE RING OF FIRE

*'Kevin asked me, when he was a
youngster in South Africa, about playing in
England. I thought he meant club cricket.
He clearly had bigger fish to fry.'*

Nasser Hussain

Pakistan provided quite a contrast to the Ashes. From the euphoria of one of the greatest summers of cricket this country has ever seen, to the gritty reality of a tough tour of the subcontinent that left us coming up short of what was required.

Looking back now, maybe we weren't as mentally attuned to our task in Pakistan as we might have been. I felt 100 per cent ready for action in Pakistan and I gave absolutely of my best, which I know for a fact was true of every member of our side. Yet maybe it was psychological. We had given so much and achieved so much to win the Ashes that maybe, without even knowing it, we were a little short of our best in Pakistan – that, emotionally, the whole Ashes experience had taken its toll.

It certainly did take a hell of a long time to come down from the high of the Ashes. As I have said, it changed all our lives and it is something that is unlikely to be repeated in all our careers. Even if we win the next seven Ashes series – now wouldn't that be nice! – it is unlikely that any of them could provide the drama and the highs of clinching the urn at the Oval. So maybe it was inevitable that it would take a little something out of us when we went back to work.

It was time to draw a line under our achievement and move on. We had thrown the Pakistan series away, to all intents and purposes, in the first Test at Multan, and we had to learn from that and put it right on the second half of our winter business in 2005/06, the equally tough visit to India.

But first came the final word on the Ashes. The final acknowledgement of what we had achieved. And the last time we would all celebrate together before finally consigning the greatest experience of our lives to our memories. And in many ways the best was saved to last.

For we, as an England team, had a date with the Queen at Buckingham Palace to pick up the honours we were awarded in the aftermath of the Ashes, which, in mine and most of the guys' cases, meant an MBE. Yes, I was to become a Member of the British Empire. Less than two years after making my debut for England. Fairy-tale stuff.

This was a huge deal for me and my family. Mum and Dad and my brother Gregg flew over for the event, which came a few days before we were due to leave for India in February 2006. Mum was like a kid in a candy store. It was the best thing in the world for her. As it was for all of us. It was a day to take it all in and reflect on the enormity of it.

To get into the palace was an event in itself. Such was the security, understandably so, that we had to undergo several checks before we made it inside and were shown to a massive hall in the palace for a pre-event drink. Water and orange juice were on the menu. No alcohol this time, which was not a bad thing when you consider the state of the boys when we went to Tony Blair's house!

Then we had a talk and were shown a video explaining how things were going to happen and what we were meant to do before the big moment came and we were invited up to receive our MBEs in groups of four. My four-ball included Marcus Trescothick, Andrew Strauss and Simon Jones, and the Queen had a few words for each of us. She said to me that cricket must be a fun game to play and watch and I replied that it certainly was to play but that I'm not sure how much fun it was to watch the

Ashes, so tense and dramatic was it for English supporters. We had a giggle and that was it for me until we had a team photo done with the Queen and the Duke of Edinburgh, who I understand was a bit of a cricketer in his day, which is a wonderful souvenir to keep.

Afterwards the Queen mingled with everybody and it struck me how well informed she seemed to be and how easy she found it talking to everyone. She was also a beautifully elegant 80-year-old lady. Her Majesty had a lovely chat with my family, talking to them for about ten minutes about Africa, and my mum was absolutely beside herself. It was like talking to your granny except she was more famous and powerful! The Queen then asked Gregg if he played cricket and he said, quick as a flash, 'No, but I taught him everything he knows!' We all had a good giggle about that and it was pretty much a perfect day.

If that was the time to draw a line under the Ashes, we couldn't have been given a more disappointing return to reality virtually as soon as we arrived in India for the second leg of our winter tour a few days later. India really is one of the toughest tours a cricketer can encounter, possibly the toughest. India is a big, amazing country, fascinating to visit but also very demanding for a cricketer. Conditions are not at all what we are used to, and India is a formidable side at home in those conditions. The country is, obviously, similar to Pakistan but there are big differences, noticeably the sheer scale of India and how many people there are in the country. Pakistan, I suppose, offers less for the western visitor, but it is also a bit calmer and a less frenetic place to go about your work.

We knew it would be even tougher than Pakistan but what we didn't know was that we would lose three key members of our side even before we reached Nagpur for the first Test. Our captain

Michael Vaughan had had problems with his knee in Pakistan but now he found himself struggling to be fit again. So much so that it quickly became evident that we were probably going to have to undergo the toughest of tours without him.

To make matters worse came a cruel blow for my good mate Simon Jones. Simon, of course, has had so many problems with injuries and had to miss the final Ashes Test at the Oval and the whole of the Pakistan tour through his latest misfortune. He has become such an important bowler, such a match-winner, and England is now a much better side when Simon Jones is playing. Yet here he was in India, having worked so hard to get himself fit, breaking down in the nets with a knee complaint and facing another painful journey home before bowling a ball in anger.

To cap it all came the sudden and very sad departure from our tour of Marcus Trescothick, one of the key reasons why England has become such a successful side in the last few years. It really came out of the blue. We had won our first warm-up game against the Cricket Club of India in Mumbai by 238 runs, a routine and reasonable enough start, even though, as I've already said, not too much can ever be taken from warm-up games these days.

We then moved on to Baroda where it became clear that Vaughan and Jones would have to come home and I wasn't in the greatest shape myself, struggling with a rib injury that forced me to retire hurt after scoring 47 against a President's XI. It was a minor thing, certainly compared to the problems of my team-mates, and there had already been a fair bit of sickness around the camp, with perhaps the worst afflicted my Hampshire team-mate Shaun Udal, who found himself having to make a brief visit to a Baroda hospital, so ill was he with 'Delhi belly'.

Then, from nowhere came the Trescothick affair. Marcus had appeared to be his usual self when he was batting in Baroda in that last warm-up game before the first Test. Nothing seemed to be amiss and, as far as I'm aware, he didn't say anything to any of the boys to make us concerned about his condition.

Yet, suddenly he was gone. We were all told that Marcus was having to leave the tour to deal with certain issues and that we all had to respect his privacy and ask no further questions. It goes without saying that we all were 100 per cent supportive of Marcus. He is and always has been an extremely popular member of the England cricket team. Not only that, but he is a really selfless person who will do anything for anybody and has contributed so much to the team and the cause.

There was not one person who questioned Marcus Trescothick's right to leave that tour for whatever reasons he had, and as far as I'm aware not one person felt the need to ask any more questions over what it was all about. I texted Marcus later that day just to ask if he was OK and to offer my full support and he thanked me and got on with whatever it was he had to sort out.

I sent other occasional texts to Marcus as the tour developed but was careful never to pry. I just wanted to make sure he knew we were all thinking of him and that we were there for him if he needed us, and I'm sure he was aware of that anyway.

Trescothick was welcomed back into the England fold before our first Test against Sri Lanka in May 2006 and he looked better than ever. I know when Marcus talked about his absence in India he mentioned that he had a virus which had got to him, and he also alluded to burnout, which is a very real worry for cricketers these days because of the sheer scale of the amount of cricket we play and touring we do. At the moment I can't get enough cricket but who's to say that itineraries won't take their toll on even the most energetic of us, like me, as time goes on.

The most important thing for English cricket is that Marcus

Trescothick appeared fit and well at the start of the 2006 season and that can only be a good thing. I repeat, it's none of my business why Marcus left that tour and I have never asked him. I never will. All I knew was that, before we played the first Test against India in Nagpur, we were having to cope without four of our Ashes heroes, Ashley Giles having failed to make the trip with hip problems that had surfaced in Pakistan.

But when one door closes, another opens, and the loss of Vaughan, Trescothick and Jones meant that opportunities were provided for three members of the A party who were touring the West Indies: Alastair Cook, Owais Shah and Jimmy Anderson. This would tell us how strong English cricket was in terms of its depth.

They were not guys I knew particularly well but they clearly had talent. And lots of it. In Cook's case this was quite a journey. He was summoned at short notice from Antigua, where he was playing with the A team, to be in Nagpur for the start of the first Test. Now that is a long way and a lot of time zones to come for a Test debut but the young Essex left-hander clearly had a bit about him when he arrived and I had no doubts that he was going to fit in well with our side.

It actually may have helped Alastair that he had no time to feel nervous or fret over his debut. He was thrown straight into the deep end and he took to Test cricket like a duck to water. By this time, of course, we were under the captaincy of Freddie Flintoff in the absence of Vaughan and Trescothick, and Freddie also took to captaincy with gusto and added it to the many jobs he carries out for the England cricket team seemingly with ease.

I was delighted for Freddie that he should receive this honour and it was clearly one he was chuffed to bits to receive. It did mean, however, that he was faced with a very tricky decision. At the start of the tour, Freddie had intended to go home for the birth of his son towards the end of the Test series, as Andrew Strauss had done towards the end of the Pakistan trip. Again, no problem as far as the lads were concerned. Some traditionalists may take issue with people leaving tours to be at the birth of their children but you have to remember that times have changed and we are away from home for an awful long time these days. It makes absolute sense from a team point of view to be sympathetic to the demands of a family man because he will return to the team invigorated and grateful for everyone's understanding. It is very good for team spirit.

Now, though, it was tricky for Flintoff because he was suddenly the captain and it is much harder for the captain to leave his ship. Typical of the man, Freddie talked to his wife, Rachael, and together they quietly decided he should stay with the team. The management, meanwhile, tried to ensure that Freddie would be allowed to go home briefly at the end of the Test series and before the one-day internationals to see his new arrival, a boy called Corry.

For now, because of our injuries, we were taking on a team who rarely lose at home, with three Test debutants, spinners Ian Blackwell and Monty Panesar joining Cook, and a new captain. So clearly this was going to be difficult, just as difficult in many ways as the Ashes.

Monty is an interesting character. He was someone else I barely knew before this trip but it became clear to me that he was a lovely lad who was determined to take his chance with England. He is an English lad from Luton with Indian parents, and in many ways was facing a similar situation to the one I found myself in when I toured South Africa on my first trip. Only the Indian people were very pleased to see Monty and gave him a hero's welcome wherever he went!

That was lovely for him but it also added to the pressure on a young lad making his way in international cricket. It was clear from the start that Monty was already an accomplished left-arm spinner, but the reservations about him as an England player concerned his batting and fielding, which he clearly had to work on. And work the lad did. Very hard. Panesar made a good impression on his first England tour, not least when he took his first Test wicket in the game at Nagpur.

Freddie had won his first toss as captain and put a decent score of 393 on the board, with Paul Collingwood demonstrating his class by scoring 134 and Cook making a dream start with 60. This was a big innings for Colly. He has had to cope with people thinking of him as a one-day specialist but I think the England camp had always been sure he could do it at Test level too, given the opportunity, and here he was showing that indeed he could. I was fit after my little rib scare but could only contribute 15 to the cause on this occasion.

Then came Monty's big moment. He had said that his hero was Sachin Tendulkar, one of the greatest batsmen the game has seen, and here he was not only bowling at his hero but getting him out as our bowlers bowled really well in the unforgiving conditions in India. Panesar trapped Tendulkar for 16 and was so happy he didn't know what to do with himself. He ran around and leapt in the air as we tried to catch him to congratulate him. It was a lovely moment in the young man's career.

Monty got another wicket, too, but the real star of the show as India were dismissed for 323 was Matthew Hoggard, who showed that he is far more than just a conventional swing bowler with an expert display of bowling that earned him six wickets and us a first innings lead.

And life was to become even better for Cook. In our second

innings the young lad scored a century, the first to do so on debut since a certain Graham Thorpe in 1993, many of them scored with me at the other end in a partnership of 124 for our third wicket. It was tremendous to be at the other end watching this lad doing so well. Alastair is clearly accomplished, cool, well organised and an accumulator, something you could say our batting has lacked in these frenetic and exciting times.

Alastair gave us a platform from which I could attack as we tried to set up a declaration, and I played my best innings of the tour, racing to 87 from 100 balls. Yes, I had a stroke of luck when I appeared to be caught and bowled in the 20s only for the third umpire to rule that it was a bump ball, but I took advantage of that good fortune to really enjoy myself.

I suppose I should have gone on to a hundred myself but the point was that we were looking to get on with it as quickly as possible, and it was one of those occasions when the interests of the team were absolutely more important than those of the individual. It's how it always is and always should be. I am an attacking player and was out trying to force the pace but not before I had hit a six and 14 fours. I know people again started to say that sometimes I gave my wicket away too easily but, honestly, I wouldn't have done anything any differently on this occasion. Cook and I between us provided the perfect double-act of attack and stability and I like to think both of us played a big part in enabling Freddie to declare in his first Test as captain, a luxury some England captains have gone years without enjoying, with us on 297 for three.

India surprised us by, at one stage, having a bit of a go at reaching their enormous target but in the end they finished on 260 for six and we were extremely happy to earn a very creditable draw. Not least because, in addition to our Ashes heroes, it was clear that there were other players bursting to get into this England side. Not least Alastair Cook and Monty Panesar.

Events off the pitch were, to a large extent, better than those on it for me in Mohali, venue for the second of our three Test matches against India. For this was where Jess was able to join me during a break in her own busy schedule with the pop band Liberty X and my parents were also able to come out from South Africa for the game. Mum and Dad have always supported me throughout my cricket career and it really gave me a boost to see them. I really think cricketers are in a much better frame of mind on tour when they have their loved ones around them.

Freddie again won the toss – he was enjoying this captaincy lark – but we fell a little short in capitalising on our leader's good fortune when we were bowled out for 300. I managed to score 64 and Freddie hit 70, but one of us should have gone on to a big hundred to put us in the driving seat.

Anil Kumble is one of the greatest spin bowlers the game has seen. Not in Shane Warne's class but a formidable competitor and servant of Indian cricket, and he made sure we realised he was still a potent force by taking five wickets in our innings.

Yes, we should have scored more runs but we were very much still in the contest when our bowlers dismissed India for 338 with that man Flintoff taking four wickets, but unfortunately we let ourselves down in slipping to 181 all out in our second knock. That left India with just 144 for victory, which they achieved with just one wicket down.

This was a big disappointment for us. Our young team had battled so well and had shown so much promise in Nagpur. We were so keen to show that our defeat in Pakistan was merely an aberration and that we were back on the right road, and then this happens. Cricket teams have bad matches. It happens and we had to remember both the quality of the opposition and also the fact that we were a weakened outfit.

Yet it still hurt. I would have loved us to put on a great show for Jess and my parents and but I couldn't score a hundred for them either, falling to Harbhajan Singh for just four in the second innings.

It was clear we had to improve in the final Test in Mumbai but our problems with injuries and illness were to resurface, this time on the team bus going to the ground for the first day's play. Alastair, who had done so well deputising for Trescothick, was ill with food poisoning and it became clear he wasn't going to be able to make it. Step forward Owais Shah, a guy who has been around the English scene for a while but who had only played one-day international cricket up to that stage.

How he took his chance. Indian captain Rahul Dravid had, perhaps surprisingly, put us in to bat upon winning the toss and we responded with 400, Shah being the latest debutant to make a mark with 88 and Andrew Strauss scoring his first hundred on the subcontinent.

Now step forward Jimmy Anderson, a bowler who made quite an impact when he first came into the England side but one who had endured a bit of a frustrating time on the sidelines while our awesome foursome of Harmison, Flintoff, Hoggard and Jones had become the pace attack to win the Ashes.

Jimmy is a quiet lad who has worked hard to win another chance and he bowled brilliantly on this occasion as India were dismissed for 279, Jimmy taking four wickets. The Mumbai pitch was becoming harder to bat on and we could only manage 191 in our second innings, which still left India a formidable victory target of 311 for a 2–0 series win.

They never came close. Now I have talked about the young players who seized their chances in this series, but I must give credit to a veteran performer who came to our aid during India's second innings with a noticeable contribution of his own.

American singer Johnny Cash had never been known for his cricketing prowess and, to be honest, if the guy was still alive he would probably be totally bemused at his role in the England cricket team's victory in Mumbai. But he was a key man. Cash was a key man because during a break in play someone put on his song 'Ring of Fire' on their iPod. It became a bit of an anthem on this trip and, I think, it was one of Freddie's favourites, even though Hoggard later claimed it was his iPod that was being played. Anyway, people were quick to ask whether 'Ring of Fire' was any sort of comment on the illness problems we experienced on our trip and I could not possibly comment about that ...

What I do know is that as soon as it was put on, as people were going about their business in the dressing room, we all started joining in until we were all having one great big team singalong. It was excellent and we went out with a spring in our step to demolish the Indians, who crashed to 100 all out, giving us one of our most famous overseas victories in recent years and a share of the series.

You could tell how much it meant to the coach because Duncan Fletcher had rarely been so animated as he was when we all went back into the dressing room for another few verses of 'Ring of Fire' afterwards. And there was one guy in our ranks who was particularly relieved that it had all been wrapped up so convincingly.

Poor Monty had made a real pig's ear of missing a chance offered in the field off the bowling of Shaun Udal by India's big-hitting keeper Mahendra Dhoni as we chased our victory. Dhoni hit the ball high into the Mumbai sun, Monty looked at it, looked at it again and then seemed to just let it thud gently back to earth. It was like something you would see on the village green.

If it had been anyone else making that mistake they would have been crucified, but as it was Monty, who had become so popular in our team, he got away with it. I found it hilarious. It just looked so funny and by that time we were well on our way to victory so I was pretty certain it wouldn't be costly. I was fielding near the boundary and after Monty had missed the chance I turned round to face the crowd and tried so hard not to burst out laughing. There were quite a few English supporters in the crowd and you could see them all looking at me as if to say: what on earth does he find so amusing? but I couldn't help it. It was so comical.

And we could all laugh two balls later when, unbelievably, Dhoni played the same shot, it stayed in the air for what seemed like an eternity, and Monty caught it. Cue pandemonium again. The serious point is that Monty does know he has to work on his fielding so it was very important for him that he clung on to that catch, as it was for my mate Shaun who ended up with figures of four for 14, a wonderful experience for him after so long in the game. But I couldn't resist telling Monty that my money was most certainly on the ball as it came back down to earth that second time. Thankfully, I was wrong.

It was a great result for England, great for Freddie who by this time had become a father for the second time and had yet to see his son, and great for Duncan Fletcher, who followed up the Ashes with a significant success in India, our first Test win in the country for something like 20 years. I was delighted and reasonably satisfied with my contribution even though I hadn't scored a century in the series, something I always want to achieve. My average was pretty good but in future three-match series I will be aiming for nothing less than 300 runs and at least one century, and unfortunately on this occasion I fell a bit short of that.

The subsequent one-day series was largely a disappointment

for us as we went down 5–1 in the seven-match series with one match rained off. But I would like to make a few points here. Firstly, I don't accept that our one-day team is any the less effective than our Test one. Yes, our form has been much better in Test cricket in recent years but what you have to remember is that we have invariably struggled to put a full-strength team out in one-day series, which invariably come at the end of a very tough Test series.

I remain convinced that we are serious contenders for the 2007 World Cup in the West Indies if we can just get everybody fit and firing by the time we get there. Our full-strength team, I am sure, will be more than a match for the rest of the world if we can get them on to the park in the Caribbean, and I for one am really looking forward to that challenge.

In India my contribution wasn't helped by an illness that struck me in Goa after I had been out for a lovely meal of prawns and lobster, with Jess, who had come out again to see me during the Goa and Cochin legs of our one-day journey. Jeez, I was so ill with food poisoning after that fish meal, and it was awful that it should happen when Jess came to see me but she was truly amazing in looking after me and the whole experience made us even closer.

During the series I became the quickest Englishman, and the joint quickest man ever along with the great Viv Richards, to reach 1,000 one-day international runs, which was something of a consolation, and my overall tally of 290 runs in five one-day international innings was not too far away from my South African form. I also hugely enjoyed my first international wicket, which came in Jamshedpur towards the end of a very demanding trip. Now I had been nagging for a bowl during the whole tour as I had been bowling a lot in the nets and was determined to give my off-spin a comeback but, although Freddie kept on promising me a bowl, it never materialised for whatever reason.

I had to wait until Andrew Strauss was in charge, with Freddie being rested, before I got my chance. Out of the blue, he shouted to me, 'You're on next over.' I asked Straussy if he was kidding and I wondered if the excessive heat had got to him, but he told me he needed me to bowl one over while he sorted out his allocation for the other bowlers and I was happy to oblige.

Well, you could say my over went pretty well. My first ball was a bit of a long hop and luckily it wasn't hit out of the ground, but the second ball was a case of 'see you later'. It came out of my hand really well, turned and hit Harbhajan Singh's off and middle stumps. Now Harbhajan was clearly even more surprised and shocked about this than me because he refused to go anywhere. It must have been the first recorded case in cricket of a batsman refusing to walk after being bowled!

There was no doubt about it in my book, but as I celebrated Harbhajan was still there. I said to him, 'Get off the field, you've been bowled,' while he stood there looking at the umpires and for some reason they conferred. Clearly the batsman must have thought Matt Prior behind the stumps had knocked the bails off but the off-stump was there at an angle so I'm not sure how our keeper was supposed to have managed that. Harbhajan, meanwhile, was swearing away and I said to him, 'There's no point swearing, you've been bowled.' He eventually left the crease and I guess got his own back on me by dismissing me later and copying my celebration routine, but that didn't concern me. Whatever happens now I've taken an international wicket and I rather hope it might be the start of the occasional bowl for me. It would be nice to bring that dimension back to my game.

So, all in all, a fairly productive tour of India. Nasser Hussain, the former England captain, watched the trip in his new media role. Here's how he assessed my game at the end of the tour.

Nasser Hussain: *I still laugh when I think back to my first tour as England captain, to South Africa in 1999–2000, when this young lad, bold as brass, came and sat beside me in the visiting dressing room. He had just taken four wickets against us with his off-spin playing for Natal and here he was asking me about playing possibilities in England. His name was Kevin Pietersen.*

Now I had enough on my plate to worry about with my own team at that stage, so probably I wasn't thinking straight, but to my subsequent embarrassment I gave Kevin the phone number of my brother Mel and told him to try Fives and Heronians, Mel's club, in Chigwell. I got the completely wrong end of the stick. I thought Kevin wanted to play club cricket, but he had his eyes on much bigger fish and was more interested in Essex. I don't think my old county will be particularly pleased to hear that they could have signed the young Pietersen if I had had my wits about me!

The more I see of Kevin now, watching him play for England, the more excited I get about his future. I felt at times he sold himself a little short with his shot selection in Pakistan and India but he rectified that problem in the home series against Sri Lanka in 2006. I think he is the best English batsman since Graham Gooch.

His technique is looking a lot stronger than when he first came into the England side, and he is out-thinking bowlers as well as giving out an aura that says, 'I'm coming to get you.' Even now he sometimes goes and gets himself out but that is just part of the package with KP.

I know some people will say we cannot have it all ways. That we cannot praise Pietersen for being positive and criticise him when he gets out. Well, if we want him to be just another good England player we can think that way. But this guy is different. He could be fantastic. He could even be one of the greats of the game. He just needs to realise that there are times in Test matches when you must accept going without scoring.

Viv Richards could keep the ball out. He knew when he had to defend and would do so when necessary in a text-book fashion. There is no reason why Kevin should not learn how to do it. I would not be saying these things if I didn't think Kevin could do it and if I didn't hold him in a very high regard. I know there will be the odd soft dismissal. I just want him to eliminate as many of them as possible. Then we truly will be seeing the most amazing talent.

21

AIMING FOR NUMBER ONE

'KP's switch-hit off Murali was
outrageous. I hope he tries that on me.
It might help me get him out!'

Shane Warne

My biggest objective at the start of our three-Test home series against Sri Lanka in the early part of summer 2006 was to go on and get big scores once I'd made starts. I was aware of people criticising me for not going on to score big hundreds once I'd made starts in both Pakistan and India, and the critics had a point. In the tour reviews I read people gave me nine out of ten and said it would have been ten if only I had turned my decent scores into big hundreds. No one was more aware of that weakness in my game over the course of that winter than me.

In any three-match series you don't have too many opportunities and I'd missed out in the first Test of both the Pakistan and India rubbers. I want to average 50 in every series I play in so it was vital to me that I got off to a good start this time, so I could kick-start my series.

I made it quite clear what my aim was at the start of the series in my *News of the World* column – I wanted to be the best batsman in the world.

I have always set targets for myself. I have talked about them in this book. And I hope I have made it clear that I want to go as far in this game as it is possible for me to go, with hard work, application and perhaps a little luck.

So it didn't seem strange to me to point this out in the paper. Some people said I was creating pressure for myself, or that headlines spelling out my ambitions might not do me any favours, but

I really don't know where they are coming from because all I was doing was reiterating my desires and my aspirations. If I achieve those over the next few years then fantastic, and if I don't I do not want it to be for want of trying.

Basically, I want to give myself the best chance possible to be number one. There is no point in saying I want to be 15th best batsman in the world. I want to be the best and that's how it is. If I don't, so be it – but at least I tried!

The best news for the England team as we gathered in London before the first Test at Lord's was that Marcus Trescothick was back in our ranks. It was fantastic to have Tres back in the team, it really was. His departure from our tour of India was in the past and forgotten. From the word go he seemed much happier, much more chatty and much more bubbly than when I last saw him in Baroda. England could only be the stronger for his return.

We had a team meeting a couple of nights before taking on the Sri Lankans and it was quite clear to me that Duncan Fletcher, our coach, was thinking in similar terms to me when I was telling myself of the absolute need to get big scores. Duncan raised the bar when he said to all us batsmen, 'When was the last time any of you got a double hundred? It's about time you did. When you get a start, make sure you make the most of it.' I was determined to follow those words to the letter.

That, mind you, was easier said than done. Because waiting to face us at Lord's was one of the best bowlers of all time. A spinner who has been equally successful, if not more so, than the great Shane Warne, but one who provides an almost unique challenge because of his unusual action. Muttiah Muralitharan.

Murali, as everyone in cricket knows him, provides one of the toughest challenges for batsmen in world cricket. He is so tough to face because he is almost double-jointed and his wrist action is like nothing I had ever faced before.

Let me try to give you an insight into what it is like to take on Murali. Normally, when a bowler is bowling to me, I watch the ball, right the way from the start of his run up, through his delivery stride, and then through the air before it reaches me. My eyes are always on the ball. Not the bowler's hand, his wrist, feet or anything else.

But Murali, for all his variations, is tricky and difficult because you can watch the ball as much as you want but it is his wrist that does everything. Watching the ball counts for nothing because it doesn't give you any clue as to what direction the ball will turn, or what ball he is going to bowl.

I can pick him occasionally but not nearly as much as everybody seems to think I can. I believe you have to pick Murali through the air, you just can't do it out of his hand. What I did decide to do when facing him was play a lot more for the ball that turned away from me rather than the one that came back in to me. My thinking was that if I picked it wrong and the ball moved into me then I would be able to react because of my leg-side dominance. And if I missed the ball it would hit my pads and I would probably be OK. To me, regularly playing for the ball that turns away from the right-hander, the doosra, gave me a 99 per cent chance of hitting every Murali delivery. If the ball then turned into me, a conventional off-spinner, my shape and whole posture was such that I was in the right place to hit the ball anyway, even if I had misread the delivery.

I'd seen a lot of Murali over the years before the series but decided not to watch too much of him on video in the build-up to Lord's because I don't feel you can learn too much that way. You have to actually stand there and face the little genius. Watch his wrist and watch everything he does. It is a heck of a difficult thing to do.

It is totally different to facing Shane Warne because he's a wrist-spinner who bowls leg-spin and bowls it brilliantly. But his variations are not as massive as Murali's. Shane has a googly but he doesn't bowl it too often these days because of problems with his shoulder, whereas Murali turns the ball sideways, both ways, and to face him on the fourth or fifth day of a Test, when the pitch is worn, can be almost impossible.

He bowls with a scrambled seam, too, just to make it even harder. With orthodox off-spinners you can see the seam coming down at you but Murali is all over the shop and that makes it even more difficult. So it's a question of working out scoring options. Yes, you can sweep him, but that's a hazardous business so I vowed I wouldn't be doing too much of that. Just try to pick him through the air, that's what I told myself.

The sun was shining and Freddie Flintoff, still leading the side in Michael Vaughan's absence, had no hesitation in batting after winning the toss on the first day of the first Test. Yes, it was, with an 11 May start, the earliest Test in English cricket history, but perfect batting conditions overrode any considerations of trying to take advantage of Sri Lanka's traditional weakness against the moving ball in an early English summer.

We were given a fantastic start by the returning Trescothick, whose hundred was greeted with much enthusiasm in the England dressing room. It was an important knock for Marcus and his family and it was a return to business in the best possible way. We were hugely delighted for him.

When my turn came to bat I decided to be as patient as I could possibly be and grind out every single run. I accumulated steadily and felt good and was extremely angry with myself when I was caught off a no-ball in the fifties. I was in and I could have easily thrown it away if I hadn't been luckily reprieved. After that little let-off I was determined to reach three figures and I remember clearly looking up at the Lord's scoreboard and seeing that I was on 72, then 86. I thought to myself: you're in now. A hundred is not enough.

The hundred came on the second day of the Test and it really turned out to be a fantastic day for me. The Sri Lankan attack, with the exception of Murali, is not the strongest in the world, and I wanted to bat on and on, to get the double hundred that Duncan had sought from us and to add it to the ones I scored for Notts.

It was not to be but I couldn't be unhappy when I was out for 158 – at least I wasn't that unhappy until I realised it was the same score as I'd reached at the Oval in the momentous Ashes-clinching Test, my previous Test innings in England. It would have been nice to better it but if 158 is going to be my score then I can think of a few that are worse. That number changed my life so I am not going to argue with it.

By the time I got back to the dressing room someone had already put up a temporary piece of sticking plaster on the famous Lord's honours board and written 'K Pietersen, 158 *v* Sri Lanka, 2006' on it, which was amazing to see. It's one of the biggest achievements in our sport to get your name up there. And the temporary one looked just as good to me as I'm sure the real thing will when I next go back to Lord's.

After the match I think I surprised the press by saying this was a better innings than my 158 at the Oval, but I stand by that statement. My knock at the Oval was played on adrenalin and emotion. I was dropped twice or even three times, whereas at Lord's with the exception of the catch off a no-ball it was a chanceless innings. I started off rock-solid, and I made sure that I played straight and that my concentration levels were perfect throughout the whole innings.

David Graveney, the chairman of selectors, had said to me before I batted, 'Just play it straight for 20 minutes.' I said, 'Grav, I'll give you ten minutes!' But as it turned out I played it very straight and very watchfully for a good 45 minutes before I started to play my natural game. In fact, I grafted my backside off and afterwards I was really, really happy with what I'd achieved.

The best thing for me was that my mum and my brother Tony had flown over for the match. Tony can't afford to come over to England too often so Dad paid for his ticket and I put them up in my apartment in Chelsea where I looked after them for a week before it was time for the Test.

It was wonderful for me to have them there. On the third morning of the game, after we had reached 551 for six declared, I took Tony out to the middle so he could look at the wicket and take in Lord's from the middle, that privileged place where we players see it from. I also took him up to the England dressing room, where he took pictures of the masking tape with my name on it on the honours board for Mum and Dad to see, and then took him on the walk out of the dressing room in the Lord's pavilion, down the stairs, through the Long Room and out on to the pitch, making sure we didn't go down one flight too many stairs and end up in the toilets!

I know how important Mum and Dad feel it is for my brothers to see and understand the life I lead, and it was a real blessing for Tony to come over during that match. Gregg has been over, Bryan lives here and now Tony has come too and seen the whole deal and how it works. It's funny, because when I first started to do well at cricket, Tony was always the one who would ring me asking, 'Can you do this, can you do that,' but now he is more inclined to be defensive on my behalf, telling people, 'No, he's too busy,' if they want a piece of me. He has seen what my life is like now and can relate to the pressures it brings. He has seen with his own eyes what the story is.

We were in a dominant position at Lord's but I'm afraid we didn't win the match because we dropped far too many catches and the Test was drawn. Drops happen. They happened to me during the Ashes series and now it was the turn of some of my team-mates to suffer. We're not robots. We're human beings. Nobody means to drop catches. Nobody went out there thinking: right, I'm going to drop a catch. There are times when there is no real explanation for it and there's nothing you can do about it.

We had to move on to the second Test at Edgbaston and put it behind us. Edgbaston was fun. I wanted more runs. I wanted to be hungry and selfish in terms of getting another big score. I knew I'd batted well in getting that hundred at Lord's and I wanted to do it again in Birmingham. As it turned out I scored 142 out of our score of 295 after we had bowled out Sri Lanka for 141.

I look at it as an innings where I grafted and did what I do best, and that's score runs. I played Murali the way I had at Lord's and tried to be as positive as I could until I got to another hundred. That's when I decided to be more expansive and enjoy myself. I also played a shot that became hugely debated in the days and weeks after the match.

Simply speaking, I played a slog reverse sweep off Murali that I caught on the full and middled so well that it went for six. I suppose it was talked about because, in baseball terms, it was more of a switch hit. I turned round and hit it left-handed into the crowd, a shot I guess you could call audacious. Even I admitted afterwards that it was a bit naughty.

To give you an insight into why I played the shot, you need to know that I'd just come down the wicket three times to Murali and hit him over mid-off for four, through mid-off for four and then cut the doosra for four. So Murali moved his mid-off and mid-on back and put men deep at cow corner and at deep square leg. All my options for big shots had been blocked. But to me, as I was so established, I needed to hit boundaries and I needed to hit big shots. As he was running up I decided to do it. I just turned round and backed my eye and my ability, but I must confess to being surprised at how far it travelled. Murali certainly didn't see it coming. I know that because he told me afterwards that if I ever try that against him again he will beam or bounce me!

I had played a similar shot once before in a match and had had a net in India with England where I just reverse-swept everything, but I had never reverse-swept a six before. Yes, I called it a naughty shot at the time but now I think of it as an interesting one. I'm not saying I will never play it again but I will need to have a lot of runs on the board before I try that again.

After I played the shot Freddie came down the wicket and said to me, 'What was that?' But I didn't think at the time it was anything that unusual. Certainly, I was more concerned with getting a guy who was moving in front of the sightscreen to sit down! Unfortunately I was out two balls later, completely unconnected to the shot, and it didn't take long before I received messages from my dad and brother Bryan, both saying, 'You used to play that shot at home when you were a kid in the courtyard. Now you're playing it in Test cricket!'

The most important thing is that we won the second Test – the first time I had scored a hundred in a Test that England had won. I'd been beginning to worry it wouldn't happen! The third Test at Trent Bridge, however, was a disappointment.

We didn't get as many runs as we should have done. I got out slogging. Unfortunately it will occasionally still happen if I try to be positive, and the match was just one of those occasions when a genius takes over. In this case the genius of Muttiah Muralitharan.

In the hot and dry conditions we faced in Nottingham there is no better bowler in the world. I honestly don't think a batsman exists who could have conquered Murali in the final innings at Trent Bridge. The ball was keeping low, spinning both ways, and it was extremely hard for anyone to survive. Murali was awesome.

In this game he bowled differently to me than any other player. It was, in fact, similar to the way he bowled to me at Lord's defensively from the start. Murali bowled straight, didn't give me any width and put pressure on me to create my own freedom. I know that will happen more and more to me the more bowlers see me in Test cricket and the more successful I become.

I will have to adapt to that and rise to any new challenges it creates for me but for the moment I have concluded that the best way to play Murali is to watch him bowl at somebody else from the other end! He can't get you out when you are at the non-striker's end.

We lost at Nottingham with Murali taking eight for 70 to dismiss us for 190. A drawn series is not what we wanted nor what we expected but we will learn from the experience. Not least that we have to be a lot more ruthless as a team.

I felt that I took my game, in the first two Tests at least, to a new level and I have got to maintain that now. After the series people started comparing me to the great Viv Richards and, while that was flattering, I don't like being compared to anybody. I just want to be successful for England, be successful for Kevin Pietersen and contribute to a successful England team.

Comparisons will happen but I don't really listen to them because I just want to be the best player I can possibly be. I want to train as hard as I can, be as successful as I can and be as good mentally and physically as I can be. I don't want to be anyone else. I don't want to be like Viv Richards. I hardly ever saw the bloke play. I just want to be me. Expressing myself on a cricket field.

22

THE SPECIAL ONE

'It is the best I have ever felt with a girl in my life.

I love her to bits! She's sensational.'

Kevin Pietersen on Jessica Taylor

Looking back on my life up to now, I couldn't have asked for more and I couldn't be happier. When I think back to the biggest and best decision of my life, to come to England, and reflect on the years spent at Nottinghamshire, the little room above a squash court in Cannock, the many and varied experiences I have been through and my first couple of years of international cricket, I can honestly say I do not have a single regret.

I am a contented man, but I know this is just the beginning. Hard work has got me to where I am and I am absolutely aware that I will have to work just as hard to stay there and continue to prosper with the England cricket team.

Off the field, too, I could not be happier and that is down to the presence in my life of a very special person. Jessica Taylor is well known to lovers of pop music as a member of the group Liberty X, the band who emerged from the original *Pop Stars* television programme, and which is made up of people who narrowly failed to make the line-up of the group the programme created, HearSay. Only Liberty X have been a lot more successful! Jess is the best thing ever to happen to me.

I met Jess through her manager, someone I have got to know in the last couple of years. One day, joking around, I said to him, 'You must have some good-looking girls on your books, can you get me any numbers?' He mentioned Jess straight away. I knew who she was, had heard the band, and knew she was beautiful. So I immediately said, 'Get me sorted.'

He asked Jess if I could have her number, gave her mine and we started texting each other, getting to know each other pretty well before we had even met. We then went on a couple of dinner dates and clicked instantly, to the point where we were speaking to each other on the phone all day, every day, within weeks of meeting in the autumn of 2005.

I introduced Jess to my mum and dad when they came over to go to Buckingham Palace and they liked her straight away, which was important to me. Jess also came to India twice when I was on tour and, as I have said, had to look after me the second time when I became ill.

Now I try to see her every day. It is the best I have ever felt with a girl in my life. It's absolutely sensational. Jess is such a supportive girl, a committed girl, successful and independent. She is a family-orientated person from Preston and is so caring. I love her to bits! She's sensational. She's the one for me. She's awesome. Fantastic!

My friends and family always said I was the type of person who would know immediately when the right person came along and that things would move pretty quickly when she did, and they have been proved absolutely right. I could definitely see marriage in the offing right from the start, and I'm happy to say we got engaged in June 2006.

I planned it all right down to the finest detail. We had just finished our series against Sri Lanka and I told Jess we were going to this romantic castle – I won't say where because it is going to be our special secret place – for dinner. Only we were going by helicopter!

During the meal I got down on one knee, got out the diamond and platinum ring I had had specially made for the occasion, and asked Jess to marry me. She didn't guess at the proposal, which was pretty amazing because all the signs were there. I had made sure I had asked permission of Jess's parents beforehand because I think that's the respectful thing to do. They were delighted about it and gave me their blessing.

When I popped the question Jess burst into tears of joy and immediately said yes – over and over again. She was as happy as anything. Everything was perfect and the ring fitted perfectly. I was relieved – but I'd have been very surprised if she'd said no. About two minutes before I did it I went through a very nerve-racking time but I was 100 per cent sure she would say yes.

Everyone is ecstatic. My parents, Jess's family, everybody. We haven't even thought about details of the wedding yet but we will be doing so soon.

Jess has made me so much happier and so much more at peace with myself. She also likes my hair short, so you may have seen the last of my eye-catching hairstyles. It's terrific to know that all the stupid stories and bullshit about my private life that were in the papers during the Ashes series are hopefully a thing of the past and I don't have to worry about the tabloids any more. I was affected by those stories and so were my family. Stories invading your privacy can ruin people's lives. The worse thing was that so much of it was made up, but it was still my fault in that I was mixing with people who would be likely to let me down. Not any more. They say that there's no smoke without fire. Well, I won't be lighting any matches any more.

I know how happy I am with Jess. I know how much I've learnt about myself in terms of getting in trouble and getting out of trouble, and I couldn't be more contented now. I want to be with her all day every day, and I know she feels exactly the same about me. Jess has added a new dimension to my life. She has also eased the pressure on me because all the nonsense has gone out of my life.

I can get on with my cricket knowing I have a great girl, and as well as her being supportive of me I'm supportive of her because I'm very interested in her industry and know a lot of people in it. It's fascinating to watch Jess at work and see how she goes about things. I love learning about her way of life and the music industry. I've always loved music and been fascinated by the music world.

I've been to see Liberty X in concert and I think they are absolutely brilliant. I was totally proud watching Jess, knowing I had a girl I could support and one in whose career I've got a real interest. That has never happened to me before. In past relationships I've had to be the money-winner but Jess is totally independent, and I also know the support I give her means a lot to her. I'm there for her 24/7. I've dropped her off at a gig and picked her up and even that I find awesome. Jess is busy and successful and I've met the other members of the band too and they're really nice people.

I see my life now at a stage where it's just a case of keeping the ball rolling. I do the right things by the right people and do the right things by myself. I know what's got me to the happy place I'm in right now. I know it's down to hard work, the training, the treadmill, the net sessions, the hard yards. That's what has got me to where I am and it's a case of keeping in tune with that.

I realise that where I am now means there's an increased level of expectation on me and I have to improve as a cricketer by at least another 20 per cent. I still love playing and training and I'm sure that will always be the case.

I know I will continue to work hard because I want to be a successful player for a long time to come. I don't want to be a flash in the pan, and I have to prove to people that I'm not. I've got to consistently achieve. I'm doing OK as a batsman but I know I can be more consistent and I know I can score a lot more hundreds. I also know I can be a lot more consistent in the field too.

There will always be areas where I can improve, mentally and psychologically, in getting in tune for a Test. You can never ever be too good, or good enough. I want to improve, I want to get better, and I won't stop until I get as good as I can be.

Batsmen mature around 27 or 28 years of age, so I reckon I'm a little bit away from my best. The reason I have done so well so quickly, I feel, is that I had that apprenticeship with Notts. I moved to this country and had to do everything for myself and stand up for myself. I had to make myself cocksure and mentally in the right place to be successful. I've learnt so much over the last few years. And I'm learning more every day.

What do I need to do to improve? Well, I have to be more solid and defensive in certain situations and more attacking in certain other situations. I can still learn more about certain shots, like the sweep. I played the sweep a lot more in India than I'd done previously in my career and it's a case of adding that and other shots to my armoury, putting them all together, making them gel and becoming the player I want to be. That could take another two years. I just don't know.

I am an instinctive, positive, attacking player and I've been successful that way, so that basic truth will not change. I'll listen to constructive criticism, and if it works for me it works; if it doesn't, I'll ignore it. I'll leave it at that and will always try not to get too hung up about people who blocked the ball their whole career telling me to block it now. That just won't happen. I've got to where I am because of the way I play. I know I'm not the best, I know I'm not great but I know I have been successful because of the way I have thought about my approach to batting and the way I go about things. It's a case of keeping those things going now.

My immediate ambitions centre on the Ashes in 2006 and the World Cup in early 2007. They are massive. To do well in the Ashes in Australia and to be one of the leading players in the World Cup would be fantastic goals to achieve.

Can I be a great player? I really do hope so. It depends on how hard I work and how committed I stay and I don't think that will change. I'm as committed and hungry as ever. I made runs in Pakistan and India without having great series and I started the international summer of 2006 with a big hundred in the first Test against Sri Lanka at Lord's to take me past 1,000 Test runs in my 23rd innings.

I want to go that bit further now, to do that extra bit to get myself up the rankings. Every time I play in a three-Test series I want to score at least 300 runs and I won't settle until I'm doing that consistently.

Every person can always improve and do things better on a day-to-day basis. I want to improve not only as a cricketer but also as a person and in my relationships and family commitments.

Clive Rice, one of the most important people in my development, has been kind enough to say in this book that he thinks I'm already one of the top five batsmen in the world. That is very nice of him and it may be true in one-day cricket but I know I need to be more consistent in Test cricket for it to truly be the case. I want to average 40 or 50 throughout my career and I want people to say, 'Hell, he's a good player.'

I want to make my parents, who have given me everything, proud, and I want to be a leading figure in an England team that goes on to become the best in the world. I have crossed many boundaries already in my life but, hopefully, the best is yet to come.

23

FROM ASHES HEROES TO ZEROS

'From the start I realised things were different with Shane. He called me Kevin in front of the Aussies rather than KP or PK. He wasn't friendly any more. He meant business.'

Kevin Pietersen

The build-up to the much-anticipated Ashes rematch of 2006–7 went pretty much as well as we could have hoped. At home, England managed to defeat Pakistan convincingly in a series that was marred by the controversy of the forfeited Test at the Oval. Yet we had already won the series before those unbelievable few days in London so we were happy with our form as we turned our minds to taking on the old enemy again and attempting to retain the Ashes.

We were confident, and we knew we had the Ashes, but we also knew that Australia would make us work twice as hard to retain them. So we worked very hard prior to the tour during the ICC Trophy in India and tried to get as fit as we could for the challenges ahead. When we arrived in Australia, however, we didn't make the greatest of starts, but then England rarely do on tour. The Aussie press got stuck into us from the word go, as is their wont. I was soon hearing that I was going to be subjected to a bouncer barrage, stuff like that. It was material I was expecting, to be honest, and it did little to affect my mood. I was excited. I was about to play in possibly the biggest Ashes series of all time, and nothing was going to spoil it for me. They thought, too, that they could get me out hooking, particularly after the game we had in India in the ICC Trophy, but I didn't mind. It was all part of the psychological battle. It was all part of the fun.

There was one minor distraction for me in the build-up to the big day at the Gabba in Brisbane. I had made some more comments about cricket in South Africa, following on from what I said in the first edition of this book, and they didn't go down too well in the country of my birth. Basically, maybe the truth hurts. I had talked about Ashwell Prince being made South African captain in an interview with *GQ* magazine, and now came 'news' that South Africa had asked for the ICC to take disciplinary action against me for my comments. I thought it was complete nonsense. A lot of people I know in South Africa said to me that they were happy that at least one person was speaking out and saying how things really were in South Africa. I was just telling it how it is. And a lot of South African people know how it is, too. Really, it was much ado about nothing. And I certainly didn't want to make a song and dance about it. It's not nice when you hear the word 'racism' associated with your name. I just wanted to dismiss what was being said because racism had nothing to do with it. I haven't heard anything about it since.

I got a hundred in a warm-up game ahead of the first Test against an attack that contained four Australia pacemen, so I was reasonably happy with my form as 23 November, the first day of that first Test, approached. I was really enjoying the wickets in Australia. Again, people tried to say they would be too quick for me, but I love quick wickets! I went into my second Ashes series, my first in Australia, pretty confident. Yes, there were nerves, but you have to be nervous to get the best out of yourself. In the England team, we minded our own business and backed our own ability.

And then we were into action in Brisbane. Much has been made of Steve Harmison's first ball at the Gabba, which was so wide it went to second slip, but I just think he was nervous. Nerves affect people in different ways. Yes, Harmy delivered a poor first ball, but so much was made of it. I just thought it was funny. It was a mistake by a bowler. If a batsman plays and misses, nothing more is made of it; yet if a bowler bowls and misses, a lot of fuss is made.

I have to admit, though, that we had a poor first Test. There were encouraging signs in our second innings, Paul Collingwood playing particularly well, and me also contributing runs, so it wasn't all doom and gloom. But we lost the Test match, and that was a huge disappointment for England. Australia really attacked us. You could see it in their eyes. I knew straight away that they had changed. They had a completely different attitude to 2005. I think the tone was set pretty early on at Brisbane, and I think Australia wanted it much more than we did. You only had to look at them, to talk to them, to realise that. You could sense venom and passion in everything Australia did, and perhaps they didn't have that in 2005. I knew right away that this series was going to be tough.

I also knew that things had changed between Shane Warne and me. We were close friends, we genuinely were, as has been documented often, and as was demonstrated when Shane agreed to write the foreword to this book. But Shane had copped a lot of stick in Australia for being friendly with me and others in the England side. Now he wasn't laughing and joking with me. He called me Kevin for a start, which he has never done before. Before then it was always KP, or even PK. It was his way of being matey with me. So I thought, 'OK, fair enough, two can play at that game.' I was going to show respect to Shane, as I would always do, but I decided to play with venom too.

There has always been sledging between us and Australia, and between me and Shane, and that's something I have always enjoyed. I enjoy conflict: it gets me going; it gets me concentrated and focused. Better that than cruising when you are at the crease. Then, while I was batting during that first Test, Shane chucked a ball right at me. I just thought it was wrong. You don't throw a ball at a mate. It just wasn't right. Yes, be aggressive, but I thought the extent to which Shane took that aggression was ridiculous. Players of his calibre should not be doing things like that. I hit back. I wasn't going to back down. I swore at Shane. I went hard at him. It did feel strange to be involved in such a conflict with such a mate, but this was real Test cricket – as tough as it gets. As I said, after the Ashes series of 2005, a lot of people said we were too pally, so I thought things were going to be a bit different this time. But not like this. I guess, though, that all it really did was inspire me and make me all the more determined.

I spoke to Shane afterwards, and we sorted it all out. From what I can gather, Shane was told to be fierce with me by the powers-that-be within the Australia set-up. He was told there was to be no laughing or giggling. Cricket Australia basically instructed Shane to be like that with me. He never actually told me that himself, but it is true, I am sure about that. Things were pretty much OK after our talk. No more abuse, no more barracking, though there was still a bit of an atmosphere. Things were just different between us. I was really upset about it when it happened. The old red mist came down. But I guess it was done in the heat of the battle, and time is a great healer in these things.

We did so much right in the second Test at Adelaide, so much to get ourselves back into the series. Paul Collingwood did fantastically well to score a double hundred. I was with him for much of the time he was batting. The real ferocious energy with which Australia had been batting had been negated. I understand that some commentators said afterwards it was one of the first times that they reckoned Shane Warne did not know what to do when he was bowling at us. I scored 158 again, for the third time in my Test career! It's strange. I really don't know why it should be that

I keep getting out on that score. I guess I would settle for 158 whenever I go to the crease, but having said that, I'd like to push on from there and make my Test best a higher score.

For large parts of that second Test the Aussies were as quiet as mice. It was just awesome for us. There was even a stage when they just seemed to be down and out. We had them really under the thumb. But the tide seemed to turn when my great mate Ashley Giles dropped Ricky Ponting in Australia's first innings. I felt for Ashley big time. I've been there. Gilo is one of the safest fielders in the side, but it went down, simple as that. And it proved crucial. The second Test really should have been an England win or a draw after we had done so well in our first innings.

It all went wrong on the last day. It was one of those days you can't really explain. There was no reason why we shouldn't have batted through and gone to Perth just one down after it had become clear that it was going to be hard for us to force a victory. As it happened, things just started to go wrong on that last day and, as if by snowball effect, we lost wickets and sank deeper and deeper into trouble. My cheap dismissal in that second innings was, I guess, crucial. Shane did me, sweeping, bowled round my legs, a mode of dismissal I have said in the past that I just didn't think could happen. It was a poor shot from me. I made a mistake. And I just couldn't believe it. I stood there in the middle of the beautiful Adelaide Oval feeling helpless, like I'd let my side down. From there it just got worse. Somehow, after dominating the Test, we were staring the most unlikely of defeats in the face.

That was the day when the Ashes were won back by Australia, no question. It was, without doubt, the worst moment of the winter. We went two down from a position of supposed superiority, and it was just surreal. It was like, 'How did that happen? Have I dreamt that? When will I wake up?' Reality had kicked in.

From that point on it was going to be an uphill battle if we were to retain the Ashes. I know people asked how Colly, Matthew Hoggard and I felt after putting in big individual performances in Adelaide and still somehow coming out on the losing side. But it wasn't about us. We are all in it as a team. And we lost on that final day as a team.

The third Test in Perth was where the whole subject of me batting with our tail became an issue. I had been batting at five because that was where I felt I was of best use to the team, and where the management, after we talked about it, felt it was best for me to bat. I had spent much of my career there, and it had worked for me. Really, batting at five, you shouldn't be batting with the tail. You really should have time to build an innings, but I'm afraid we got to the stage where we were losing wickets quicker than we should have been and I was faced with the dilemma, quicker than expected, of whether I should hit out, try to retain the strike, or bat normally.

As one of the recognised batsmen, my job is to score runs. The majority of them. And it was up to me, the management and the rest of the boys to discuss the best policy for getting the best out of myself and the rest of the boys I was batting with. I got out slogging in the first innings and was stranded in the second, so it became clear that we had to think about this and maybe change things.

In the second innings in Perth, I was taking singles with the tail. I thought that was the best way to go, to put some faith in my team-mates and take runs when they were there. But a message came out from the dressing room basically saying that I should wait a bit longer during each over before I took singles. The advice was that I should try to monopolise the strike a bit more. It left me with a dilemma: the decision was whether I should try to be more positive and go for my shots, or should I carry on trying to keep the strike and aiming for singles towards the end of each over?

Ricky Ponting, the Australian captain, saw what I was trying to do and did his best to nullify my efforts. He started to lock the field up so I couldn't get singles. It was a massive compliment to me as far as I was concerned. I just carried on trying to get singles, trying to be positive. I got to 70, but then made the wrong decision in trying to hit Brett Lee into the Fremantle Doctor wind. Afterwards, the question was asked whether or not I'd followed the advice that had been sent out to me from the dressing room, but to me it was simply a question of taking the advice on board and playing it as I saw it for the rest of our innings.

There were other issues swirling around Perth and that third Test. The boys were all aware that there had been an outcry at home over Monty Panesar not playing in the first two Tests. From the players' point of view, such matters were up to the selectors. They picked the team they thought was best equipped to retain the Ashes, and if that meant that Monty didn't play in Brisbane and Adelaide then that wasn't an issue for us. When you are in a group of 15 or 16 players you all feel you are in it together. Whoever plays and whoever misses out, everyone supports one another.

At Perth, however, Monty came in, and he immediately did well. Everything had changed from our perspective at two down. It was going to be mighty hard to win the Ashes from there. But the one shining light was that Monty came in and took wickets for England. People love Monty. I love it when he takes a wicket and comes running, or rather bouncing, past me wherever I'm fielding. He has a fantastic natural celebration. He has enthusiasm. Monty is always smiling, but don't mistake that for any sort of lack of determination. Monty never stops learning, and he will never stop wanting to improve. I give him some batting tips now and then in the nets. He loves the challenge of the nets, and that appeals to my nature too. I try to be aggressive in the nets towards Monty's bowling, and he loves to respond to that and try to outwit me. We are similar in many ways.

But it was another defeat for us at Perth. Our feelings in the aftermath of that third Test were just horrible. At the very worst we should have been one down after three Tests, but after the dramatic reversal at Adelaide and now this loss at Perth, the Ashes were gone already. It was just incomprehensible to me.

To me, it proved how well we had played in 2005. We had beaten a great side in England with our boys playing so well. But if we thought we had turned a corner, if we thought we were now the best side in the world, then we were sadly mistaken.

The bottom line, as I have alluded to already, is that Australia came fighting back twice as hard in this series. Almost every single metaphorical punch they threw was on target. They were riding a wave. Australia not only wanted to beat us, they wanted to embarrass us. This is the mindset we need to get ourselves into. We must try to embarrass Australia when we next play them, in 2009. It comes down to energy, determination and passion. Australia wanted the Ashes so much more than us in 2006–7. In comparison, we were laughing our way through the series. The intensity wasn't there. Why that should have been I just don't know, because there isn't a single England cricketer who didn't desperately want to retain the Ashes. But our intensity levels, maybe even subconsciously, were not as good as theirs.

Australia possess some fantastic cricketers. It became an emotional series for some of them because it soon became clear that this would be their last series for Australia. The first to announce that he would be retiring, with the series won, was Shane Warne; he was to be followed by Glenn McGrath and Justin

Langer. All three were to call it a day in Test cricket after the fifth and final Test against us in Sydney. That situation had been set up for them by our failure to take the series beyond the third match, and it proved to me that when great cricketers want to do something, to put their minds to it, then they can do it.

Shane was fantastic in the fourth Test in Melbourne just after Christmas, truly amazing. I had agreed to be present at a breakfast for the Shane Warne Foundation on the morning of the first day, and it was clear to me that Shane was as excited as ever about playing in a Test match for Australia. After his retirement announcement, it was an emotional final Test for him at his home ground of the MCG. The Boxing Day crowd at the rebuilt stadium was close to 100,000, too. Shane could not have written a better script. And this was to be the match in which he took his 700th wicket in Test cricket – more victims than any other bowler in history. It could not have been more perfect for the great man.

I actually think, having faced and watched Shane bowl throughout that match, that it was the best I have ever seen him perform. When he finally took that landmark wicket he just went mental, and rightly so. I hugged Shane afterwards and said, 'Well done.' He was receptive to that, and said, 'Thanks for that.' As a mate, I was really happy for him. Our friendship had finally been fully restored. It was a great moment in the history of Test cricket. Who could possibly ask for more than to take his 700th Test wicket on his home ground just a few days after announcing that he will retire at the end of the series? Shane Warne is simply a genius, the like of which our game will never see again.

After that business with me batting with the tail in Perth there was a lot of talk about our batting order before that fourth Test. In our first innings in Melbourne I found myself batting with the tail again and again. At times I would be in two minds as to whether I should get on with it or protect the tailenders. I had another meeting with the management about it. The truth was, I was comfortable at five. I have batted there for much of my career. We all agreed that any change to that position should only be made when I was mentally ready for a switch.

Well, the time seemed right after that first innings in Melbourne. But first I had to make sure Paul Collingwood, who would move down to five in the reshuffle, was happy with me taking his slot at four, and then I had to have further discussions with the management. Paul was happy about it, which was very important to me, and the decision was made. I know it might have seemed odd to make the switch in the middle of a Test, but from our point of view it was a natural thing to do.

Of course, that wasn't the end of the matter. Australia were so desperate to beat us 5–0 that their coach, John Buchanan, dropped a bomb into our laps. He tried to separate and divide the England cricket team by suggesting that I was not a team man, that I was a man apart. Basically, that I was selfish.

It was a bit of a joke, to be honest. It just gave us something to laugh about at a very difficult time for England. It certainly didn't affect me at all. From what I could gather – so, from an outsider's point of view – the Australian team don't tend to listen much to John Buchanan anyway. If you have a team as good as theirs, it could even be argued that they don't need a coach! I thought it was all a bit of rubbish that was aimed at keeping us down. There is no point in listening to nonsense like that. I get on absolutely fine with my team-mates, thank you very much, and we are a very united England team. That goes for hard times as well as good, for it is those hard times that can keep you together, can keep you strong and united.

Sydney was a very disappointing final match of the series for us. After all the expectation and excitement, all the hopes and planning, things had gone desperately wrong. We had a meeting before Sydney and decided that we had to draw a line under the 2006–7 series and start planning for 2009 in England. Still, we tried to be upbeat. We trained hard. We tried to regain our pride.

By this time, McGrath and Langer had officially joined Warne in announcing their retirements. We didn't want the last Test to become a goodbye party for them all. Unfortunately for us, things didn't work out how we wanted – like the whole of the winter. The momentum was just too much in Australia's favour; it was too much for us to stem now. They were riding the wave, and in that New Year Test the luck went with the team that was winning, which is often the case.

I felt sorry for our batsmen. Poor Andrew Strauss got some terrible decisions over the course of the series. Things just seemed not to go our way at all. Often in an innings the more you bat, the luckier you become. We never got to that stage. It was hard to take, a bitter pill to swallow. We hated losing so much, but it got to the stage where we couldn't seem to do anything to halt the inevitability of it all. Again, it made me realise just how good Australia were and how well we had played in 2005 to beat them. We were up against a very special team. I stuck around for a bit at the crease, but it was too little, too late.

The scoreline of 5–0 was achieved for only the second time in Ashes history. We didn't spend too much time in the Australian dressing room after that Sydney Test. It was no place for us to be, and we left them to their own devices. Really, 5–0 was the last scoreline I expected. No way did any of us think we could possibly lose 5–0. To try to take that in the immediate aftermath of the final Test, and to react to it, was horrendous. The series destroyed us. We were totally drained, mentally and physically.

My analysis of the series is pretty simple, really. Australia raised the bar to a new level, and our mission now is to try to get to that level, a goal we must achieve by the time they come here again in 2009. Sydney was the toughest batting I have ever experienced. The likes of Glenn McGrath, Brett Lee and Stuart Clark hit a penny on a length every ball for two sessions. They just increased the pressure on us and got wickets with aggressive bowling that really showed us how to execute the most perfect bowling plan. In fact, they all hit their areas throughout the series, and that's what we have to learn from them. And next time there will be no Glenn McGrath, no Justin Langer, possibly no Adam Gilchrist and Matthew Hayden. But above all, there will be no Shane Warne. That is the biggest blow to them, and the biggest boost to us. The man is simply irreplaceable. He and these other great players have certainly earned their team-mates a lot of win bonuses over the last few years!

Little did I know it at the time, but my Australian summer was drawing swiftly to a close. When the Test series was over, we played Australia in a Twenty20 game in Sydney, and then travelled to Melbourne for the first one-day international. I was going well in our first 50-over innings of the series. Then, on 82, towards the end of the England innings, I advanced down the wicket at McGrath and was hit in the right side of my ribs by a short ball. It hurt like hell. I didn't know it at the time, but I had fractured my seventh rib. My one-day series was over before it had really begun.

Coming down the wicket to the great McGrath was a policy that had been successful for me throughout the Ashes, and I certainly don't regret it, despite what happened in Melbourne. Glenn doesn't like it, mainly because not a lot of people have done it to him over the years, and he doesn't handle it particularly well. The aim is to get him off his line and length. But on this occasion he saw me coming, dropped it short, and I got hit. Still, it would-n't stop me doing it again in the future.

I was distraught when I learned that I wouldn't be fit for the rest of the one-day series. Absolutely mortified. I wanted to be with my team, helping them, putting the Ashes behind us with a good one-day series. I was prevented from flying for a couple of days, but the day I finally left Australia, England beat New Zealand in Hobart to register our first win on the tour. I was so happy for the team, but it was also bad for me because I hadn't been able to be in a winning side.

The Aussies aimed a final parting shot at me when their former captain Allan Border basically accused me of getting out of the country a bit too quickly. The inference was that I wasn't that badly hurt, or that if I had hung around I could have been fit before the end of the series. I considered this a massive insult. I can promise Mr Border and everyone else that I wasn't fit to play any part in the triangular one-day series with Australia and New Zealand after fracturing my rib. My priority had to be trying to regain my fitness in time for the 2007 World Cup. No one should ever question my integrity, passion and commitment for the England cause, and nobody had before Allan Border did. I've proved how hard I play for England, how tough I am, and how hard I try for England. To say that I was gutless and wanted to get out of the country is absolute nonsense and a cheap shot as far as I'm concerned. It wasn't the way I wanted to leave Australia, but if I had tried to rush back and play before I was ready, then aggra-vated the injury and missed the World Cup, I would never have forgiven myself.

I felt humiliated, though, when I left Australia. It had been the most chastening of winters and I had been unable to help my side do anything to stop Australia winning 5–0. As I have said, we did not do nearly as well as we should and could have done. We are a quality side. We are, in the ratings, the second-best Test side in the world. Our intensity was simply not as good as it should have been, and for me, the events of 2006–7 were a massive kick up the bum. There was, of course, the not inconsiderable consolation of England winning the Commonwealth Bank one-day series against all the odds with a 2–0 finals victory over Australia. I was absolutely delighted that the lads pulled this win off. It is a tribute to their character and determination to end such a disappointing tour on the very highest of notes.

I was so disappointed I wasn't there with them to contribute to and share in this triumph but that didn't make me any less pleased about it. It didn't make up for the Ashes. We all know that. But it helped the guys recover some lost pride, gave a considerable boost to our World Cup prospects and, perhaps, sowed the first seeds of doubt in the minds of the Australians, who went on to lose a one-day series against New Zealand 3–0. Duncan Fletcher, Andrew Flintoff and the England cricket team deserve all the praise under the sun for winning that one-day series.

Australia have shown us the levels we need to play at in 2009. Just like they did in 2005, we need to remember how we feel now, and vow never to suffer these feelings again. We must come back as better players for England, and I believe we will. The Ashes tour did not go anything like how we hoped it would, but we have not become a bad side overnight. I promise you, England will hit back from this. Roll on 2009!

APPENDIX

FIRST-CLASS CAREER

CAREER DETAILS UP TO AND INCLUDING SUMMER 2006

Debut: Natal B v Easterns at Kingsmead, Durban 1998

Batting and Fielding Record

M	Inns	NO	Runs	HS	Ave.	100	50	Ct
94	154	13	7237	254*	51.32	25	30	88

Bowling Record

M	Balls	Runs	Mdns	Wkts	BB	Ave.	Econ.
94	4684	2617	160	55	4/31	47.58	3.34

SEASON BY SEASON

Batting and Fielding Record

	M	Inns	NO	Runs	HS	Ave.	100	50	Ct
1997–8 (South Africa)	1	1	1	3	3*		0	0	0
1998–9 (South Africa)	4	7	0	146	60	20.85	0	1	6
1999–2000 (South Africa)	5	5	1	104	61*	26.00	0	1	4
2001 (England)	15	26	4	1275	218*	57.95	4	6	14
2002 (England)	12	17	3	871	254*	62.21	4	0	12
2003 (England)	16	30	0	1546	221	51.53	4	11	17
2003–4 (India)	3	6	1	523	147*	104.60	3	1	4
2004 (England)	16	21	1	1044	167	52.20	4	4	19
2005 (England)	11	21	1	897	158	44.85	3	4	4
2005–6 (Pakistan)	4	8	0	205	100	25.62	1	0	3
2005–6 (India)	4	7	1	263	87	43.83	0	2	1
2006 (England)	3	5	0	360	158	72.00	2	0	4

* = not out

Bowling Record

	Balls	Mdns	Runs	Wkts	BB	Ave.
1997–8 (South Africa)	222	14	73	1	1-20	73.00
1998–9 (South Africa)	312	4	173	8	3-22	21.62
1999–2000 (South Africa)	1153	50	516	14	4-141	36.85
2001 (England)	1404	52	767	9	2-46	85.22
2002 (England)	372	13	226	5	2-54	45.20
2003 (England)	652	18	428	11	4-31	38.90
2003–04 (India)	54	0	50	0		
2004 (England)	491	7	365	7	3-72	52.14
2005 (England)	12	1	7	0		
2006 (England)	12	0	12	0		

FIRST-CLASS RECORD FOR EACH TEAM

Batting and Fielding Record

	M	Inns	NO	Runs	HS	Ave.	100	50	Ct
England	14	27	1	1250	158	48.07	4	5	8
England A	3	6	1	523	147*	104.60	3	1	4
England XI	2	3	1	51	47*	25.50	0	0	0
Hampshire	6	11	0	424	126	38.54	2	1	4
Kwazulu-Natal	5	5	1	104	61*	26.00	0	1	4
Kwazulu-Natal B	4	7	0	146	60	20.85	0	1	6
Marylebone CC	1	1	0	17	17	17.00	0	0	2
Natal B	1	1	1	3	3*		0	0	0
Nottinghamshire	58	93	8	4719	254*	55.51	16	21	60

Bowling Record

	Balls	Mdns	Runs	Wkts	BB	Ave.
England	12	0	12	0		
England A	54	0	50	0		
Hampshire	12	1	7	0		
Kwazulu-Natal	1153	50	516	14	4-141	36.85
Kwazulu-Natal B	312	4	173	8	3-22	21.62
Natal B	222	14	73	1	1-20	73.00
Nottinghamshire	2919	90	1786	32	4-31	55.81

First-class Batting and Fielding Record against each team

	M	Inns	NO	Runs	HS	Ave.	100	50	Ct
Australia	5	10	1	473	158	52.55	1	3	
Border	1	2	0	35	22	17.50	0	0	2
Derbyshire	6	9	2	809	218*	115.57	5	0	5
Durham	5	7	0	160	52	22.85	0	1	10
Durham Uni. Centre of Cricketing Exellence	2	2	0	191	133	95.50	1	1	4
East Zone (India)	1	2	0	126	94	63.00	0	1	2
Eastern Province	1	0							
Easterns	1	1	1	3	3*		0	0	0
England XI	1	1	1	61	61*		0	1	0
Essex	5	9	1	323	167	40.37	1	1	4
Gauteng	1	2	0	8	4	4.00	0	0	1
Glamorgan	4	4	0	247	126	61.75	1	1	2
Griqualand West B	1	2	0	19	16	9.50	0	0	0
Hampshire	4	6	0	160	87	26.66	0	1	3
India	3	6	0	216	87	36.00	0	2	1
Indian Board President's XI	1	1	1	47	47*		0	0	0
Kent	3	6	0	307	125	51.16	2	1	3

Lancashire	2	3	0	108	52	36.00	0	1	1
Leicestershire	4	7	0	233	95	33.28	0	2	3
Middlesex	7	13	3	768	254*	76.80	2	4	9
North West B	1	2	0	53	37	26.50	0	0	3
Northerns	1	0							
Northerns B	1	1	0	60	60	60.00	0	1	0
Nottinghamshire	1	2	0	41	41	20.50	0	0	0
Oxford Uni. Centre of Cricketing Excellence	1	1	0	62	62	62.00	0	1	0
Pakistan	3	6	0	201	100	33.50	1	0	3
Pakistan A	1	2	0	4	4	2.00	0	0	0
South Zone (India)	1	2	0	219	115	109.50	2	0	1
Sri Lanka	3	5	0	360	158	72.00	2	0	4
Surrey	1	2	0	95	79	47.50	0	1	1
Sussex	5	9	0	529	166	58.77	2	3	4
Tamil Nadu	1	2	1	178	147*	178	1	0	1
Warwickshire	5	9	0	440	221	48.88	1	2	6
West Indies A	1	1	0	1	1	1.00	0	0	0
Western Province B	1	2	0	14	10	7.00	0	0	3
Worcestershire 3	5	1	211	103*	52.75	1	1	3	
Yorkshire	2	3	0	188	167	62.66	1	0	2

First-class Bowling Record against each team

	Balls	Mdns	Runs	Wkts	BB	Ave.
Border	278	14	141	5	3-69	28.20
Derbyshire	336	10	205	2	1-26	102.50
Durham	144	5	82	0		
Durham Uni. Centre of Cricketing Exellence	325	18	119	8	4-31	14.87
Eastern Province	264	13	105	2	2-73	52.50
Easterns	222	14	73	1	1-20	73.00
England XI	335	14	141	4	4-141	35.25

Essex	257	7	133	3	2-23	44.33
Gauteng	246	7	114	3	2-75	38.00
Glamorgan	48	0	33	0		
Gloucestershire	222	2	162	1	1-53	162.00
Griqualand West B	126	3	80	1	1-38	80.00
Hampshire	396	10	284	6	3-72	47.33
Kent	81	0	87	0		
Lancashire	54	0	31	1	1-31	33.00
Leicestershire	66	1	55	0		
Middlesex	222	12	116	1	1-13	116.00
North West B	54	0	31	1	1-31	
Northerns	30	2	15	0		
Northerns B	48	0	22	3	3-22	7.33
Sri Lanka	12	0	12	0		
South Zone (India)	54	0	50	0		
Surrey	24	0	22	0		
Sussex	252	9	167	0		
Warwickshire	360	13	216	6	3-95	36.00
Western Province B	84	1	40	3	3-40	13.33
Worcestershire	120	3	73	3	2-46	24.33
Yorkshire	24	1	6	1	1-6	6.00

Wicket Breakdown

	Batting	Bowling
Bowled	18	14
Caught	59	32
LBW	32	5
Caught and Bowled	4	3
Run out	2	0
Stumped	2	1
Not out	10	
Total	127	55

First-class centuries

100	Nottinghamshire v Kent at Trent Bridge 2003
100	England v Pakistan at Faisalabad 2005
103*	Nottinghamshire v Worcestershire at Worcester 2001
103*	Nottinghamshire v Derbyshire at Derby 2002
104	England A v South Zone at Gurgaon 2004
107	Nottinghamshire v Derbyshire at Trent Bridge 2004
115	England A v South Zone at Gurgaon 2004
116	Nottinghamshire v Gloucestershire at Trent Bridge 2002
125	Hampshire v Kent at Canterbury 2005
126	Hampshire v Glamorgan at Southampton 2005
133	Nottinghamshire v Durham Uni. Centre of Cricketing Excellence at Trent Bridge 2002
139	Nottinghamshire v Sussex at Trent Bridge 2003
142	England v Sri Lanka at Edgbaston 2006
147 (ret. hurt)	England A v Tamil Nadu at Chennai 2004
150	Nottinghamshire v Derbyshire at Trent Bridge 2001
153	Nottinghamshire v Derbyshire at Derby 2004
158	England v Australia at The Oval 2005
158	England v Sri Lanka at Lord's 2006
165*	Nottinghamshire v Middlesex at Lord's 2001
166	Nottinghamshire v Sussex at Horsham 2003
167	Nottinghamshire v Essex at Southend 2004
167	Yorkshire v Nottinghamshire at Headingley 2004
218*	Nottinghamshire v Derbyshire at Derby 2001
221	Nottinghamshire v Warwickshire at Edgbaston 2003
254*	Nottinghamshire v Middlesex at Trent Bridge 2002

ONE-DAY CAREER

International Batting and Fielding Record

M	Inns	NO	Runs	HS	Ave.	100	50	Ct
30	24	6	1179	116	65.50	3	8	16

International Bowling Record

Balls	Runs	Mdns	Wkts	BB	Ave.	Econ.
18	26	0	1	1-4	26.00	8.66

SEASON BY SEASON

Batting and Fielding Record

Season	M	Inns	NO	Runs	HS	Ave.	100	50	Ct
2004–05 (Zimbabwe)	4	3	2	104	77*	104.00	0	1	3
2004–05 (South Africa)	7	6	3	454	116	151.33	3	1	3
2005 (England)	10	6	1	228	91*	45.60	0	2	8
2005–06 (Australia)	2	2	0	18	16	9.00	0	0	1
2005–06 (Pakistan)	2	2	0	84	56	42.00	0	1	0
2005–06 (India)	5	5	0	291	77	58.20	0	3	1

One-Day International Batting and Fielding Record for each team

	M	Inns	NO	Runs	HS	Ave.	100	50	Ct
England ICC	28	22	6	1161	116	72.56	3	8	15
World XI	2	2	0	18	16	9.00	0	0	1

One-Day International Batting and Fielding Record against each team

	M	Inns	NO	Runs	HS	Ave.	100	50	Ct
Australia	9	7	1	223	91*	37.16	0	2	8
Bangladesh	3	1	0	23	23	23.00	0	0	1
India	5	5	0	291	77	58.00	0	3	1
Pakistan	2	2	0	84	56	42.00	0	1	0
South Africa	7	6	3	454	116	151.33	3	1	3
Zimbabwe	4	3	2	104	77*	104.00	0	1	3

One-Day International Bowling Record against each team

	Balls	Mdns	Runs	Wkts	BB	Ave.	Econ.
India	6	4	0	1	1-4	4.00	4.00
Zimbabwe	12	22	0	0			11.00

One-Day Batting and Fielding Record

M	Inns	NO	Runs	HS	Ave.	100	50	Ct
132	117	22	4394	147	46.25	8	27	58

One-Day Bowling Record

Balls	Runs	Mdns	Wkts	BB	Ave.	Econ.
1930	1689	3	35	3-14	48.25	5.25

Wicket Breakdown

	Batting	Bowling
Bowled	4	1
Caught	11	0
LBW	1	0
Caught and Bowled	1	0
Run out	0	0
Stumped	1	0
Not out	6	
Total	18	1

Twenty20 Batting and Fielding Record for each team

	M	Inns	NO	Runs	HS	Ave.	100	50	Ct
England	1	1	0	34	34	34.00	0	0	3
Hampshire	10	10	0	256	67	25.60	0	2	0

Twenty20 Bowling Record for each team

	Balls	Mdns	Runs	Wkts	BB	Ave.
Nottinghamshire	108	0	136	6	2-9	22.66

Twenty20 Batting and Fielding Record against each team

	M	Inns	NO	Runs	HS	Ave.	100	50	Ct
Australia	1	1	0	34	34	34.00	0	0	3
Derbyshire	2	2	0	34	32	17.00	0	0	0
Durham	2	2	0	92	67	46.00	0	1	0
Lancashire	2	2	0	65	58	32.50	0	1	0
Leicestershire	2	2	0	21	21	10.50	0	0	0
Yorkshire	2	2	0	44	44	22.00	0	0	0

Twenty20 Bowling Record against each team

	Balls	Mdns	Runs	Wkts	BB	Ave.
Durham	36	0	37	1	1-20	37.00
Lancashire	18	0	18	2	2-9	9.00
Leicestershire	18	0	28	2	2-28	14.00
Yorkshire	36	0	53	1	1-27	53.00

Wicket Breakdown

	Batting	Bowling
Bowled	2	1
Caught	5	4
LBW	3	0
Caught and Bowled	0	0
Run out	0	0
Stumped	1	1
Not out	0	
Total	11	6

THE ASHES 2005
FIRST TEST, LORD'S, 21–24 JULY

Australia won by 239 runs

Australia won the toss

Umpires: Aleem Dar and RE Koertzen

Man of the Match: Glenn McGrath

Close of Play

Day 1: Australia 190, England 92/7 (Pietersen 28*)

Day 2: Australia 190 & 279/7 (Katich 10*); England 155

Day 3: Australia 190 & 384; England 155 & 156/5 (Pietersen 42*, GO Jones 6*)

Australia 1st Innings

JL Langer	c Harmison	b Flintoff	40
ML Hayden		b Hoggard	12
*RT Ponting	c Strauss	b Harmison	9
DR Martyn	lbw	SP Jones	2
MJ Clarke	lbw	SP Jones	11
SM Katich	c GO Jones	b Harmison	27
AC Gilchrist	c GO Jones	b Flintoff	26
SK Warne		b Harmison	28
B Lee	c GO Jones	b Harmison	3
JN Gillespie	lbw	b Harmison	1
GD McGrath	not out		10
Extras	(b 5, lb 4, w 1, nb 11)		21
TOTAL	(all out, 40.2 overs)		190

FoW: 1-35, 2-55, 3-66, 4-66, 5-87, 6-126, 7-175, 8-178, 9-178, 10-190

Bowling	O	M	R	W
Harmison	11.2	0	43	5
Hoggard	8	0	40	1 (2nb)
Flintoff	11	2	50	2 (9nb)
SP Jones	10	0	48	2 (1w)

England 1st Innings

ME Trescothick	c Langer	b McGrath	4
AJ Strauss	c Warne	b McGrath	2
*MP Vaughan		b McGrath	3
IR Bell		b McGrath	6
KP Pietersen	c Martyn	b Warne	57
A Flintoff		b McGrath	0
GO Jones	c Gilchrist	b Lee	30
AF Giles	c Gilchrist	b Lee	11
MJ Hoggard	c Hayden	b Warne	0
SJ Harmison	c Martyn	b Lee	11
SP Jones	not out		20
Extras	(b 1, lb 5, nb 5)		11
TOTAL	(all out, 48.1 overs)		155

Fow: 1-10, 2-11, 3-18, 4-19, 5-21, 6-79, 7-92, 8-101, 9-122, 10-155

Bowling	O	M	R	W
McGrath	18	5	53	5
Lee	15.1	5	47	3 (4nb)
Gillespie	8	1	30	0 (1nb)
Warne	7	2	19	2

Australia 2nd Innings

JL Langer	run out (Pietersen)		6
ML Hayden		b Flintoff	34
*RT Ponting	c sub	b Hoggard	42
DR Martyn	lbw	b Harmison	65
MJ Clarke		b Hoggard	91
SM Katich	c SP Jones	b Harmison	67
AC Gilchrist		b Flintoff	10
SK Warne	c Giles	b Harmison	2
B Lee	run out (Giles)		8
JN Gillespie		SP Jones	13
GD McGrath	not out		20
Extras	(b 10, lb 8, nb 8)		26
TOTAL	(all out, 100.4 overs)		384

FoW: 1-18, 2-54, 3-100, 4-255, 5-255, 6-274, 7-279, 8-289, 9-341, 10-384

Bowling	O	M	R	W
Harmison	27.4	6	54	3
Hoggard	16	1	56	2 (2nb)
Flintoff	27	4	123	2 (5nb)
SP Jones	18	1	56	0
Giles	11	1	56	0
Bell	1	0	8	0

England 2nd Innings

ME Trescothick	c Hayden	b Warne	44
AJ Strauss	c & b	Lee	37
*MP Vaughan		b Lee	4
IR Bell	lbw	b Warne	8
KP Pietersen	not out		64

A Flintoff	c Gilchrist	b Warne	3
GO Jones	c Gillespie	b McGrath	6
AF Giles	c Hayden	b McGrath	0
MJ Hoggard	lbw	b McGrath	0
SJ Harmison	lbw	b Warne	0
SP Jones	c Warne	b McGrath	0
Extras	(b 6, lb 5, nb 3)		14
TOTAL	(all out, 58.1 overs)		180

FoW: 1-80, 2-96, 3-104, 4-112, 5-119, 6-158, 7-158, 8-164, 9-167, 10-180

Bowling	O	M	R	W
McGrath	17.1	2	29	4
Lee	15	3	58	2 (1nb)
Gillespie	6	0	18	0 (2nb)
Warne	20	2	64	4

SECOND TEST, EDGBASTON, BIRMINGHAM, 4–7 AUGUST

England won by 2 runs

England 1st Innings

ME Trescothick	c Gilchrist	b Kasprowicz	90
AJ Strauss		b Warne	48
MP Vaughan	c Lee	b Gillespie	24
IR Bell	c Gilchrist	b Kasprowicz	6
KP Pietersen	c Katich	b Lee	71
A Flintoff	c Gilchrist	b Gillespie	68
GO Jones	c Gilchrist	b Kasprowicz	1
AF Giles	lbw	b Warne	23
MJ Hoggard	lbw	b Warne	16

SJ Harmison		b Warne	17
SP Jones	not out		19
Extras	(lb 9, w 1, nb 14)		24
Total	(all out, 79.2 overs)		407

Bowling	O	M	R	W
Lee	17	1	111	1
Gillespie	22	3	91	2
Kasprowicz	15	3	80	3
Warne	25.2	4	116	4

Australia 1st Innings

JL Langer	lbw	b SP Jones	82
ML Hayden	c Strauss	b Hoggard	0
RT Ponting	c Vaughan	b Giles	61
DR Martyn	run out (Vaughan)		20
MJ Clarke	c GO Jones	b Giles	40
SM Katich	c GO Jones	b Flintoff	4
AC Gilchrist	not out		49
SK Warne		b Giles	8
B Lee	c Flintoff	b SP Jones	6
JN Gillespie	lbw	b Flintoff	7
MS Kasprowicz	lbw	b Flintoff	0
Extras	(b 13, lb 7, w 1, nb 10)		31
Total	(all out, 76 overs)		308

Bowling	O	M	R	W
Harmison	11	1	48	0
Hoggard	8	0	41	1
SP Jones	16	2	69	2
Flintoff	15	1	52	3
Giles	26	2	78	3

England 2nd Innings

ME Trescothick	c Gilchrist	b Lee	21
AJ Strauss		b Warne	6
MJ Hoggard	c Hayden	b Lee	1
MP Vaughan		b Lee	1
IR Bell	c Gilchrist	b Warne	21
KP Pietersen	c Gilchrist	b Warne	20
A Flintoff		b Warne	73
GO Jones	c Ponting	b Lee	9
AF Giles	c Hayden	b Warne	8
SJ Harmison	c Ponting	b Warne	0
SP Jones	not out		12
Extras	(1 lb, nb 9)		10
Total	(all out, 52.1 overs)		182

Bowling	O	M	R	W
Lee	18	1	82	4
Gillespie	8	0	24	0
Kasprowicz	3	0	29	0
Warne	23.1	7	46	6

Australia 2nd Innings

JL Langer		b Flintoff	28
ML Hayden	c Trescothick	b SP Jones	31
RT Ponting	c GO Jones	b Flintoff	0
DR Martyn	c Bell	b Hoggard	28
MJ Clarke		b Harmison	30
SM Katich	c Trescothick	b Giles	16
AC Gilchrist	c Flintoff	b Giles	1
JN Gillespie	lbw	b Flintoff	0
SK Warne	hit wicket	b Flintoff	42

B Lee	not out		43
MS Kasprowicz	c GO Jones	b Harmison	20
Extras	(b 13, lb 8, w 1, nb 18)		40
Total	(all out, 64.3)		279

Bowling	O	M	R	W
Harmison	17.3	3	62	2
Hoggard	5	0	26	1
Giles	15	3	68	2
Flintoff	22	3	79	4
SP Jones	5	1	23	1

THIRD TEST
OLD TRAFFORD, MANCHESTER, 11–15 AUGUST

Match drawn

England 1st Innings

ME Trescothick	c Gilchrist	b Warne	63
AJ Strauss		b Lee	6
MP Vaughan	c McGrath	b Katich	166
IR Bell	c Gilchrist	b Lee	59
KP Pietersen	c sub	b Lee	21
MJ Hoggard		b Lee	4
A Flintoff	c Langer	b Warne	46
GO Jones		b Gillespie	42
AF Giles	c Hayden	b Warne	0
SJ Harmison	not out		10
SP Jones		b Warne	0
Extras	(b 4, lb 5, w 3, nb 15)		27
Total	(all out, 113.2)		444

Bowling	O	M	R	W
McGrath	25	6	86	0
Lee	27	6	100	4
Gillespie	19	2	114	1
Warne	33.2	5	99	4
Katich	9	1	36	1

Australia 1st Innings

JL Langer	c Bell	b Giles	31
ML Hayden	lbw	b Giles	34
RT Ponting	c Bell	b SP Jones	7
DR Martyn		b Giles	20
SM Katich		b Flintoff	17
AC Gilchrist	c GO Jones	b SP Jones	30
SK Warne	c Giles	b SP Jones	90
MJ Clarke	c Flintoff	b SP Jones	7
J N Gillespie	lbw	b SP Jones	26
B Lee	c Trescothick	b SP Jones	1
GD McGrath	not out		1
Extras	(b 8, lb 7, w 8, nb 15)		38
Total	(all out, 84.5)		302

Bowling	O	M	R	W
Harmison	10	0	47	0
Hoggard	6	2	22	0
Flintoff	20	1	65	1
SP Jones	17.5	6	53	6
Giles	31	4	100	3

England 2nd Innings

ME Trescothick		b McGrath	41
AJ Strauss	c Martyn	b McGrath	106
MP Vaughan	c sub	b Lee	14
IR Bell	c Katich	b McGrath	65
KP Pietersen	lbw	b McGrath	0
A Flintoff		b McGrath	4
GO Jones	not out		27
AF Giles	not out		0
Extras	(b 5, lb 3, w 1, nb 14)		23
Total	(6 wickets dec, 61.5 overs)		280

Bowling	O	M	R	W
McGrath	20.5	1	115	5
Lee	12	0	60	1
Warne	25	3	74	0
Gillespie	4	0	23	0

Australia 2nd Innings

JL Langer	c GO Jones	b Hoggard	14
ML Hayden		b Flintoff	36
RT Ponting	c GO Jones	b Harmison	156
DR Martyn	lbw	b Harmison	19
SM Katich	c Giles	b Flintoff	12
AC Gilchrist	c Bell	b Flintoff	4
MJ Clarke		b SP Jones	39
JN Gillespie	lbw	b Hoggard	0
SK Warne	c GO Jones	b Flintoff	34
B Lee	not out		18
GD McGrath	not out		5
Extras	(b 5, lb 8, w 1, nb 20)		34
Total	(9 wickets, 108 overs)		371

Bowling	O	M	R	W
Harmison	22	4	67	2
Hoggard	13	0	49	2
Giles	26	4	93	0
Vaughan	5	0	21	0
Flintoff	25	6	71	4
SP Jones	17	3	57	1

FOURTH TEST
TRENT BRIDGE, NOTTINGHAM, 25–28 AUGUST

England won by 3 wickets

England 1st innings

ME Trescothick		b Tait	65
AJ Strauss	c Hayden	b Warne	35
MP Vaughan	c Gilchrist	b Ponting	58
IR Bell	c Gilchrist	b Tait	3
KP Pietersen	c Gilchrist	b Lee	45
A Flintoff	lbw	b Tait	102
GO Jones	c & b Kasprowicz		85
AF Giles	lbw	b Warne	15
MJ Hoggard	c Gilchrist	b Warne	10
SJ Harmison	st Gilchrist	b Warne	2
SP Jones	not out		15
Extras	(b 1, lb 15, w 1, nb 25)		42
Total	(all out, 123.1 overs)		477

Bowling	O	M	R	W
Lee	32	2	131	1
Kasprowicz	32	3	122	1
Tait	24	4	97	3
Warne	29.1	4	102	4
Ponting	6	2	9	1

Australia 1st Innings

JL Langer	c Bell	b Hoggard	27
ML Hayden	lbw	b Hoggard	7
RT Ponting	lbw	b SP Jones	1
DR Martyn	lbw	b Hoggard	1
MJ Clarke	lbw	b Harmison	36
SM Katich	c Strauss	b SP Jones	45
AC Gilchrist	c Strauss	b Flintoff	27
SK Warne	c Bell	b SP Jones	0
B Lee	c Bell	b SP Jones	47
MS Kasprowicz		b SP Jones	5
SW Tait	not out		3
Extras	(lb 2, w 1, nb 16)		19
Total	(all out, 49.1 overs)		218

Bowling	O	M	R	W
Harmison	9	1	48	1
Hoggard	15	3	70	3
SP Jones	14.1	4	44	5
Flintoff	11	1	54	1

Australia 2nd Innings

JL Langer	c Bell	b Giles	61
ML Hayden	c Giles	b Flintoff	26
RT Ponting	run out sub		48
DR Martyn	c GO Jones	b Flintoff	13
MJ Clarke	c GO Jones	b Hoggard	56
SM Katich	lbw	b Harmison	59
AC Gilchrist	lbw	b Hoggard	11
SK Warne	st GO Jones	b Giles	45
B Lee	not out		26
MS Kasprowicz	c GO Jones	b Harmison	19
SW Tait		b Harmison	4
Extras	(b 1, lb 4, nb 14)		19
Total	(all out, 124 overs)		387

Bowling	O	M	R	W
Hoggard	27	7	72	2
SP Jones	4	0	15	0
Harmison	30	5	93	3
Flintoff	29	4	83	2
Giles	28	3	107	2
Bell	6	2	12	0

England 2nd Innings

ME Trescothick	c Ponting	b Warne	27
AJ Strauss	c Clarke	b Warne	23
MP Vaughan	c Hayden	b Warne	0
IR Bell	c Kasprowicz	b Lee	3
KP Pietersen	c Gilchrist	b Lee	23
A Flintoff		b Lee	26
GO Jones	c Kasprowicz	b Warne	3

AF Giles	not out			7
MJ Hoggard	not out			8
Extras	(lb 4, nb 5)			9
Total	(7 wickets, 31.5 overs)			129

Bowling	O	M	R	W
Lee	12	0	51	3
Kasprowicz	2	0	19	0
Warne	13.5	2	31	4
Tait	4	0	24	0

FIFTH TEST
THE OVAL, LONDON, 8–12 SEPTEMBER

Match drawn

England 1st Innings

ME Trescothick	c Hayden	b Warne	43
AJ Strauss	c Katich	b Warne	129
MP Vaughan	c Clarke	b Warne	11
IR Bell	lbw	b Warne	0
KP Pietersen		b Warne	14
A Flintoff	c Warne	b McGrath	72
PD Collingwood	lbw	b Tait	7
GO Jones		b Lee	25
AF Giles	lbw	b Warne	32
MJ Hoggard	c Martyn	b McGrath	2
SJ Harmison	not out		20
Extras	(b 4, lb 6, w 1, nb 7)		18
Total	(all out, 105.3 overs)		373

Bowling	O	M	R	W
McGrath	27	5	72	2
Lee	23	3	94	1
Tait	15	1	61	1
Warne	37.3	5	122	6
Katich	3	0	14	0

Australia 1st Innings

JL Langer		b Harmison	105
ML Hayden	lbw	b Flintoff	138
RT Ponting	c Strauss	b Flintoff	35
DR Martyn	c Collingwood	b Flintoff	10
MJ Clarke	lbw	b Hoggard	25
SM Katich	lbw	b Flintoff	1
AC Gilchrist	lbw	b Hoggard	23
SK Warne	c Vaughan	b Flintoff	0
B Lee	c Giles	b Hoggard	6
GD McGrath	c Strauss	b Hoggard	0
SW Tait	not out		1
Extras	(b 4, lb8, w 2, nb 9)		23
Total	(all out, 107.1 overs)		367

Bowling	O	M	R	W
Harmison	22	2	87	1
Hoggard	24.1	2	97	4
Flintoff	34	10	78	5
Giles	23	1	76	0
Collingwood	4	0	17	0

England 2nd Innings

ME Trescothick	lbw	b Warne	33
AJ Strauss	c Katich	b Warne	1
MP Vaughan	c Gilchrist	b McGrath	45
IR Bell	c Warne	b McGrath	0
KP Pietersen		b McGrath	158
A Flintoff	c & b Warne		8
PD Collingwood	c Ponting	b Warne	10
GO Jones		b Tait	1
AF Giles		b Warne	59
MJ Hoggard	not out		4
SJ Harmison	c Hayden	b Warne	0
Extras	(b 4, w 7, nb 5)		16
Total	(all out, 91.3 overs)		335

Bowling	O	M	R	W
McGrath	26	3	85	3
Lee	20	4	88	0
Warne	38.3	3	124	6
Clarke	2	0	6	0
Tait	5	0	28	1

Australia 2nd Innings

JL Langer	not out		0
ML Hayden	not out		0
Extras	(lb 4)		4
Total	(0 wickets, 0.4 overs)		4

Bowling	O	M	R	W
Harmison	0.4	0	4	0

INDEX